The World Is Watching

Dennis Redmond

THE WORLD IS WATCHING

Video as Multinational Aesthetics, 1968–1995

Southern Illinois
University Press
Carbondale

Library of Congress Cataloging-in-Publication Data
Redmond, Dennis, 1968–
The world is watching : video as multinational aesthetics, 1968–1995 /
Dennis Redmond.
 p. cm.
Includes bibliographical references and index.
1. Video recordings—Social aspects. I. Title.
PN1992.945.R43 2003
384.55'8—dc21
ISBN 0-8093-2535-7 (cloth : alk. paper)   2002156348

Printed on recycled paper. ♻

The paper used in this publication meets the minimum requirements
of American National Standard for Information Sciences—
Permanence of Paper for Printed Library Materials,
ANSI Z39.48-1992. ∞

Dedicated to the memory of Katharine Gelles

Contents

Acknowledgments

Thanks are due to Atsuko Hayashi for the detailed transcript and translation help with *Evangelion;* to the members of the Department of Comparative Literature at the University of Oregon for their energy and inspiration; to Wolf Sohlich, who actually gave me the idea for this project during a conversation at the Roma; and finally to my family, for the moral and financial support that helped make this book a reality.

The World Is Watching

Introduction

It's one of the great paradoxes of culture studies nowadays that despite the ever-increasing integration of the media culture into classrooms and seminars, and despite an impressive body of critical work on film, some of the most significant works of video culture remain untheorized, underappreciated, or simply ignored by media critics and cultural theorists. Strangely enough, this is not because the works in question suffer from artistic obscurity or commercial failure. The paucity of critical literature dealing with Patrick McGoohan's masterpiece, *The Prisoner* (1967), Krzysztof Kieslowski's *Decalogue* (1988), Hideaki Anno's epochal anime *Evangelion* (1995), and the 3D video games such as Quake and Half Life currently revolutionizing the Web culture stands in marked contrast to the extraordinary enthusiasm of audiences, artists, and culture workers themselves for all these things. This enthusiasm is by no means the product of some dubious marketing blitz but testifies to one of the most intriguing aspects of video culture, its bedrock plebianism. As we shall see, the greatest video works combine the aesthetic power and complexity of the twentieth-century modernisms with the popular appeal and revolutionary panache of the great eighteenth- and nineteenth-century realisms.

Much of the difficulty, to be sure, lies in the quicksilver nature of video as a field. Spawned in the late 1960s out of the meteorite impact of the counterculture—or what in retrospect could be defined as the unexpected collision of auteur cinema, late modernist theater, and television broadcasting—video has migrated from the film screen and TV set to the personal computer and the Web at a dizzying rate. The speed of video's evolutionary clock is matched perhaps only by the rapidity of its internal metabolism, which teleports endless quantities of images, sound tracks, and scripts across a wider and wider range of technological platforms. All this creates a number of unique hurdles for would-be critics. For one thing, theorists have to be familiar with a far broader array of cultural technologies than the concert, record, and film audiences of yore ever had to cope with. For another, video culture is really and truly multinational, in terms of its canon of aesthetic forms and its specific visual, acoustic, and scripted content. Whereas the most characteristic aesthetic form of the epoch of monopoly capitalism, the national cinema, was dominated by a relatively narrow range of American

and Western European studios, advertisers, broadcasters, and stars, and an
equally limited range of cultural forms (the symbolic landscapes of the Western, the national character systems of the war movie, the monopoly-era gender codes of the private eye and detective thriller, the scriptwriting innovations of the screwball comedy, etc.), video culture draws on a much larger
library of mediatic narratives, which circulate across the length and breadth
of the world system. To read video works means to read multinationally or,
more precisely, to read the patterns of multinational history encoded in the
work of art. This is not a license, to be sure, to write off or ignore the levels
of the regional, national, or international. Rather, to paraphrase Sartre, the
multinational is our untranscendable horizon of horizons, which qualifies
all these other levels as the local manifestations of some larger phenomenon.

If this is true, then why, one might well ask, wasn't multinational culture
on anyone's critical agenda during most of the 1990s? An intriguing shift in
critical discourse over the past two decades yields a significant clue. The
leitmotif of theory in the 1980s was unquestionably *postmodernism,* a term
that, whether you celebrated or deplored the thing, emphasized a certain
historical link to whatever modernism was (or wasn't) supposed to be. But
the buzzword of the 1990s, the term that could function as adjective, noun,
verb, and epithet all at once and instantly spark theory brawls worthy of an
on-line 3D death match, was *globalization.*[1] More is at stake here than the
upstaging of a primarily cultural concept by a crassly economic one. Postmodernism was invented in the specialized realm of literary theory, and it
only gradually conquered the sociological, political, and journalistic realms.
Globalization, on the other hand, required no such dissemination, for the
simple reason that the thing seemed to arrive everywhere, at all points of the
compass, all at once.

This suggests that the real weakness of cultural theory in the 1980s was
not its inability to diagnose the dominant economic, political, or cultural
logics of the era, for example, monetarism, Thatcherism, and postmodernism. Rather, it lacked a comparative metric capable of triangulating between
all these things—that is to say, a genuine concept of multinational capitalism.
Nor, in fairness to the critics, was creating such a metric a simple task in the
era of the cold war. Probably the only thinker of note to take the notion of
multinational capitalism seriously was Theodor Adorno, whose very complicated concept of the "total system" was largely ignored by the postmod-
ernists, with the signal exception of Fredric Jameson, who hit the nail on the
head by famously proclaiming Adorno to be the "thinker of the Nineties"
in *Late Marxism.*

One of the main subtexts of this book will be that Adorno is indispensable to contemporary culture theory, only not in the way this is usually thought of, that is, in terms of the Frankfurt School's denunciation of the culture industry and commitment to early-twentieth-century Central European modernisms (the span from Kafka and Klee to the music of the Second Viennese School). One of Adorno's most telling points was that the Eastern and Western blocs had long ago become two sides of the same coin and that the job of intellectuals was not to make false choices about which set of power elites to swear fealty to but to resist cold war tyranny on both sides of the Berlin Wall: to try, in short, to create truly democratic and humane alternatives on a global scale. Probably his greatest contribution to this project was the 1966 *Negative Dialectics,* an epochal intellectual bequest to the critics of the future. The central achievement of this text was to create the world's first concept of multinational form, or what Adorno called the constellation. These were a kind of trail or legible script created by the historical process. The job of theory was therefore to map out, interpret, or otherwise decode these scripts, thereby opening up a space for new types of praxis and new types of theory alike.

To see how this works in practice, consider the striking fact that even the most compelling media critiques of the late twentieth century—for instance, Fredric Jameson's *Signatures of the Visible* and Laura Mulvey's *Visual and Other Pleasures*—are limited to a very narrowly defined constellation. Specifically, they define video in terms of a neonational set of media tropes, micropolitical issues, or interpretive viewing positions, linked to various international networks of dissemination (CNN or MTV, the feminist music video, the Fourth World documentary, and so forth). The upshot is Jameson's famous definition of video as the depthless, hallucinatory rush of images, shorn of their national and international significations. This is a fine exegesis of that early 1980s science fiction cinema typified by Ridley Scott's *Blade Runner,* but tells us very little about the achievements of a William Gibson or Hideaki Anno.

That said, the conclusion of Jameson's 1991 *Postmodernism* offers an indispensable set of guidelines for a future theory of video. The depressing and demoralizing reality of multinational capital, Jameson tells us, is both true and untrue, both ruthless demystification and rampant ideology. As demystification, it is socially necessary appearance, the mere reiteration of our individual helplessness in the face of the vast, almost incomprehensible networks of global capital. Yet as ideology, it is an equally necessary resistance and ultimately the remobilizing injunction to create a new kind of cognitive mapping or subjective consciousness of the world system. This cognitive mapping can be thought of as the ideological equivalent of open source software, a set of theoretical models capable not only of hacking into the total system that surrounds us but also generating new forms of collective consciousness and multinational solidarity. It goes without saying that such models are neither prefabricated interpretations handed down by self-appointed central committees, nor the spam-infested blurbs of marketing bureaus, but are simply tools that each local user must reappropriate, rethink, and redeploy in their own unique way. Above all, Jameson takes a page from Adorno by insisting that we can only think *against* the total system to the extent we are willing to think *through* it. The mote in our own eye, wrote Adorno in *Minima Moralia,* is the best magnifying glass.[2] As we shall see, the greatest works of video are very much the mediatic mote in the basilisk eye of the information age.

Video and Interpretation   1

Before defining what video is, it's worth taking a moment to define what it is not. For starters, video is not simply the flickering play of random images or the televised reproduction of cinematic forms. Rather, it draws its aesthetic content from a vast multinational reservoir of icons, scripts, sound tracks, sound bites, and performances, each of which requires the most careful critical analysis. Second, video's apparent simplicity conceals enormous complexity. The iridescent surfaces, ingenious scripts, and user-friendly icons of the greatest works of video pack an astonishing amount of data into the smallest and most portable of aesthetic forms—forms that require, in turn, no less agile methods of interpretation and decoding. This is probably most obvious to those of us who teach in the university classroom and discover, to our chagrin, that our youngest students can swim effortlessly through the sort of hurricane-force media surf capable of shipwrecking a platoon of Ph.D. candidates. Still, it's worth stressing that video works are a deeply plebeian and democratic art form. Designed for maximum accessibility to a multinational audience, they display many of the best features of the global aesthetic commodities they both occasionally mimic and savagely critique: flexibility, ease of use, and sheer entertainment value.

Most of all, video culture is part and parcel of a globe-straddling consumer culture teeming with multinational contradictions. However stupefying and mind-numbing specific aspects of the consumer culture may be, multinational culture as a whole presupposes a remarkable amount of collective cultural labor, everywhere from the childhood sports scrimmage to the World Cup spectacular, and from the vast textual overproduction of email and listservs to the public domain freeware powering the server farms, hypertext documents, and telecom protocols of the Web. Where shoppers once distinguished between nineteenth-century family trademarks or waded through twentieth-century corporate acronyms, consumers nowadays confront the commodity form through plastic shells brimming with multinational icons, symbols, and data of all kinds. Browsing through this information has become both a necessary survival skill in the late capitalist marketplace and one of its most signal (if signally double-edged) pleasures.

To bring the market into the discussion, however, immediately raises some thorny questions about what role video plays in that marketplace and whether it is even permissible to speak of a truly global media culture, given the horrific social, political, and economic disparities of the present era. According to the World Bank's Year 2000 development report, as of 1998 the average rate of TV ownership in low-income countries was 76 TV sets per 1,000 people, whereas the comparable figures for middle-income and high-income countries were 257 and 567, respectively, suggesting an unprecedented expansion of TV viewership around the globe. To paraphrase the famous slogan of the 1960s, for the first time in human history, the whole world really *is* watching. On the other hand, the same report reveals that most human beings on the planet can only dream of owning a telephone, let alone a computer or an ISP connection; billions must survive on less than two dollars a day, and they lack the most rudimentary access to health care, employment, housing, and clean water.[1]

Just because the technomillennial hype of the wiring of the planet is wildly overblown, however, is not a license to write off the concept as a mere media stunt or passing craze. Globalization may be kilometers wide and only millimeters deep, but those few millimeters are packed with the densest socioeconomic circuitry imaginable. The World Bank's own data prove, beyond the shadow of a doubt, that the end of the cold war has brought not prosperity for all but a pitiless economic struggle for pole position on the food chain of information capitalism. The neoliberalism and neocolonialism of the 1990s are the direct heir of the Manchester liberalism and colonialism of the 1890s, the only difference being that whereas Victorian rentiers extracted their Imperial textile rents from the labor of the Great Unwashed, their postmodern analogues on Wall Street speculate on the viewing rents of the Great Unwatched. The global in its most pejorative, polemical sense is simply the word we use to describe the meat hook realities of this struggle, namely, the hideous swathe of social and ecological destruction spawned by flagrantly ill advised IMF structural adjustment packages, toxic World Bank lending practices, all-around neoliberal deregulation across the planet, and the corresponding enrichment of select North American, East Asian, and EU business interests.[2]

We will argue that video culture at its radical best is far more than just an urgent corrective on the global; it is the meditation and self-critical reflection upon such. Itself the site of truly planetary political and social conflicts, video culture is also the staging grounds for new forms of multinational solidarity and community, being reinvented on a daily basis. The Ur-form of this process can be traced back to the micropolitical movements of the 1980s, when groups such as Amnesty International and Greenpeace discovered that local struggles against polluters and human rights abusers could not really be separated from the systemic struggle against globe-trotting oil, timber, and mining companies and neocomprador governments under the thumb of IMF neoliberalism. One of the most memorable video images of the 1980s, for instance, was a satellite photo graphically illustrating the annihilation of the Brazilian rain forest by cattle ranchers; the local had gone irrevocably global. By the 1990s, this process was accompanied by its logical and complementary corollary, the localization of global issues—something visible everywhere from free trade deals administered on behalf of the supply chains of multinational corporations (hereafter referred to as "multis") to the creation of transnational networks of trade unions, and from the packs of well-heeled corporate lobbyists prowling the corridors of Washington, D.C., to the citizens' movements, trade unions, and peasant associations fighting against ecologically toxic and economically wasteful World Bank–financed dam projects in rural India.

Our own version of the local and global, adapted specifically for the field of video, will be the micrological and the geopolitical. The micrology is borrowed wholesale from Theodor Adorno's negative dialectics, a set of concepts designed to locate the smallest gaps, fissures, and nonidentities buried within commodities, works of art, ideological formations, or what have you in order to map the totalizing dynamics of late capitalism as a whole.[3] Geopolitics is taken from Jameson's notion of the geopolitical aesthetic of cinema, which is deployed here in the context of the dissolution of the cold war power blocs and the rise of a different configuration of power blocs and economies in their stead (a polite synonym for the decline of the Pax Americana and the rise of the European Union and East Asia). One needs nanometric lenses to read the cosmological constellations of video, so to speak, and a theory of constellations in order to properly calibrate those lenses.

The rise of video accompanied another significant event worth exploring in some detail, namely, the globalization of cultural theory generally. This is closely connected to the rise of a multinational theory market, not to mention the institutional hothouse of the post–World War II university system in which the theory market emerged. Pierre Bourdieu's *Homo Academicus* has blazed an impressive new trail here, by outlining in compelling detail how the specific contradictions of a massively expanding French university system generated the sociological basis for the May 1968 uprising, uniquely catalyzing the specific mind-sets, life histories, and psychological affiliations by which that uprising was concretely lived, felt, and rhetorically justified (or symbolically repudiated). Rather than attempting to single out one over-riding element—say, the economic—as the "meaning" or fundamental cause of May 1968, Bourdieu asks that we think through the economic, the political, and the psychological all at once. The historical event functions, in essence, very much like Adorno's notion of the constellation, effectively mediating between the objective set of social relations and symbolic capitals (what Bourdieu terms the field), and the subjective set of positions, position taking, and strategic maneuvers in that field (the Bourdieusian habitus). Just as each field is in constant motion, as various schools, class fractions, or aesthetic formations compete for internal forms of symbolic capital, status, and prestige as well as external position vis-à-vis other fields, so too does each habitus offer a range of dynamic positions and possibilities, as individuals, groups, or institutions ascend or descend in the competitive hierarchy, grabbing or relinquishing market share as best they can.[4] The point isn't to denounce the grimy realities of competition or the existence of the theory market per se, but to ask why they exist, to analyze how they work, and to invent ways they might be changed for the better (by increasing public access to the field in question, greater solidarity and cooperative ventures in lieu of ruinous competition, and so forth).

Abstract as all this sounds, Bourdieu's work will be enormously helpful to us in the next chapter, which will take the position that Patrick McGoohan's series *The Prisoner* was to the national mass media very much what May 1968 was in the field of national politics: the zero hour of the multinational. But for now, we need to return to the question of theory and ask some hard questions about the role of the theory market in the post-1968 period—the trajectory from the theory booms of the 1970s and 1980s to the theory bust of the 1990s. Although a full explication of all the factors involved would require a book in its own right, two general features of the process need to be mentioned here. First, there is a powerful element of social geography at work in the theory market: The Francophone thinkers (Pierre Bourdieu, Jacques Derrida, Michel Foucault, Julia Kristeva, and Jacques Lacan, to name just a few) were very much concerned with discursive issues, that is to say, the mediatization of the French state and the emergence of the European Union. By contrast, the leading North American thinkers (Fredric Jameson, Judith Butler, Eve Sedgewick, Gayatri Spivak, and others) were much more attuned to the cultural sphere, particularly the politics of the media culture and Wall Street neoliberalism, that is, the ideology of global finance capitalism.

Second, there is no question but that the speculative drive of the post-structuralisms and postmodernisms harmonized, on some deep level, with the real-life financial speculations of Wall Street. At their best, the post-modernisms were the critical meditation and reflection upon those specu-lations (as with Jameson's classic essay on postmodernism). At their worst, they were little more than the media chatter of academic superstars shielded from the grim realities of economic austerity, skyrocketing tuition, and ram-pant privatization—realities that had begun to undercut the very existence of autonomous national literary, philosophical, and cultural departments, as tenured and full-time positions were slashed to make way for vast pools of contingent and adjunct academic workers.

The culture workers of the 1990s were thus confronted with an unprec-edented contradiction: While the total stock of conceptual and theoretical capital in their specialized fields kept right on increasing, each person's spe-cific symbolic capital—that is, the advanced degree or tenure-track univer-sity position—was being devalued, privatized, or downsized out of existence. The upshot was a phase of excruciating personal demoralization and dis-content, followed by the sweeping repoliticization of the cultural field, vis-ible everywhere from a remarkable upsurge in graduate employee and fac-ulty unionism (involving, among other things, the establishment of grad unions throughout the University of California system) to new and interest-ing work in media studies, postcolonial studies, and comparative literature. Suddenly, the most obscure zones of cultural theory had shockingly relevant things to say about the marketization of the planet, the rise of media multis like AOL Time Warner, Sony, and Bertelsmann, and the blossoming media cultures of the European Union and a rapidly integrating East Asian polity. In classic Marxian fashion, the marketization of the university forced the toilers of academe to construct zones of extra-academic solidarity, in a man-ner similar to that of the programmers and technicians of the information culture, who struck back against the pernicious greed and privatizing ma-nia of the silicon rentiers by creating the electronic commons of open source software and the Web.

This is why any theory of video culture has to do more than simply take the realities of economic and social polarization seriously. To really do its job, it also has to touch base with the ways in which people are creatively rethinking or otherwise resisting that polarization, by means of a range of covert and overt solidarities. As Adorno would have put it, gloomy denun-ciations of the totally mediated society are not gloomy—or mediated—enough. This, of course, is to defer to Adorno's invaluable definition of the total system as a totality that is never at rest: It is dynamic, and it *moves* in multiple and contradictory directions (not all of which are progressive, but not all of which are regressive, either). Just as solidarity cannot be simply imposed from without or ordained by fiat, but emerges out of the complex interactions of class consciousness, identity politics, and legislative and juridical struggles, neither can theory peremptorily exempt itself from its own analyses or wall itself off from whatever it is attempting to investigate. Rather, it must grapple with the messy micrological resistances and uneven geopolitical solidarities of the contemporary world system, both accessing the global history buried in local forms as well as doing justice to the localized content bound up in global forms. To paraphrase Adorno once more, cultural theory need not privilege itself over cultural praxis, any more than the latter has priority over the former; rather, each is the necessary and indispensable corrective on the other.[5] Theory must learn, in order to teach.

There is no more striking confirmation of Adorno's insight than the literature on one of the most innovative subcategories of video of them all, namely, the aesthetics of the Web. There has been a tidal wave of books, reports, and articles on cyberculture, both in the mainstream business press and in academia. But one cannot help but notice that the first book-length study of video games to do justice to its subject, Steven Poole's excellent *Trigger Happy*, appeared in 2000—more than thirty-five years after the very first video games were written by minicomputer programmers, and fifteen years after video games became a multibillion dollar industry, with revenues rivaling those of TV and film. More is at work here than the usual time lag between the emergence of a work of art and its critical reception or canonization (centuries in the case of the novel, decades in the case of film). Rather, the field of Web aesthetics is only mirroring a much broader set of social tendencies, namely, the all-pervading influence of a Wall Street culture that favors speculative frenzies of form over the production of content. At the peak of the Wall Street bubble of the 1990s, the stock market value of high-tech companies—that is, their speculative or potential value twenty and thirty years down the road—was inflated wildly beyond their actual revenues (let alone minor details such as profits).

All too many accounts of the media culture in the 1990s suffer from a similar fetishism, by overvaluing the dissemination of music, images, or other signifiers at the expense of what is actually being transmitted. In the musical field, this has resulted in countless analyses of how Madonna, MTV, or the latest VJ cites or samples auteur film, rhythm and blues, and funk music, that is to say, the video marketing of music, at the expense of anything like musical content.[6] Something similar is at work in all too many analyses of the global news media, which tend to confuse the video clips of the uprisings, rebellions, and revolutions of Eastern Europe and Southeast Asia rebroadcast by the mass media with the underground networks of local and regional media cultures in those regions that spurred those rebellions in the first place (what could be called the cybersamizdat of media artists such as Poland's Andrzej Wajda, the Czech Republic's Jan Svankmajer, China's Yimou Zhang, and countless others).

That said, contemporary media theorists such as Michael Parenti, Ben Bagdikian, and Robert McChesney have done a commendable job of critiquing the ownership structures of the media, the relentless concentration of media outlets, the gutting of U.S. public television and radio, and the fire sale of the radio spectrum to well-heeled media multis. What we have been lacking, however, is a theory of how video works resist the dictates of the media business around them, on the immanent level of aesthetic content. And resist they do, clawing, scratching, and biting for their own semiautonomous space, everywhere from pointed satires of multinational media executives (the malevolent president in *Fall Out,* the final episode of *The Prisoner*) to the creative reappropriation of marginalized or peripheral aesthetic forms (science fiction, fantasy, and horror narratives) evident in the best Japanese anime.

Probably the best way of grasping the problem is to highlight video's emergence in the late 1960s from its constituent national and international predecessors, most notably cinema. Ella Shohat and Robert Stam offer this intriguing meditation on the subject:

> Contemporary video and computer technologies facilitate media jujitsu. Instead of an "esthetic of hunger," video-makers can deploy a kind of cybernetic minimalism, achieving maximum beauty and effect for minimum expense. Video switches allow the screen to be split, divided horizontally or vertically with wipes and inserts. Keys, chroma-keys, mattes and fader bars, along with computer graphics, multiply audiovisual possibilities for fracture, rupture, polyphony. An electronic "quilting" can weave together sounds and images in ways that break with linear character-centered narrative. In such texts, multiple images can be "hung" on the screen like so many paintings in a gallery, obliging spectators to choose which image to contemplate, without losing themselves in any single image. All the conventional decorum of dominant narrative cinema—eyeline matches, position matches, the 30 degree rule, cutaway shots—is superseded by proliferating polysemy.[7]

The insight into the multilayered nature of video works, heavily mediated by a multinational technological matrix, is well taken, but the recourse to the trope of the gallery of paintings is problematic for two reasons. First, video images do not directly invoke filmic space in that sense, any more than film directly invokes painted or photographic space; rather, they occupy what might be called informatic space—most apparent in the graphics interface of the average home computer, the framing techniques of the news broadcast, or the on-screen box score of the sports event. Second, the crucial question of how one aesthetic mediation can negate or otherwise turn the tables on another is forestalled by the notion of "polysemy," that is to say, a formalized aesthetics or semiotics of the rupture or break, which never quite rises to its (latent) multinational content. Put another way, Shohat and Stam are outlining a theory of national cinematic forms, whereas the field of video is inherently multinational and thus requires a rather different set of critical instruments.

We will suggest that any account of multinational content must deal with the fundamental reality of multinational consumerism, in its broadest sense as a source of narratives of all kinds. In contrast to the great films of high modernism, which combed through mass-cultural subgenres such as the murder mystery, the romantic melodrama, the adventure thriller, and the costume epic for their raw materials, the earliest video sequences cycle through a much broader array of noncinematic visual forms and genres. Some of the most memorable protovideo clips in the films of the late 1960s, for example, mobilize the specific visual forms pioneered by that decade—the countercultural street poster, the graffiti tag or protest slogan, and of course the earliest video games—against the narrative machinery of the Hollywood blockbuster. In the case of the Western, the obvious example is Sergio Leone's *The Good, the Bad, and the Ugly,* with its thinly disguised allegories of bureaucratization, the crucial writing of names that unlocks the secret of the buried gold (narratives of credit accumulation, rather than land accumulation), and the stylized close-ups of the gunfighters that displace the panoramic shoot-out. Kubrick's *2001* did something similar vis-à-vis the visual forms of the cold war space opera: thus the poignant scene of televisual mail, the suggestive span from the hand-drawn sketch that an astronaut displays to the computer HAL to the glowing, disembodied circuit maps the astronauts later scan for faults, and of course the false-color panoramas and close shots of the astronaut's faceshield during the celebrated psychedelic sequence.

During the 1970s, video techniques began to break out of the cinematic forms in which they had emerged, by constructing their own freestanding framing and editing techniques. From a narrowly technological standpoint, one could easily assume that the crucial influence here was the emergence of the VCR, invented by Ampex all the way back in 1956 and commercialized by Sony in 1965. In reality, models affordable to the average First World consumer—as well as a corresponding infrastructure of videocassette rental stores—did not arrive until the late 1970s. What this meant was that the major visual innovations of early video did not materialize in the field of videotaped material per se, but rather in those marginalized cultural zones of cinema excluded, for whatever reason, from the Hollywood studio system. Two of the most striking examples of this dialectic are the Hong Kong films of the late 1960s and 1970s, typified by innovative directors such as Zhang Che and Lau Kar-leong and the emergence of global superstars like Bruce Lee and Jackie Chan, and the low-budget U.S. horror film whose greatest expression was Tobe Hooper's classic *Texas Chain Saw Massacre.*

As Stephen Teo points out, the Hong Kong film industry pioneered the use of extended editing techniques for quite pragmatic reasons—namely, to make up for tiny special effects budgets, overworked production crews, and short production runs.[8] The result was a quantum leap in framing techniques, something most obvious in the multiple tight shots of the martial arts contest, capable of either shrinking down the panoramic space of the Western into a kinetic field of moving objects or else telescoping small spaces into dramatically larger ones, via stylized combat sequences and slow-motion stunts. By contrast, Hooper's shot techniques radically accelerated or decelerated the flow of time, most notably in the use of chase sequences and the twin themes of a terrifying bodily incarceration (most notoriously, the scene where the video work symbolically "watches" the modernist horror film, as when we are forced to watch someone forced to watch *someone else* being carved up by Leatherface) and exhilarating escapes (hinted at by the close shots of Sally's eye, juxtaposed against the moon, and sealed by the concluding reverse tracking shot of Sally aboard the fleeing truck, reflexively realizing her liberation).

Although the sheer visual energy of the Hong Kong films certainly exceeds anything found in the toolkit of the horror film, it is significant that the latter manages to compensate by much more effective use of the sound track (something that can be traced back to the trademark shock theme of Hitchcock's *Psycho,* and forwards to the electrifying sound track of Kubrick's *The Shining*). This is the genesis of *Texas Chain Saw*'s clattering machines, sputtering engines, and, of course, the sussurating chain saw, that household item of consumer technology that gruesomely consumes its erstwhile consumers. Put another way, where the Hong Kong films answered for a lack of expensive scenery and set designs with ingenious stunts and rapid editing techniques, the horror film answered for a lack of studio musicians and theme music with a bone-jarring, technological sound track, with profound affinities to the acoustic palette of 1970s punk rock.

In fact, the affinity between the horror film and punk rock runs much deeper than one might think. The horror film showcased downscaled or proletarianized teenagers and students, who experienced the freezing shock of economic austerity as low-wage workers in suburban malls and convenience stores rather than as apprentices in factories or mines. Punk rock was similarly scripted by London's service-sector working class, historically excluded from the counterculture by deindustrialization and Thatcherism. Both explicitly turned the logic of the media culture against itself, by politicizing not merely the production of culture but its networks of distribution and dissemination as well: Where horror films negated the special effects–laden Hollywood monster and occult blockbuster, punk rock repudiated a predatory record and concert industry. Finally, each almost single-handedly invented two of the most lucrative cultural niche markets of the 1980s, the slasher film and heavy metal music.

Such affinities tell us a great deal about why—and how—video works differ from cinematic ones. For starters, video works are clearly the product of a much more complex division of aesthetic labor. Whereas the filmic auteurs operated under any number of constraints, ranging from the technological dependence on live actors (or, in the case of animation, hand-drawn cels) and raw film stock to the economic dependence on Hollywood studios or national film agencies, video works can electronically sample, alter, or pastiche a vast library of prerecorded media. The price paid for this increase in complexity, however, is a much tighter degree of integration with the multinational media and consumer culture as a whole—something that has incalculable consequences for the vocation of cultural politics. Unlike film in the heyday of modernism, video does not have the option of what might be termed national-autarkic strategies of aesthetic development—the creation of specialized filmic languages or genres, ranging from the Soviet documentary montage to Italian neorealism, and from the Japanese samurai adventure to the American screwball comedy. This is because culture (defined as the sum of the tourist, media, entertainment, sports, and gaming industries) has become one of the biggest, fastest growing, and most multinational consumer markets of them all. The upshot is that the cultural politics of mobilization endemic to the modernist period, where the point was to persuade, shock, or otherwise bestir the audience to think and act on a monopoly-national level, has acceded to the cultural politics of interpretation, where the point is to get the audience to think and act multinationally. Put another way, whereas the filmic modernisms narrated the seismic conflicts of fascism, communism, and the New Deal in terms of one's allegiance or antipathy to a fairly restricted set of nation-states, national political parties, or corporate brand names, video is directly tied to the political conflicts of a genuinely global geopolity, that is, multinational states, political movements, and corporations.

To see how such an interpretive politics might work, one need look no further than the musical field of the 1970s. Two of the greatest sources of musical innovation in that decade were (1) the reggae compilations of Bob Marley and the Wailers (*Legend* and *Exodus*), which transformed Jamaican folk music, African American rock and roll, and the technologies of the electronic studio into the reggae dub; and (2) the Sex Pistols' stunning *Never Mind the Bollocks, Here's the Sex Pistols,* which retrofitted working-class blues and rock music with cutting-edge studio mixing and processing technology. Whatever their other differences, reggae and punk music were crucially dependent on their location in the world system for their lyric content: for Marley, the resistance movement of Rastafarianism, with its diasporic links back to the African fatherland and the African American and Jamaican communities scattered across North America and Britain; for Johnny Rotten, the Cockney accent, urban camaraderie, and volatile class-consciousness of the London proletariat. Each unites a radical neonational identity cut loose, exiled, or otherwise cast adrift from its traditional moorings in the traditional nation-state by means of a multinational musical palette, thereby creating a kind of "liberated zone" or space of postcolonial cultural solidarity with *other* neonational identities. Put another way, the Sex Pistols and Bob Marley set the musical materials of the First World working-class and Third World peasant liberation movements into motion toward one another, the former from postcolonial London and the latter from postcolonial Jamaica, thereby creating a genuinely multinational musical aesthetics.

Applying this insight to our previous discussion, it is therefore no accident that the Hong Kong films were spawned in a British colonial entrepot turned export-platform heavyweight, while *Texas Chain Saw Massacre* was produced as an independent film project in Austin, Texas, one of the leading university towns in the blossoming service-sector economy of the New South. In Hong Kong's case, the crucial elements here were (1) a displaced or otherwise deeply compromised Chinese national culture, (2) a dynamic and restless population of urban immigrants who experienced a massive economic boom but no corresponding political decolonization, and (3) direct access to the English-speaking film markets of the Chinese communities of the Pacific Rim. For the horror film, the key ingredients were clearly

(1) a displaced or otherwise compromised Southern culture located at some distance from Hollywood, (2) a dynamic and restless population of students at the University of Texas at Austin, during the transition from the great student and civil rights mobilizations of the 1960s to the micropolitics of the 1970s, and (3) direct access to the post-1968 youth market, in the form of the slasher film genre.

Now, at last, we can put all the pieces of the puzzle together. For just as the horror film is the visual analogue of the punk album, so too does reggae have a formal visual equivalent: nothing less than the space of postcolonial video. The obvious example here is Bruce Lee as the breakthrough Asian American superstar, who single-handedly blazed the trail for John Woo, Chow Yun-Fat, the Chinese Fifth Generation filmmakers, and countless other luminaries. But one could also point to Richard Roundtree and Mario van Peebles, who blasted open the door for the African American actors and directors of the future; or indeed the Polish "cinema of moral anxiety" of Wajda, Zanussi, and others, which achieved something similar for Eastern European media producers.

This suggests, in turn, that the great anticolonial and revolutionary films of the 1960s have more in common with the video works of the 1970s than is commonly presupposed. Both Gillo Pontecorvo's *Battle of Algiers* (1965) and Tomás Gutiérrez-Alea's *Memories of Underdevelopment* (1968) culminate in the collective spectacle of national mobilizations, wherein an urban space (the comprador city turned revolutionary citadel) is occupied by a new kind of micropolitics. This is closely linked to a revolutionary politics of gender, loosely aligned with a kind of Second Wave or juridical feminism: thus the women dressed in European garb smuggling weapons to the rebels in *Algiers,* or the love affair subplots of *Memories.* Each reappropriates the shot techniques, editing, and composition of the documentary, the existentialist-era thriller (especially film noir), and the newsreel, creating what amounts to the postcolonial version of telejournalism. The limits of this strategy were therefore the limits of telejournalism as a cultural form, or put another way, whereas telejournalism broadcasts the symbolic capital of the news announcers, broadcasters, executives, and news firms involved, its postcolonial reappropriation could be said to broadcast the symbolic capital of the national-revolutionary mass party or anticolonial movement to international markets.

During the 1960s, the latent antinomies of this strategy were not really an issue, thanks to the brutal power politics of the U.S. and Soviet national security states, which crushed or derailed fledgling democracies and nascent developmental states everywhere from Guatemala, Chile, and Vietnam to Czechoslovakia, Poland, and Hungary. By the 1970s, however, in the context

of political decolonization and the winding down of the cold war, this particular aesthetic solution was no longer a viable option. The experience of
the newly independent countries was especially bitter, as the relentless pressure of the world market transformed erstwhile revolutionary movements
and parties into cash machines for neocomprador elites, little better than the
colonists they once chased out. Political decolonization, in short, turned out
to be the flip side of electronic neocolonization.

The political stakes of this transformation are probably easiest to grasp
in the context of what is most dated in Alea and Pontecorvo's classics: This
is the trope of the existentialist urban intellectual, whose painful vacillation
between the high culture of the colonial metropole and the urgent demands
of the anticolonial resistance can be said to symbolize the desperate choices
of Third World nationalism and identity formation. The national intellectual thus incarnated a particular national identity politics in much the same
way that the national mass party embodied those broad coalitions of peas-
ants, agrarian workers, and urban comrades and intellectual sympathizers
who energized the national and anticolonial movements of the post–World
War II period. Each is an allegorical narrative designed to reorganize and
reconfigure a host of local, regional, and international narratives into a single
coherent code or set of ideologemes, or what amounts to the creation of a
national cultural currency, if you will, roughly analogous to the economic
kind. It is striking that the later, more radicalized works of Third World cinema (Ousmane Sembène in the 1970s, or Yimou Zhang in the 1980s) explicitly critique such codes, in what amounts to a nascent solidarity with that
strange new thing, the neocolonial proletariat spawned by capitalist neoliberalism and Communist industrialism alike. These are the residents of the
rapidly swelling favelas and shantytowns, who are as ruthlessly exploited and
politically marginalized by the postcolonial nation-state as the landless peas-
ants once were by the colonial authorities, but whose habitus is heavily in-
fluenced by First World consumer goods and media culture. Culturally
speaking, the vast migration from the farms to the factories in the Third
World did more than just broaden the base of urban culture. It also transformed the natural world into an object of aesthetic contemplation—most
famously, in the gorgeous outdoor panoramas and eroticized bodies of
Yimou Zhang's *Red Sorghum,* which fluoresce with the global energies unleashed by Chinese rural industrialization.

This immediately raises the question of how multinational class structures, ideologies, and identities relate to video culture. The simple answer
is that there *is* no simple answer here. As Adorno noted long ago, the proletariat is an object of domination in capitalist societies, a situation that can-

not be remedied by simply snapping one's fingers or issuing Party ukases. Rather, the consciousness of people who work for a living will be as varied as their modes of work and as complex as the division of labor itself, registering everything from the crassest xenophobia and consumerism to quite sophisticated scientific and cultural critiques (not to mention the ubiquitous micropolitics of gender, ethnic affiliation, and family structures). This is true even of those societies that notoriously claimed to have abolished class, such as the Communist regimes, which promulgated the ideology of proletarian rule while practicing the reality of autarkic proletarianization.

What differentiates the contemporary experience of class from anything in the past is the fact that, for the first time in human history, the majority of human beings on the planet live in cities and exist outside of the agrarian economy. Significant enclaves of rural and peasant culture do, of course, continue to exist, but they are far more tightly integrated with the urban centers of accumulation than ever before, something that has led to new types of popular mobilizations *against* formerly revolutionary one-party states and crossing all manner of national borders, everywhere from Ken Saro-wiwa and the Ogoni people in Nigeria to the Uw'e people of Colombia locked in struggle against Occidental Petroleum, and to the Zapatistas of southern Mexico. Urbanization also transformed the one-party state from within, spurring both its complete abolition (as in the case of the Eastern bloc) as well as its drastic modification. Thus in 1949, the Chinese Communists were the leading expropriators of the landlord class, while the Nationalists were its leading defenders; five decades later, both parties had evolved into astonishingly similar developmental technocracies.

Probably the best strategy here is to think of multinational class identity as a hazy, provisional habitus, locked into struggle with its more organized monopoly and national analogues, and located in a multinational cultural field littered with monopoly-national and neonational forms. This enables us to avoid overly simplistic questions about the immediate political stance of a given aesthetic work (for or against the Party, for or against neoliberalism), by grasping the fact of geopolitical location as a crucial structural feature of video culture. The leading cultural works of postcolonial video, for example, had to sublate the broadcasting monopoly and cinematic heritage of the one-party state and Third World nationalism alike in order to create their own cultural space. The rather different location of the earliest First World video works, situated in the core economies of consumer capitalism, dictated a rather different strategy; but to see how different, we need to turn to Patrick McGoohan's classic series, *The Prisoner*.

Mapping the Global Village   2

> For all the pleasure his fans have given him, Schulz is a prisoner of his
> fame as well. He worries some about the lunatics who sometimes stalk
> celebrities. "Sometimes I'll be walking across the parking lot of the
> shopping mall and I'll think about how easy it would be for somebody to
> get at me. Or I'll think about a white van with men with machine guns
> jumping out the back. For some reason, it's always a white van."
>
> —Rheta Grimsley Johnson,
> *Good Grief! The Story of Charles M. Schulz*

Paranoia, white vans, and beneficent technologies of consumption and distribution that turn out to be the mask of an omnipresent, seething cauldron
of violence. This terrifying glimpse into the heart of the Pax Americana's
imperial darkness is surely the last thing one would ever expect from the
mild-mannered Charles Schulz, creator of the *Peanuts* comic strip and one
of the most underappreciated artists of the 1960s. But as Johnson's biogra-
phy reveals, the cartoonist was in exactly the right position to know what he
was talking about. As a canny artist-entrepreneur who parlayed a daily comic
strip into an enormously lucrative global merchandising empire, Schulz was
uniquely qualified to register the deep-seated social contradictions of 1960s
consumerism. On a certain level, Schulz's paranoia bespeaks a kind of over-
compensation for the subjective anomie of the new spaces of suburban consumption in the 1960s, or what Sartre would diagnose as the class aversion
to the swarming multiplicity of white service vans and the electricians, car-
penters, and postal and delivery workers who drive them.

As we shall see, white vans, the agents who operate them, and the politics of consumerism are all key components of Patrick McGoohan's classic
1967 TV series, *The Prisoner,* which at first glance seems to be nothing more
than a spy thriller with a twist: Instead of trying to break into the villain's
fortress to uncover hidden secrets, the mysterious No. 6, protagonist of the
series, is trying to escape from a mysterious Village with his mind (and secrets) intact. Still, one might well ask, what on earth does the world of *Peanuts* have to do with the world of the Village, which is part psychedelic fable,
part paranoid thriller, part James Bond parody, but most of all a kind of

televisual theater worthy of Brecht and Genet—a theater that does not simply denounce suburbia, mass tourism, and the consumer society but reappropriates these things from the standpoint of a new and hitherto unknown politics of consumerism?

One would have to retrace the whole development of the comic strip, from its distant roots in the eighteenth-century engraving to the urban caricatures of the nineteenth-century mass periodicals, all the way to the surrealism of early Disney, and finally to George Herriman's high modernist *Krazy Kat,* in order to appreciate the true magnitude of Schulz's aesthetic achievement. Suffice to say that Schulz's greatest single contribution to the cartoon was to grasp the contradiction between an archaic set of existential coordinates (such as the biblical quotations of Linus, Charlie Brown's role as permanent antihero, and scattered but regular references to World War I, Beethoven, and other monuments of a vanished or neutralized modernism) and postmodern or multinational ones in a new kind of visual language. This is the genesis of Snoopy's smoothly rounded, bubblelike build, probably the single most memorable shape of the 1960s, all set against that Lacanian reservoir of the Symbolic, Snoopy's abstractive doghouse. Just as Snoopy's name is a significant mediatic pun in its own right, suggesting a harmless "snooping" or prying with secret affinities to the cold war spy thriller and the existential voyeur or film noir detective, it is surely not an accident that Snoopy's boon companion—that eternally wordless but constantly twittering bird, who zigzags through airspace with the gusto of Emily Dickinson's bee, and who looks like a miniaturized version of Snoopy—should be named Woodstock. But where Woodstock denotes the countercultural outer limit of Schulz's work, Snoopy resembles nothing so much as a freeform scansion of the design ethos of the refrigerators, washing machines, vacuum cleaners, and other household appliances of the 1960s consumer culture—the so-called "white goods" that replaced a feminized or household labor with electrical machines encased in white or off-white plastic shells of various kinds.

If this is even halfway to the mark, and Schulz is narrating the domestic mythology of early consumer society (something apparent in Snoopy's role-playing skits, which ingeniously reprise almost every professional-class activity or mediatic spectacle imaginable), then our white van might conceivably be related to quite another visual feature of the suburban household. This is nothing less than the ubiquitous off-white interiors and painted and plastic surfaces encasing the wiring, plumbing, ventilation, and other subsystems of the average house. It is as if these surfaces have been peeled off like a sticker and made over into an autonomous, three-dimensional construct in their own right, bristling with potential menace or, at the very least, the necessity of continual capital investments. What advertises itself as a stable, securely immutable interior turns out, in reality, to be just another exterior, requiring all sorts of bothersome maintenance and a knack for the do-it-yourself job.

Although this particular constellation of an anxiety-laden cold war consumerism and the nascent postmodernism of the comic strip no longer has much resonance for us today, in the full flood of the information age, the example sheds a significant light on the mass cultural moment of McGoohan's masterpiece. Whereas Schulz derived his visual materials from the American domestic sphere of the 1950s, and thus was able to articulate a 1960s consumerism well in advance of the actual thing (Snoopy's Joe Cool is not quite the leather-jacketed rocker but not yet the hippie college student), McGoohan will reappropriate one of the first genuine documents of the transnational media culture, namely, the TV spy serials and Bond blockbusters of the 1960s, and set them in motion toward the nascent counterculture. In fact, *The Prisoner* will go much further than simply reinventing the spy narrative as a psychedelic fable. The series inaugurates a veritable revolution in the fields of scriptwriting, set design, sound editing, and editing. Such technical innovations are more than matched by the amazing versatility and stellar quality of McGoohan's contributions; he was not only the main star of the series but also wrote and directed the more significant episodes, successfully bargained for its financing and distribution, and even recruited a truly stellar technical and support staff, including writers such as Terence Feely and co-stars such as Leo McKern. In stark contrast to Hitchcock's television series or Rod Serling's early 1960s *Twilight Zone*, which bespeak a cinematic specialization of labor still organized around the strict specialization of the functions of the writer, director, and actor (Hitchcock's lapidary comments and Serling's moralizing conclusions refrain from interfering with the plot at hand, however much they obviously would like to do so), McGoohan's position as executive producer of the series allowed him to employ a qualitatively new division of aesthetic labor, wherein the fields of visual production, distribution, and consumption begin to interact in new and surprising ways.

None of this would have been possible, to be sure, if McGoohan had not already built up an enormous store of personal and social capital in the TV business. Thanks to his starring role in the long-running and highly acclaimed series *Secret Agent* (originally titled *Danger Man* in the U.K. but renamed for U.S. distribution), he had the requisite experience and personal connections to launch his own project, hiring some of the best scriptwriters, directors, and actors of the era. Yet the true inspiration for *The Prisoner* was not so much McGoohan's position within the Anglo-Saxon culture industry per se, but the contradiction of the latter with the specific circumstances of his own specifically Irish identity, or what Bourdieu would term the clash of a neonational Irish habitus with an Anglo-Saxon cultural field.

McGoohan was born in New York City in 1928 to a family of recent Irish immigrants. They soon returned to their home country, possibly as a result of the Depression, though little biographical information is available here, and of course it is a significant clue in its own right that McGoohan has consistently refused to advertise his past or otherwise pander to the Hollywood publicity machine. McGoohan worked his way up the ladder of the Irish and British stage, and after playing bit parts in various films, he finally struck it rich in the then fairly new industry of television, catapulting virtually overnight into fame and fortune to become one of the highest paid actors of 1960s British television.

On the surface, such a career would seem to be none too extraordinary for the mass media. Sean Connery's ascent from bodybuilder to Bond superstar also leveraged a previously marginalized cultural form (the sports and fitness industries) in tandem with a no less marginalized neonational identity (nicely signified by Connery's Scotch burr), while the underrated mid-1960s American TV series *Get Smart* offers still another version of cultural upwards mobility: the rise of Mel Brooks from series scriptwriter to one of the all-time great comedy film directors.[1] What distinguishes McGoohan's trajectory so radically from either of these cases was the complicating presence of a third element, namely, the irreparable social and political divide between postcolonial Ireland, still culturally and economically subordinate to Britain, and the vibrant culture industry of a somnolent postmodern Britain, its decrepit industrial base fading in the heat of the American, Continental European, and East Asian competition.

Probably the closest equivalent to McGoohan's position was the situation of the African American artists of the late 1960s and the need to invent a multinational cultural praxis somehow able to evade the Scylla of a regressive neonationalism and the Charybis of a multinational consumerism. Certainly, one can argue that McGoohan catalyzed the invention of video in much the same way that Jimi Hendrix engineered the emergence of hip-hop. Whereas Hendrix reunited the deepest impulses of late jazz modernism with the mass cultural innovations of the rhythm and blues, and thus created the world's first multinational musical vocabulary, McGoohan fused the spy and adventure serial with the most progressive tendencies of Western European mediatic and theatrical modernism. This is a complicated way of saying that *The Prisoner* and, by extension, the dimension of scriptwriting in video generally owe a tremendous debt to the pioneering work of Ireland's greatest postcolonial playwright, Samuel Beckett.

It would not be an exaggeration to say that the original concept of McGoohan's series is, from the standpoint of form, basically *Endgame* starring 007. Certainly, in episodes such as "Once upon a Time," McGoohan will graciously acknowledge his predecessor in a number of ways, ranging from the wheelchair upon which No. 6 is rolled into No. 2's office, to the childhood toys and eerily exposed culture-industrial machinery of the Embryo Room. In terms of content, however, Beckett's influence is far more subtle, and consists less of any presumed similarities in set design or characterization—the windows and household objects of *Endgame* are not really analogous to McGoohan's television screens and household technologies, and the Village's number hierarchy is light-years away from Beckett's quasi-theological, punning surnames—than in the realm of the theatrical gesture.

Beckett's dialogues react allergically to the debased language of mainstream cinema not by simply proclaiming the impossibility of speech but by intermittently crystallizing around what truly cannot be spoken, rather like a series of snapshots of a self-acting machine tool. The gestural function of the plot functions as a set of repetitions whose exact tempo and execution can never be quite predicted in advance, rather like the early slapstick cinema of Chaplin, which compensated for the lack of a sound track by gestural improvisation. This is why Beckett's late modernism comes closest to postmodernism, surprisingly enough, not in the negation of the mise-en-scène per se, something that is better ascribed to the magnificent oeuvre of Heiner Müller's mature plays, but in its emancipation of the theatrical gesture via the stage improvisation: thus Watt's famous counting-stones, or the hilarious exchange of hats in *Waiting for Godot*. In so doing, Beckett extends the central insight of Brecht's epic theater, namely, the imperative of turning the aesthetic division of labor typical of monopoly capitalism against itself via the somatic vocabulary of the nascent consumer society (the stark visual contrasts of the A-effect demanding not a lesser effort from the actors but correspondingly more: The players become coproducers, cowriters and codesigners of the entire production), via the somatic vocabulary of the nascent consumer society. The wheelchair jaunt in *Endgame* already invokes the inner immobility of the fully automobilized society, in the same way that Hamm's unwieldy grapple gives a whole new meaning to the term *writer's block,* or, less humorously, the way the garbage cans signify the festering expanses of those gray-in-gray postwar cement blocks into which people were literally thrown away.

This is something *The Prisoner* will invoke not in the terms of a modernist culture of moving vehicles or commodities with visibly motorized parts but in an unmistakably postmodern one of information-processing commodities. In effect, McGoohan will relocate the function of theatrical gesture away from the specific consumer commodity or species of cultural capital at hand, such as the specific mass media, film genre, or theatrical citation, and toward the ensemble of mediatic effects that repackage or otherwise enclose the specific scene, in what amounts to a primordial video form. This is the moment we are asked to watch the process of watching, via those wall-sized video monitors and screens by which the Village's rulers attempt to keep tabs on No. 6 and the other inmates—a reflexivity that then generates its corresponding political content, as No. 6 gradually learns to derail this constant surveillance, by misleading or otherwise manipulating his would-be manipulators. Not the least brilliant aspect of the series is its steadfast refusal to speculate on whether the consumer culture drove the totalizing paranoia of the cold war, or whether cold war paranoia was itself merely the plutonium soft-shoe of the total theater of global consumerism. Rather, both of these social tendencies converge in a politics of information, as relayed by the stunning opening sequence or "tag" of the series, worth analyzing at some length.[2]

The very first shot we see is a thunderstorm gathering overhead, followed by a series of thunderclaps (the first in a series of ecological and meteorological symbols and metaphors) and then a vista of an open freeway. The thunder fades away, and we hear the Doppler effect whine of a passing overhead jet, our first explicitly transnational acoustic signifier. Finally McGoohan himself roars into view in a custom-built Lotus Seven (license plate KAR120C) in synchrony with another peal of thunder, while the superb theme music of the series (composed by studio artist Ron Grainer, renowned for writing the memorable synthesizer-charged musical opening for the *Doctor Who* science fiction series in 1963) rises up from the background. Whereas the opening sequence of the Bond films offset the silhouette of the business-suited secret agent with the famous opening bass theme derived from an African American R&B band, *The Prisoner* complements a series of peals of thunder with a Latin drumbeat, a much lighter, nimbler horn section, high-pitched marimbas, and an electrical harpsichord. The effect is one of extreme aural polarization, between a very low, dense set of bass registers and very high-pitched overtones, or what amounts to the negation of John Barry's superb musical scores for the Bond films, which typically deployed amplified big band and swing tropes (most notably, the use of blaring, overproduced trumpets) to signify the sexual swagger and military bluster of its hero.[3] Although we will have more to say about the role of the sound track later on, for now it should be noted that *The Prisoner* deploys a remarkably sophisticated set of aural coordinates that will, by the very end of the series, converge literally and figuratively with the musical palette of the counterculture.

The view then shifts to historic central London and the Parliament building, where McGoohan cruises to the underground parking lot of what is presumably a top secret government agency. After a determined stroll through a darkened passage, he opens a pair of double doors and tenders a letter to an official, while the sound track reverberates with a peal of thunder. This fascinating relocation of the exterior thunderstorm into an interior bureaucratic space turns out to be the prelude to his official resignation from some sort of top secret job. Deliciously, the official McGoohan is talking to is portrayed by George Markstein, the actual script editor with whom he had a real-world falling-out over the direction of the series. The office also contains two significant symbols that will acquire more and more meaning as the series progresses: a cup of tea on the desk and a map of the world on the wall. We also catch a glimpse of a computerized file cabinet where McGoohan's computer punch card (the highest of high tech in 1967) is stamped "Resigned" by the anonymous typewriter so beloved of the spy genre. Upon leaving the office, he drives to his apartment, tailed by a pair of agents. There he packs his belongings in preparation for what seems to be a vacation trip (the camera zooms in on a photo advertisement of a glorious tropical beach). At that moment the agents pump sleeping gas into his room, and McGoohan looks up briefly through the window at the visual equivalent of the jet engine we heard at the beginning of the opening tag. An array of glass skyscrapers tilts hazily in front of his eyes like the quintessential monuments to the postmodern they indeed are, before he loses consciousness.

This amazing conjunction between McGoohan's upturned, hooded glance and the blank, faceless glass boxes housing the multinational overlords of the global village—that primal political tocsin of the New Left from Prague to Peking, and from Mexico City to Chicago, captured as much by the memorable line, "The whole world is watching," as by the heady days of May 1968, when students and workers alike flashed to the insight that Gaullist France was a capitalist workhouse like any other on the planet—turns out to signify as well a significant rupture in the prevailing spy thriller narrative. This is the moment when McGoohan's character wakes up, opens the blinds, and discovers to his astonishment that he is in an exact replica of his room, located in the middle of a nameless, placeless Village. As the Bond series transformed scenic vistas and tourist locales from around the world into movie sets, McGoohan turned an actual resort hotel on the Welsh coast into the set for the entire series, ingeniously adopting what appears at first glance to be a quaintly medieval architecture to highlight the hyper-modern equipment and deadly power bureaucracies housed within. At the same time, the action-adventure sound track is replaced by a subtle, eerie, almost psychedelic background noise, or high-pitched overtones sounded randomly, while the following densely interpolated set of shots and dialogue takes place. (Note that each of the following scene changes occur during the previous spoken dialogue, resulting in a smooth, rhythmic cycling of images.) The spy movie turns into a protomorphic video:

> *Steel doors open to reveal No. 2's office situated in the Green Dome, a cavernous, high-tech bubble of steel girders and translucent glass panels; No. 2 sits in a revolving, black bubble-shaped chair at the center of the room.*
>
> NO. 6: Where am I?
>
> NO. 2: In the Village.
>
> NO. 6: What do you want?
>
> NO. 2: Information. *(Visuals cut to No. 6 walking across the main lawn of the Village.)*
>
> NO. 6: Whose side are you on?
>
> NO. 2: That would be telling. We want information. Information. Information. *(The scene cuts to No. 6 running across the sandy beach, attempting to escape.)*
>
> NO. 6: You won't get it. *(Scene cuts to an underwater sequence of air bubbles spawning the Village's main security device, the giant white security bubble called Rover [actually, a giant weather balloon]; we hear the bubbles as well as what sounds like scuba gear.)*
>
> NO. 2: By hook or by crook we will. *(Scene cuts to close-up of the new No. 2 [played by a different actor in almost every episode]).*
>
> NO. 6: Who are you? *(The scene cuts to No. 2 watching Rover hunt down and trap NO. 6 on the beach on a giant movie screen, which is the other notable feature of NO. 2's office; we also see a control panel and three upright objects on the desk, which turn out to be handheld mobile phones.)*
>
> NO. 2: The new No. 2.
>
> NO. 6: Who is No. 1? *(The scene cuts to the central mechanical eye of the Control Room, a clearly Expressionist trope, and pans back to reveal another bubble-room, this one with strange machines, a central, rotating camera device, and extensive wall maps.)*
>
> NO. 2: You are No. 6.

NO. 6: I am not a number. I am a free man! *(The scene cuts to a shot of No. 6 on the beach; the camera alternately pans far back and zooms in, silhouetting McGoohan as he raises his fist to the sky in defiance. Cynical laughter from No. 2.)*

This celebrated three-minute sequence, one of the great video productions of all time, disproves the widespread fallacy that video amounts to the mere acceleration of cinematic images, whose sheer overproduction elides the function of criticism altogether (what Jameson described elsewhere as postmodernism's depthless rush of images). In reality, video works involve a significant compression and abstraction of the image, and the displacement of photographic coordinates or cinematic tropes (collages of photographs) by a heterogenous set of viewing levels or windows (collages of cinema, if you will). The tag scene of the open road, for example, which we at first expect to highlight a typical automotive panorama, flashes by so quickly that the eye cannot fix on any specific object and is forced to lock onto the close-up of McGoohan behind the wheel, the wind roaring in his face. Where Stanley Kubrick's *2001* spends two and a half hours making the transition from the modernist trope of the moving or flying vehicle to the postmodern one of mobile environments (thus the psychedelic conclusion, which elides the spacecraft altogether and counterpoints the astronaut's dazed expression with the celestial light show), *The Prisoner* accomplishes the same feat in roughly two and a half seconds. The same is true of the underground spy agency, where the shots of McGoohan's car are upstaged by a series of increasingly faster-paced close-ups; thus the superficially personal explosion of the resignation scene turns out to herald the information age close-up of the typewriter X-ing out McGoohan's photo (the photo is McGoohan's very own, real-life publicity shot from the *Danger Man* series!) or the chase scenes replayed on No. 2's monitor in the above quotation, which illustrate No. 6's ceaseless escape attempts and invariable recapture by Rover. Over and over again, kinetic or movement-based narratives turn out to be merely a pretext or blind for the far more interesting and important story of the production, delivery, and consumption of information.

The question then arises as to why McGoohan chooses to divide the title tag from the credits tag as definitively as he does. A moment's thought will show that the four visual spaces of the title tag—the open road, London, the spy agency, and No. 6's residence—are not just spaces but also specific viewpoints (the panorama, the aerial shot, the underground shot, and the scene from the window). What McGoohan is doing, in effect, is transforming these national and international tropes into the multinational ones of the surveillance screen, the space of the Village, the interior of the Control Room, and of course, No. 2's office in the Green Dome, respectively. What makes the effect even more stunning is the fact that, contrary to the first impressions of the casual viewer, the Village is by no means a medieval landmark but is in fact the Portmeirion Hotel, a famous resort in Penrhyndeudraeth, North Wales. Constructed in 1926 by renowned architect Sir Clough Williams-Ellis, Portmeirion is characterized by a wide-ranging ensemble of styles and periods, and certainly there is something deeply provocative about staging the pitiless power struggles of the Village not in some secret base or mountaintop fortress, or even in the swanky hotels or tourist monuments favored by the Bond films, but in a quirky resort that might be said to be the *avant la lettre* emblem of postmodern pastiche.

In fact, Portmeirion will set two intriguing visual precedents for the series: first, a sense of teeming visual overproduction or scenic density that is too compartmentalized to be a traditional urban space, but which is also too explicitly historical and refers to altogether too many architectural periods to be a suburban one; second, the displacement of the automotive registers of the spy thriller by battery-powered white electrical carts, bubble-shaped helicopters, and of course sheer walking. If the Village seems closer to the jumbled heterogeneity of the Second and Third World favela than to Jameson's great example of postmodernism, the Bonaventura Hotel, this is only because the latter is primarily about an internalized architecture, the exotic innerspace of the people-moving lifts and shrubbery-lined atrium, or what amounts to the transplanted aesthetic of the enclosed shopping mall as opposed to the walkable outdoor arcades of metropolitan Europe or the street festivals of Japan. The true social model for the Village would thus be a kind of elite favela, or a zone where the utopia of unlimited leisure time advertised by late capitalism is, for some reason, turned into a hideous compulsion. In the context of the 1960s, this might refer to the apparatus of psychiatric wards, mental hospitals, and hormone injections by which both cold war power blocs disciplined their political and sexual dissidents; it could also, as in the case of the Old People's Home highlighted in "Arrival," refer to that newly expanded population of pensioners created by the welfare state and gradually increasing life spans, which has not yet organized itself into a conscious political or cultural bloc.

All this is closely connected with another profound absence in the series: the utter lack of the psychological or familial registers still faintly visible in the existential and mystery thrillers, most typically via the dynamics of voyeurism and the Hitchcockian fetish of juridical evidence. Yet the Village is ruled neither by the villainous father figures of the action-adventure drama nor by the national agencies of the cold war, nor by any combination of these things (as with the invariably Teutonic and Nipponese villains of the Bond series), but rather by a thoroughly impersonal, devious, and universalized number bureaucracy. This not only allows McGoohan to portray female characters with an unusual degree of depth and complexity, free from the worst excesses of Bond-style sexism (as with the supposedly Lithuanian female agent in "The Chimes of Big Ben" or the upwardly mobile taxi maid who turns out to be the new No. 2 in "Free for All"). This also permits the series to outflank a whole range of cold war nationalisms by means of a powerful aesthetic multinationalism, whose ultimate consequence will be to displace questions of agency onto the thematics of identity. It is not the formal ownership of the Village that is really at stake but the fact that nowhere on the planet (as No. 6 discovers on those occasions when he does physically leave the Village, as in "Many Happy Returns") can one really escape it.

One need not be an aficionado of Kafka nor have memorized chapter and verse of Weber's description of the rationalizing function of modern bureaucracies to guess that the positively global reach of the Village ought to have something to do with the social realities of globalization—the grim, meat hook realities of the capitalist world market. In fact, McGoohan will make the task much easier for us by constantly harping on the autarkic, self-contained nature of the Village, which has its own hospital, stores, dwellings, sports facilities, political spaces, and even television station, and thus qualifies as a genuine microcosm of the late 1960s world system. Putting all the pieces of the puzzle together, the Village is clearly not an allegory of the cold war but a metaphor of something else: a social phenomenon that is not a conspiracy per se but often acts like one; something associated with a brazenly open and multinational architecture rather than the hidden bunkers of the Pentagon, while somehow being just as deadly as the latter; something organized as a totalizing bureaucracy not reducible to the cold war national security states themselves but not averse to borrowing and refining their tactics (bridging, in effect, the divide between the Hegelian Mind of the State and the Californian state of mind); and something conversant with the latest mass media and advertising techniques. That something, as we shall see, can be nothing less than that qualitatively new historical subject birthed by the 1960s, the multinational corporation.

Witness an early scene in "The Chimes of Big Ben":

> NO. 2: There are some people who talk and some people who do not. There are some people who leave this place and some people who do not leave. You are obviously staying.

NO. 6: *(Lightly.)* Has it ever occurred to you that you're just as much a prisoner as I am?

NO. 2: *(Apologetic.)* Oh, my dear chap, of course, I know too much. We're both lifers. I am definitely an optimist. That's why it doesn't matter who No. 1 is. It doesn't matter which side runs the Village.

NO. 6: It's run by one side or the other.

NO. 2: Oh, certainly. But both sides are becoming identical. What in fact has been created: an international community. A perfect blueprint for world order. When the sides facing each another suddenly realize that they're looking into a mirror, they will see that this is the pattern for the future.

NO. 6: The whole Earth as the Village.

NO. 2: That is my hope. What's yours?

NO. 6: *(Ponders.)* I'd like to be the first man on the moon.

The deliberate repetition of the opening tag, and the unusually direct mention of No. 1 by Leo McKern's unexpectedly sympathetic No. 2, culminates in the playful reappropriation of the Apollo project (undoubtedly the premier symbol of scientific and technological progress of the day), allowing us to grasp the astronaut as the cosmological equivalent of the terrestrial secret agent. This refunctions the "alien invaders" trope so beloved of cold war science fiction, where various and sundry entities indulge in the cosmic bad taste of attempting to do to the U.S. empire exactly what American corporations were doing to the Third World, into a parable worthy of William S. Burroughs: The astronaut is really an intergalactic political refugee, seeking egress from the Earth. The same principle is at work in such scriptwriting gems as the Orange Alert by which No. 2 summons up Rover from the deep. Any other color besides red would be an effective enough parody, but orange is so outrageously inappropriate, reminiscent as it is of Florida, sunshine, and the tropical beach to which No. 6 would like to escape, that one cannot help but make the logical link between the permanent rhetoric of crisis endemic to the cold war era and the no less permanent assault of the global mass media and the advertising industry on our eyes and ears.

Cold war science fiction is relevant in one other respect, and that is the basic visual apposition of the series, namely, the contrast between a set of curvilinear, smoothly molded bubblelike interiors containing the latest in information collection, and jumbled postmodern exteriors studded with the latest sensor and videocamera technology. Where the original *Star Trek* series displaced the contradiction between the battle-ready interiors of the Enterprise (essentially the interstellar version of the World War II aircraft carrier) and the apparatus of extended visual reproduction symbolized by the bridge's viewscreen onto a series of suspiciously neonational alien cultures—the visual clichés of the sleekly aerodynamic, flying-saucer-plus-twin-booster-rockets Enterprise, set against the Sovietized hyperphallus of the Klingon Warbird—McGoohan foregrounds the extended reproduction of images in precisely those plasticized, somatically overcharged surfaces of the 1960s consumer culture that *Star Trek* takes such pains to literally and figuratively alienate. Such surfaces do not simply distort or fragment the cinematic surface, as a visual modernism might do. They are sites that constantly reproduce *other* surfaces: as with the endless plasticity of the Village lava lamps, the wall-sized television screen in No. 2's office, or the monitors on which we watch the crews in the Control Room watch No. 6.

This drastic expansion and extension of the processes of viewing is underlined as much by the double-edged Village refrain "Be seeing you" (something accompanied by the Village's curious salute: a hand-gesture based loosely on the "OK" symbol, formed by using the right thumb and the right forefinger to form a circle over one's eye and bunching the three remaining fingers together; the result looks like an ingenious mime of the number six) as by the visual formatting of the Control Room, where No. 1's central mechanical Eye peers at land maps, star constellations, and the activities of the supervisors. The content of this Eye finds its content only elsewhere, however, in the curious central rotating pivot or seesaw contraption located in the center of the Control Room. Two supervisors are seated on either end of the seesaw, which has counterpoised videocameras on each end. This is something we might write off as simply another form of camera technology if it were not for the superabundance of other metaphors of confined, circular motion and enclosed movement of all kinds, everywhere from the dizzying scene in "Free for All" when No. 6 confronts the Town Council and is spun around and around to the beat of No. 2's hammer, to that arch symbol of all Village symbols, the penny-farthing or high-rider bicycle. There is an actual copy of this relic of the Victorian era, invented in 1879, in No. 2's office, where it seems to serve much the same function as the obligatory Greek statue, Renaissance painting, or high modernist lithograph in the corporate boardroom, invoking an archaic mode of technology rather than an archaic mode of aesthetics (rather like a hologram of Charles Babbage's difference engine in the midst of a semiconductor factory). Less understandable, however, is the ubiquity of the symbol, which is printed on all manner of lapel buttons, newspapers, and the like. Adding to the mystery, McGoohan imprints the high-rider forever in our viewing consciousness via the credits that conclude every episode except for the very last ("Fall Out"). The high-rider does not appear all at once but piece by piece, in tandem with the names of the cast and crew, while the opening theme music thunders in our ears.

This might seem to be mere whimsy or a peculiarly British visual motif, were it not for the fact that something else is being repeated, too, and not just the fact of No. 6's continuing imprisonment: an element so obvious that, as in the classic Poe detective story, we fail to notice it precisely because it is right in front of our eyes. This is the universal Village font in which the show's opening and closing credits, subtitles, and on-screen signs, numbers, newspapers, and posters are routinely printed: a variation of the Albertus letterset, best described as a kind of streamlined or high-tech Gothic script, whose visual Brechtianism is the perfect foil for the wonderfully devious poster-slogans we glimpse around the Village. (My own favorites are "questions are a burden to others, answers a prison to oneself" in "Arrival" and the triple-edged "music says all" in "Hammer into Anvil.") The point is not only that there is no real difference between the late 1960s mass media and the world of the Village, but that we are to read this particular video script not figuratively—that is, as simply a metaphor for the spy film—but absolutely literally, as the incarnation of the corporate icons, logos, trademarks, brand names, and visual and aural motifs that constitute a henceforth multinational culture. This is confirmed by the closing credits, which depict a wheel spinning round and round, which freezes into the lower wheel of the high-rider, while the logo of ITC (the entertainment firm that bankrolled McGoohan's project) appears to the upper right. Additional pieces of the bicycle appear in lockstep with the mention McGoohan's own company, Everyman Films Limited, the names of the cast and crew, and MGM Studios.

This suggests the two-person video carousel in the Control Room is not so much a cipher of viewing as a cipher of the re-viewing of prerecorded materials: the space, in short, of the extended visual editing process of video. The Control Room is really the Editing Room. It should be emphasized that this is merely the potential space of such, and not yet the realized thing itself, in the sense that the vocabulary of video techniques in the series is still directly linked to cinematic and late modernist forms. Again, the parallels with Hendrix, who was as extraordinary a studio technician, mixer, and sound engineer as he was a pure musician, are instructive. Hendrix's greatest works, "If a Merman I Should Turn to Be" and "1983," from the 1968 *Electric Ladyland* album, which transformed the aural heritage of the blues, R&B, and the sonic palette of the early counterculture into soaring hip-hop soundscapes, project a revolution of musical form that nevertheless did not go beyond the neonational materials of the dissonant R&B 9th chords patented by James Brown and the psychedelic guitar palette. Just as the sampling and scratching techniques of hip-hop could not truly be born until mass cultural works, tapes, cassettes, and recording machinery became available to the public, so too would the furthest possibilities of video sketched out by *The Prisoner* be realized only much later, in the video techniques inaugurated by the Hong Kong action-adventure films of Bruce Lee and Tobe Hooper's *Texas Chain Saw Massacre*.

McGoohan's two most significant visual innovations are the subjective viewing fragment or informatic icon and the multinational field of viewing levels of those icons, which we'll call the video cut and the video frame, respectively. The video cut is conveyed by the most characteristic shot technique of the series, an accelerated zoom that first frames an outdoor sequence and then zeroes in, sniper-style, on the telltale videocamera, sensor-unit, loudspeaker, or other incriminating detail in question. Meanwhile, the video frame is relayed by the symbolic editing machinery of the spinning Lego-style children's blocks on the desk of the psychologist in "Arrival" and "Free for All," and of course the Judge sequence in "Once upon a Time." The video frame also has an acoustic supplement, in the form of the spinning magnetic sound tracks and other culture-industrial equipment that litter the background of "Once upon a Time." If the carousel is very much the substantive synthesis of these two elements, the place where the process of recording and a library of prerecorded materials are brought into contact, then the double wheels of the high-rider might well signify a double editing process, with the larger wheel standing for the visual reel and the smaller one for the sound track. The seemingly archaic carriage of the bicycle, on the other hand, is a dead ringer for the sunroof of the average Village taxi, suggesting that perhaps a modularized or miniaturized transport machinery is the real issue at stake here.

But the closing credits have one more puzzle for us, without which we cannot fully solve the enigma of the high-rider: This is the ominous line of statues behind the high-rider, another significant reference to the Village statuary, whose stone eyes are actually video-sensors connected to the Control Room. The crucial scene here, in "Arrival," depicts No. 6 searching wildly for a way out of the Village, while Rover hunts him down and the distorted visages of the statues careen wildly back and forth. The statues seem to be the usual assortment of dead white males, radiating the power and authority of a repressive society that presumably attempts to speak in their name. What, then, are we to make of the glimpse of a Buddhist statue in the midst of the pandemonium, which seems to intermediate between No. 6's panic-stricken flight and Rover closing in for the kill? As it turns out, McGoohan will refashion this puzzling non-European reference into an increasingly powerful oppositional theme as the series progresses. This is the progression from No. 8's supposedly Lithuanian allies in "Chimes," who turn out to be Village agents, to the authentic but peripheralized Gypsies by the seashore of "Many Happy Returns"; and finally to the professionalized Haitian technical assistant in "Schizoid Man," the French Madame Engadine in "A, B, and C," and the honorably pacifist Swiss scientist of "Do Not Forsake Me, Oh My Darling." Still later we encounter genuinely multinational games, such as the fictional Asian game of kosho (a kind of martial arts involving trampolines, another amazingly prescient nod in the general direction of the future Hong Kong films) featured in "It's Your Funeral" and "Hammer into Anvil."

This tends to undercut the otherwise tempting notion that *The Prisoner* is motivated by a progressive neonationalism, wherein a postmodern Irish culture-entrepreneur symbolically repudiates a claustrophobic British mass culture on its own mediatic grounds (what amounts to a McLuhanite neoliberalism, and it is worth noting that McLuhan's perspective was that of a Canadian mass culture under assault by its better capitalized American competitor). There are indeed specifically Irish themes located in the series, most notably in "It's Your Funeral," which unmasks the nascent practice of the IRA as the mirror image of the repressive system it claimed to oppose, or the hilarious moment in "The Girl Who Was Death" when the mad scientist's minions turn out to be the Welsh marshal, the Scottish marshal, and the Irish marshal. (Naturally McGoohan will take advantage of the Irish marshal, the de facto weak link in the chain of Empire.) But the series as a whole will insist, quite correctly, that the system is neither British nor American nor Soviet per se but rather the totality of all those things. This suggests that the high-rider symbolizes more than just the perversion of a specific cultural technology, but incarnates a totally mobilized, mediatized, and modernized—and for that very reason utterly immobile, invisible, and archaic—multinational consumer society with the same visceral power as the peace symbol that signified the 1967 countercultural resistance to such.

Just as the counterculture symbolically negated the totalizing superhighways, bunkered concrete housing projects, and political witchhunts of the cold war secret police of whatever national provenance by means of freefloating happenings or gatherings, so too will *The Prisoner* negate the spy thriller by means of an increasingly complex multinational network of spaces. The trajectory from the office of the underground psychologist in "Arrival" to the brief shot of Rover in an underground cavern at the end of "Free for All," and from the settlement of Harmony (truly the town of one's dreams) in "Living in Harmony" to the ballroom dream sequence in "A, B, and C" is more than just the simple extension of mediatic coordinates to the action-adventure genre. By constantly recycling and reprocessing the available palette of shot techniques and scripted dialogues, and squeezing more and more allegorical content out of less and less material, McGoohan carries out one of the central formal principles of video, namely, the conjunction of accelerated shot innovation with the ever-increasing repetition of the thing being shown (generally by means of unusually intense montages or varieties of slow-motion or half-motion close-ups, most familiar to us from the resplendent video epics of John Woo). This aporia between innovation and repetition runs far deeper than what the 1960s saw as the struggle between the Organization Man and the individualistic rebel ("IBM vs. Tarzan"), and what the 1970s glossed as the poststructuralist apposition of the linguistic signified amid the echoing, decentered field of signifiers. It is the site of a genuine social contradiction between the extended reproduction of the commodity form and the innovation rent by which that form is valorized on the marketplace.

Where McGoohan decisively bolts from the mainstream corporate ideology of our own day—that incessant admixture of manic Wall Street speculation, silicon industrialism, and Web-babble, which is so busy reinventing itself from millisecond to millisecond that it never has time for a single concrete thought, let alone an authentic political or cultural meditation—is that delightfully Brechtian insouciance (one thinks of Brecht's anti-Stalinist poignard, that the only way to abolish the curse of bureaucracy was to make everyone an administrator) by which a multinational aesthetics stages its own reflexive self-decolonization from the world of the multinationals that created it. This is the genesis of No. 6's most insistent and telling gesture, the fact that he has *resigned*—not because he doesn't care but precisely because he does; and not because he isn't playing the role of the secret agent anymore but because he really does play one on a television screen, which we are suddenly forced to acknowledge, against all our preconceived notions and ideological conditioning, to be a new kind of political and cultural battlefield. No. 2's infamous opening line is a double gambit: The Village does not really want information, of course, only obedience. (From their point of view, information is an exchange value, not a use value.) In fact, it is No. 6 who truly wants information: information on who No. 1 is, where the Village really is, which side runs it, and how it might be possible to escape.

The very first shots fired in this informatic battle are no more than sniper rounds. At the very beginning of "Arrival," when No. 6 wonders why the only maps sold are local ones, depicting only the Village, the shopkeeper responds cheerily, "There's no demand for any others." Microsoft's marketing bureau could not have put it better themselves. Likewise with No. 6's first meeting with No. 2, where he gives his date of birth as March 19, 1928—actually McGoohan's own, real-world date of birth, and the one moment of genuinely personal information he will ever impart throughout the series—thus lending an especial poignancy to the classic line: "I will not make any deals with you. I've resigned. I will not be pushed, filed, stamped, indexed, briefed, debriefed, or numbered. My life is my own." What might be taken for the classic bourgeois or Enlightenment defense of the propertied individual is belied, however, by No. 6's unusual mien—an air of utter simplicity, devoid of even the slightest hint of false humility or paranoid grandeur—and no less unusual garb. He wears not the business suit favored by Bond but extremely dark clothing, no tie, and patent leather shoes. Interestingly enough, No. 6's normal Village attire comes very close to the latter, with the exception that his jacket is completely black with a single thin white stripe emblazoned around the lapels and wrists, and the shoes are replaced with that postmodern article of footwear par excellence, a pair of sneakers. By contrast, the ultimate symbol of the Village, Rover's floating bubble surface, is pure white. In between these polar opposites are the Village inmates, who are generally dressed in segmented blocks of alternating primary colors, strongly reminiscent of zebra-striped prison garb, as well as customized capes and bubble-shaped hats. The visual effect is one of an incessant streamlining, of smoothly rounded curves and jumbled planes of color that comprise the sartorial complement to Portmeirion's picturesque backdrop: clothes that are neither work suits nor leisure garb, but an ominous blend of both (in the same way that the Village is simultaneously an interrogation center and vacation resort).

Two other significant visual symbols need to be mentioned here: the giant multicolored umbrellas of the Villagers, which combine Rover's distinctive shape with a clearly televisual form (No. 6 never has one, while No. 2

never does without one), and the mysterious Butler, played to quiet perfection by Angelo Muscat. The Butler is particular interesting, both for his constant propinquity to No. 2 (by continuously serving breakfast or tea or performing other symbolic tasks) and the fact that he utters not a single word throughout the entire series. All the other characters of the series have an explicit acoustic content: the Villagers with various marching bands; No. 2 with the hazy, psychedelic background music of No. 2's office; No. 6 with the series theme music, and so forth. Nor does the Butler ever seem to take sides in the battles between No. 2 and No. 6, preferring to hold his black-and-white umbrella with an air of solemn indifference. Given that the Villagers' umbrellas are associated with a specific kind of movement, the whirling effect created by spinning the handle, this suggests that the Butler is the site of a kinetic as well as chromatic and acoustic austerity.

If the Butler is always silent, it is noteworthy that there is one character who never fails to kick up a commotion. This is our old friend Rover, whose inimitable roar of rage and aggression drowns out whatever else is going on in the same way that Rover's white surface blots out the faces of its victims with a rubberized death mask. This visceral horror of packaging, of the seamless white surfaces of the 1960s consumer culture suddenly revealed to be gruesomely embodied labor, whose torment is visually annihilated but rendered audible via the anonymous scream of the victim, is more than just a Kafkaesque parable of the nightmare of bureaucratic oppression and the horror of arbitrary state power. For one thing, Rover's electronicized howl is set against a whirring, reverberating sonic background, strongly reminiscent of an electronically altered version of an exploding blender or another appliance gone haywire. For another, Rover is always spawned in the ocean deep and centrally associated with the sea. According to the recollections of those associated with the series, Rover was originally supposed to be a white, bubble-shaped battery-powered cart, resembling a stack of pancakes topped by a flashing police siren. In McGoohan's telling of the story, the contraption was supposed to be seaworthy, but it sank into the sea during a test run and was replaced at the very last second by a giant weather balloon.[1] This suggests that Rover does indeed have something to do with the Rover Company, one of the leading British vehicle manufacturers of the 1960s, though probably less in the sense of an automotive or transport technology than in the export-driven reality of the world market. Some crucial moments in "The Chimes of Big Ben" do indeed revolve around scenes of a shipping line and then airline transport. No. 6 and No. 8, supposedly a Lithuanian defector, are to be smuggled into England inside a shipping crate, tacit acknowledgment of those twin sinews of the newly globalizing economy, waterborne and airborne containerization. The remote-controlled, bubble-shaped helicopters of the Village are certainly another example of postmodern air mobility.

On the other hand, it is probably significant that the idea of the flashing siren is divested from Rover's immediate corpus and relocated onto the circular overhead lights and pulsating beam projectors by which the various No. 2s attempt to hypnotize No. 6, that is to say, as the limit point of various light sources or visual technologies. The most intriguing of these is the eerie light machine of "Free for All" and "Fall Out," where the camera zooms in and out at a rapidly rotating theatrical light surrounded by gyroscopic gears of various kinds, while the sound track replays a kind of high-tech, oscillating whine somewhat similar to the acoustic backdrop of Rover, only without the latter's roar. During the resuscitation of the deceased No. 2 in "Fall Out," the light machine kicks into gear while President remarks enthusiastically, "A revolution!" to the seated No. 6, and we see a brief clip of the death sequence put into rewind, clearly a dead giveaway for the video recorder (an extremely expensive high-technology item in 1967). This suggests that one of the key strategies of the series will be to turn the extended reproduction of the televised image against the extended reproduction of consumable surfaces signified by Rover. This may explain the (seemingly) shell-shocked Dutton's white toy balloon in the trial scene of No. 6 in "Dance of the Dead," which contrasts nicely with the period costumes of those attending the ball. (The judges are dressed as a Roman emperor, Marie Antoinette, and Napoleon, while No. 2 is dressed, perversely enough, as Peter Pan, suggesting a properly American continuation of certain inglorious Imperial traditions.) This is also the genesis of the moment in "Free for All" where No. 6 announces, as part of his election campaign, "I am not a number. I am a *person*." The camera cuts briefly to a bright yellow balloon with the word *Vote* scrawled on it, and then we hear the sound of it being popped and the scandalized laughter of the crowd. In "Once upon a Time," the two themes are finally conjoined in an early scene where No. 6 rocks back and forth on a rocking chair while No. 2 fires questions at him, with the crucial word *pop* interpolated between shots of a glowing overhead light (the "bubble" No. 6 would like to burst).

This disruption of plastic surfaces is the flip side of a no less thoroughgoing recuperation of nonplastic surfaces, ranging from Portmeirion's racy architectural modernism to the art exhibition in "The Chimes of Big Ben," where No. 6 wins first prize due to the fact that his entry, an abstract sculpture hewn by hand, is the only one that does not have No. 2's visage somehow imprinted, carved, woven, or stamped upon it. The resulting dialogue is priceless:

> FIRST JUDGE: We're not quite sure what it means.
>
> NO. 6: *(With a pixieish grin.)* It means what it is.
>
> NO. 2: *(Hovering in background.)* Brilliant. It means what it is. Brilliant. *(All affability to judges.)* Oh, you mustn't let me influence your decision. *(Moves away.)*
>
> NO. 6: This piece . . . what does it represent to you?.
>
> SECOND JUDGE: A church door?
>
> NO. 6: Right first time.
>
> THIRD JUDGE: I think I see what he's getting at.
>
> NO. 6: Now, this other piece here, the same general line, something more abstract as you'll notice, representing freedom—or a barrier, depending on how you look at it. *(Moves behind sculpture.)* The barrier's down, the door is open, you're free, free to go, free to escape, to escape to this . . . symbol of human aspirations. Knowledge, freedom, escape.

The sculpture is actually part of the frame of a boat he will use for the escape attempt. There is a roughly analogous scene in "It's Your Funeral," where an inmate who is painting No. 6's portrait discusses the "jammers," eccentrics who give so much false information to the Village that eventually the authorities ignore them. "What do you think?" says the artist, turning the canvas to the camera. It is an abstract painting, essentially a series of smudged boxes and a circle, vaguely Cubist with Abstract Expressionistic touches. "A perfect likeness," responds No. 6, and indeed it is. This significant leap from the merely formal rebellion of the art exhibition to the genuine content of the radical modernisms of Klee, Kandinsky, and Picasso marks a formal mutation in the story line away from the purely privatized or psychologizing escape from the Village envisioned at the beginning of the series, and toward the collective resistance movement mapped out at the end.

One of the crucial elements of this movement is the subterranean transformation of the gender ideology of the 1960s spy thriller, and in particular the erasure of the clearly sexist antagonism No. 6 displays toward the Villagers in some of the earlier episodes (in "Dance of the Dead," he remarks, in reference to No. 2's black cat, "Never trust a female, even the four-legged variety") by a more complex set of gender ideologies. Of course, the men are even less trustworthy, and given that the whole point of the Village is that blindly trusting anyone, least of all yourself, is a sure recipe for disaster, No. 6's comment reads as an interesting variant of male resentment, wherein the sudden, disorienting plethora of female service workers, drivers, and technicians of all kinds disrupts the home-and-hearth ideology still latent in, say, the occupations of the household maid or nurse. In fairness to McGoohan, one of the hallmarks of the series is its insistence that there *is* no domestic sphere anymore, or at least not one even remotely autonomous from or outside the reach of the juridical and economic infrastructures of the Village. This may explain why the Village, otherwise such a detailed microcosm of global society, is largely devoid of children, at least until near the end, when the children at the conclusion of "The Girl Who Was Death" and the children's rhymes and games of "Once upon a Time" intimate the sort of utopian prison breakout visible in the finale of *Endgame,* that is, Clov's sighting of the boy outside the bunker (suggesting in turn that Clov's telescope is the primordial version of McGoohan's video cameras).

The flip side of the feminized domestic sphere was always the male monopoly on public violence. It is noteworthy that where the Bond series in its classic form sought to retain the usual patriarchal monopoly on such, and was consequently forced to stage ever vaster and more stupendous combat sequences in order to shift attention away from the aporia of female agents who could be sexually threatening but were not permitted to carry guns or engage in direct combat (a kind of symbolic arms race of the cold war patriarchy, as it were, roughly parallel to the phallic rocket fetishism of the United States and USSR), McGoohan will critique this on two levels. First, the male secret agent undergoes a self-referential or immanent deprogramming, as in "Schizoid Man," where No. 6's self-inflicted electric shock triggers the repressed memories of No. 2's brainwashing program; second, the female agent undergoes an externalized or transcendent deprogramming, as with the woman brainwashed to fall in love with No. 6 in "Checkmate," one of the most damning critiques of mass mediatic gender ideologies ever made. Her own moment of liberation arrives when she returns the locket with No. 6's photograph to him—a locket that is actually a radio transmitter designed to track his movements; tellingly, he will later use the circuitry of the device for an escape attempt. This trope of a masculinized technological self-sacrifice paired with the feminized gift of technology, the immediate negation of the masculinized elite consumerism and feminized high-tech toys of the Bond films, will be greatly expanded in the context of "A Change of Mind," where an entire cold war culture of enforced drug regimens and repressive community politics is turned against itself via No. 2's female assistant. Here it is not the gift of technology but the gift of a freely given labor-time, which allows No. 6 to turn the tables on his captors: She unwittingly takes the tranquilizer that she is supposed to administer to No. 6 and ends up as one of television's first authentic Flower Children, high as a kite and the willing accomplice to No. 6's ingenious counterstrike against No. 2.

The true gender revolution of the series, however, occurs only when this sequence of events is reversed, and No. 6 deliberately takes a hallucinogenic drug that is supposed to break him, only in a manner of his own choosing, while the female agent, previously merely a dupe of the authorities, actively assists his rebellion. This is the moment of "A, B, and C," probably the single most intriguing episode in the series outside of the double-decker conclusion, and certainly the most sophisticated in terms of gender ideology. For one thing, the female scientist, No. 14, is no hapless underling. She is an independent scientific researcher whose experimental drug permits dreams to be transformed into images displayed on a television monitor and for a limited amount of information to be piped in to the dreaming subject. The title of the episode is based on the three suspects to whom No. 2 believes No. 6 was selling out at the moment of his resignation. The first, labeled "A," evidently represents the traditional hard-nosed male secret agent, while "B" represents the relatively more glamorous female secret agent. "C" is an unknown agent, the ringer in the lineup, whose identity is a mystery even to the Village spymasters themselves. An image of each agent is fed into No. 6's chemically tranquilized mind while a background tape replays a party at a certain Madame Engadine, French socialite extraordinaire. This suggestive allegory of the editing process, wherein the body's memories are manipulated like videotape, has its primary model in a bizarre scene in "Dance of the Dead," where McGoohan discovers the body of an agent in a filing cabinet. This move is strongly reminiscent of Heiner Müller's theatrical works, which prefigure the text as a properly postmodern corpse, that is, as a bureaucratized pattern of information or mass-mediatic DNA.

But more amazing still is the content of No. 6's normal dream sequence: We see not the usual series of abstract images or surreal collages but the resignation sequence of the opening tag, namely, the opening of the double doors and McGoohan's irate delivery of his resignation to George Markstein, repeated over and over again! What makes the visual impact of this move so striking is the lack of a sound track: Instead of the thunder and theme music of the tag, we hear instead the astonished No. 2 and No. 14 wonder what could possibly motivate their captive's obdurate resistance to the Village, even (and especially) in his dreams. Such extreme contrasts of acoustic and visual registers are hardly untypical for the series, as the title shot of "Living in Harmony" with a fist fight raging in the background goes to show; one could also point to the vicious fight between No. 2's assistant and No. 6 in "Hammer into Anvil," where they practically destroy No. 6's residence while Vivaldi flows peacefully from a record player. More revealing still is the sequence of musical quotations in "Hammer into Anvil, where No. 6 plays and replays the opening of a piece by Bizet on a number of seemingly identical records as part of a cat-and-mouse game with the authorities. This is an unmistakable reference to Kurt Weill's musical parody of Bizet in the opening of Bertolt Brecht's *Threepenny Opera,* as well as a deft scansion of the musical studio technology of the nascent counterculture. "A, B, and C" will relay this theme not in terms of an interpretive system per se but as a set of characterological actants or allegories for mass media spaces out of which an interpretive system will later be constructed. Thus No. 6 represents the superstar actor playing in a new kind of video theater, No. 14 signifies the media innovator or visual technician who links this theater to (and is linked by) the actual technologies of the video screen and editing room, while No. 2 satirizes those professionals whose business it is to decode or otherwise retail mediatic images but who do not formally create or directly control the production of such—the ambiguous space of the executive producer or studio executive.

This is not to say that *The Prisoner* is just another mediatic critique of the mass media, as so much of the garden variety or Web criticism of the series tends to assume—a line of reasoning with a powerful affinity to a certain moralistic critique of capitalism, which condemns the rich for being greedy while failing to comprehend that incessant accumulation is the truly destructive feature of the system, that is, the fact that even the most garish displays of the profit motive are only the symptoms and not the cause of the hegemony of the commodity form. The limitations of such thinking are most apparent when one tries to apply mass media categories to the characters of A, B and C. In the case of A, we seem to be dealing with the standard cold war double agent. Less convincingly, B may be said to involve a variation on the detective or suspense narrative; at one point, No. 6 accuses No. 14 of being an accomplice to No. 2's latest scheme, and No. 14 says, ambiguously, "We all make mistakes. Sometimes we have to." Later, when No. 14, at No. 2's behest, employs the additional technique of piping not just images but also sound into her sleeping patient, she deliberately puts the same words into B's mouth, tipping No. 6 off to what is going on. ("Have you ever had the feeling you're being manipulated?" McGoohan bursts out at that point in his dream, one of the great moments in a series devoted to cataloging the ways the media manipulates us.) But C corresponds to no known mediatic genre whatsoever. In the story line, No. 6 uses his waking hours to discover the underground laboratory that is the site of the dream experiments. He finds the drug, but does not destroy it or the machinery. Instead, he reduces the dosage considerably and then leaves everything as it is. When No. 14 finally applies the drug, No. 6 is able to steer himself, to some degree, through the resulting psychedelic experience. (As if to emphasize the point, the camera shifts and rolls drunkenly, following No. 6 through what he knows now is a dream party, to the accompaniment of thundering horn music.) A similar mutation transpires with the mystery spy, who at first seems to be none other than Madame Engadine herself, until we learn of yet another secret agent, heretofore unknown to the Village, who apparently even Engadine works for. Although the unmasking of this super secret agent is far too delightful a scene to spoil for those who have never seen the series (suffice to say that McGoohan upstages the stage as well as the stagers), it is significant that the unmasking takes place inside a church, whose doors open to reveal not an interior but an exterior—an anonymous urban scene somewhere in Europe, garnished with the disorienting sound track of an onrushing train. This architectural inversion is nicely complemented by the following exchange: McGoohan takes the package of presumably secret information from his jacket and says, "This means a great deal to me." The hooded mystery spy responds, in best corporate manner, "It is only a commodity." "No," retorts McGoohan with a twinkle in his eye. "It's my future." Still later, McGoohan walks back to the underground laboratory—not in "reality" but in his dream, and No. 2 and No. 14 watch in astonishment as the on-screen No. 6 presents the virtual No. 2 and No. 14 with the contents of the presumably top secret information he supposedly wished to present to the mystery spy. The packet turns out to contain innocuous travel brochures, another inventive variation on the opening tag.

In fact, the travel brochure's reference to physical escape from the Village is no mere metaphor. What is at issue is the determinate negation of the homogenizing anonymity of the Village by a concrete, irreproducible place. A, B, and C are thus not symbols of mass-media genres but of mediatized social spaces. In A's case, the location in question is clearly the national embassy. For B, it is the less definable space of a garden labyrinth somehow associated with B's (hidden) family and No. 14's spoken resistance, that is, the collective solidarities of the European social democracies. For C, it is the shadowy, dimly lit urban street corner, with the obligatory church bell echoing in the background—the prototypical urban stage, in short, for that other great media-assisted unmasking of the Powers That Be, namely, the tsunami of street uprisings that would inundate downtown Prague, Paris, Chicago, and countless other cities around the globe in the spring of 1968. The signal achievement of "A, B, and C" is therefore its ability to conjoin a localized micropolitics to a globalizing mediatic space, or what Bourdieu would term that multinational class praxis that ties together the local habitus with the transnational operations of the aesthetic niche market or field in question: Visual sampling and aural dubbing converge into the art form of video editing. A little thought will show that most of the other episodes of the series involve a similar constellation of localized mediatic spaces with global coordinates. In "The General," it is the space of the university amid the ongoing computerization of knowledge. "Living in Harmony" pastiches the Hollywood set in the context of a psychedelic Western, while in "Dance of the Dead," it is the popular judgment of the carnival, which is played off against the juridical sphere of media History, and so forth.

Bourdieu's aesthetic critique includes one other term, however, which is no less important than the fields of aesthetic production and interpretation per se, and that is the field of unabashedly political power upon which the aesthetic producers, distributors, and consumers are forced by the very logic of commodity society—the unrestricted competition of all against all—to stake their respective claims, in a more or less mediated fashion (if for no other reason than the fact that even the refusal or inability to stake such a claim is itself contingent on the historically constituted autonomy of art from politics, criticism from censorship, art appreciation from commercial exploitation, etc.). In the Village, the field of power takes some very strange forms indeed, everywhere from the early scene in "Arrival," where the heliborne No. 2 informs No. 6 that the town hall is host to both a "democratically elected" council and amateur theatrical events, to the literal and figurative chess games of "Checkmate," all the way to the repressive therapeutic-pharmaceutical complex and drug-assisted insurrection of "A Change of Mind." The most direct critique of what might be called the politics industry of late capitalism, however, is undoubtedly "Free for All," both the funeral dirge for the national mass party and the unofficial founding charter of the New Left. In many ways, "Free for All" is the logical complement to the visual innovations and luminous mediatic strategies of "A, B, and C"; whereas the latter identifies the space of the editing room as a new kind of cultural zone, and thus transforms a certain visual recursion into a protomorphic video library of images, the former concentrates not on the image per se but on the messages and texts transmitted by such—or what Derrida would identify as the thematic of a dissemination that is never quite identical with what is being disseminated. But where deconstruction and poststructuralism promptly sealed off this potentially explosive insight behind the specialized ghettos of linguistics or ontological philosophy, and thus unwittingly perpetuated precisely the authoritarian monopoly over theory authorized by the ontologies in the first place, the most insightful intellectuals of the New Left (most notably, Adorno and Sartre) would insist on the necessarily mediated nature of this dissemination, that is, the fact that the narrative industries of late capitalism are hardly innocent bystanders in the business of accumulation, but play an indispensable role in creating new markets, restructuring old ones, and ceaselessly legitimating, transacting, and regulating the sway of the commodity form over society as a whole.

This may explain why McGoohan will not simply condemn the marketized election campaign as a fraud or a perversion of democracy, which merely begs the question of what a truly democratic politics *would* look like, anyway, but plays off the element of scriptwriting against the scripted endorsements, scripted media events, scripted sound bites, and scripted speeches of the political marketplace. Each of these elements is closely conjoined to a specific media technology, ranging from the opening scene where No. 2 appears on TV and on the telephone simultaneously (a nice rewriting of an early scene in "Dance of the Dead," where the new No. 2 greets No. 6 directly from the television screen), to the instantaneous press publications and megaphone-driven rallies of the actual campaign, to the wallscreen and underground bunker revealed at the very end (the model for the full-fledged videoscreen and underground political unconscious of "Fall Out"). Unlike earlier episodes, which tend to delimit the process of mediatization to two or three discrete mediatic spaces—the usual ones are the hospital or therapy center, the visual surveillance center of the Control Room, and the theatrical stage of No. 2's office in the Green Dome—"Free for All" does something new, by tagging each media technology with an appropriately subversive and semiautonomous space. Consider No. 2's delightfully Mephisphelean pitch to No. 6 concerning the chance to run for office:

NO. 2: Every citizen has a choice. Are you going to run?

NO. 6: Like blazes, the first chance I get.

NO. 2: I meant, run for office.

NO. 6: Whose?

NO. 2: Mine, for instance.

NO. 6: *(Pauses.)* You have a delicate sense of humor.

NO. 2: Naturally. Humor is the very essence of a democratic society.

One might assume that this formal counterpoint of meaning, counter-meaning, irony, and counterirony indicates that the authorities are somehow just as cognizant of the potential instability of their rule as No. 6's prototypical rebel, but in fact nothing here is quite what it seems. For one thing, the scene takes place not in No. 2's office (as was the case for the breakfasts in "Arrival" and "Schizoid Man") but at No. 6's residence. For another, in the best tradition of Brecht, No. 2 gets to deliver one of the best and most subversive lines of the series—but then, as we learn later on, even No. 2 is not quite No. 2 in this particular episode. By negating the visual motif of the initial meeting between the new No. 2 and No. 6, McGoohan opens up a space where even the script does not follow its own script. The text shears loose from the image and floats over the scene like a free-floating metacommentary or video clip of itself. Something similar is at work in the rally scene, wherein No. 2 seemingly urges No. 6 on to ever more radical anti-Village rhetoric (the space of the professional politician); or the escape attempt via the speedboat, where No. 2 looks on and directs the action from a helicopter (the space of the action-film director); or, for that matter, the flight from the Village's nonalcoholic bar (the adroitly named Cat and Mouse) to a supposedly covert still, whose drinks are spiked with a powerful set of drugs designed to break No. 6 (the space of the film noir nightclub owner). The high point of this strategy is the scene where No. 6 is "interviewed" in the back of a Village cart by news reporters from the *Tally-ho*, the Village newspaper, which can be described as Time-Warner meets Beckett in Prague's Wenceslas Square:

> NO. 113: How are you going to handle your campaign?
>
> NO. 6: No comment.
>
> NO. 113: *(Writes in reporter's pad.)* "Intends to fight for freedom at all costs." How about your internal policy?
>
> NO. 6: No comment.
>
> NO. 113: *(Writes.)* "Will tighten up on Village security." How about your external policy?
>
> NO. 6: No comment.
>
> NO. 113: *(Writes.)* "Our exports will operate in every corner of the globe." How do you feel about life and death?
>
> NO. 6: Mind your own business.
>
> NO. 113: *(Writes.)* "No comment."

The litany of double and triple puns here (the Prisoner is indeed fighting for a certain kind of freedom; he is indeed testing the Village's security system; the Village is indeed a globally exported phenomenon; and of course the whole point is that No. 6 really does have nothing to say to the Powers That Be) expertly sets off the spectacle of a mass media whose only real business is, just like that of the cold war spy agencies, retailing the business of others. Probably the only real weakness in this episode is the brainwashing sequence that follows the confrontation with the Village council (again, the significant prototype for the parliamentary assembly in "Fall Out"), an overly subjective or paranoid register that is the privatized or psychologizing flip side of the objectively schizophrenic gestures and unidentifiable language of the taxi driver assigned to No. 6 for his campaign. (The taxi driver turns out to be the real No. 2 after all; the "language" she speaks is actually a meaningless linguistic pastiche specially invented by the scriptwriters.) The conclusion of "Free for All," where No. 6 is "elected" to be the new No. 2 and begins wildly operating the controls of No. 2's office, first to see if No. 2 has really left the stage and then in a vain attempt to order the Villagers to rise up in rebellion, suggests that a more fundamental representational dilemma is involved here, namely, the problem of narrating consumer capitalism not just as a form but as a genuine content. The political version of this was the seemingly clear-cut choice before the New Left, either to transform the Establishment from within (the Long March through the institutions envisioned by the Prague Spring reformers and Western social democrats alike), or to instigate an actual revolution in the streets. History teaches us that both options were illusory; national social democracy could temporarily flourish in the hothouse export-platform economies of Central Europe, but a resurgent neoliberalism was about to strangle the effective global demand this model depended on and thus reactivate the latent class tensions smoothed over by the golden age of state-monopoly Keynesianism. Meanwhile, the national-democratic and anticolonial revolutions in the Second and Third Worlds could defeat the U.S. Empire's rampaging armies with guerrilla tactics, but could hardly be expected to counter the far more insidious enemy of falling raw materials prices on world markets. Neither international solidarity actions nor neonational political disruptions were, by themselves, really capable of challenging the henceforth global habitus of multinational capitalism; only truly transnational labor and political movements would be able to do that.

From this global perspective, the curious ending of "Free for All"—the System's necessary resort to a direct, brutish violence, seemingly at odds with the much more subtle forms of manipulation and repression No. 6 faced previously—is an example not of weak scriptwriting but of extraordinarily good scriptwriting indeed. This is the moment of naked political crisis, when the United States and the USSR, COINTELPRO and the KGB, the crushing of the Prague Spring and the police riot at the Democratic Convention in Chicago of 1968, U.S. military Keynesianism and goulash Stalinism, the FBI and the Stasi, the killing fields and torture cells of U.S.-sponsored juntas throughout Asia and Latin America and the horrors of the gulag and the laogai, all turn out to be shockingly, monstrously identical.

McGoohan's counterstrategy will cancel out the theme of the existential conflict of the alienated outlaw versus the System at the heart of the spy narrative, choosing instead to set a series of multinational subjects (for instance, the nursery school rhymes, biographical peregrinations, and Shakespearian stages of the senescence of the British Empire in "Once upon a Time") in motion toward transnational or mass mediatic objects (the American-style media executives, paranoid cold war security agencies, and countercultural uprising of "Fall Out"). Although the two final episodes of the series were televised separately, McGoohan's own editorial work here— "Fall Out" begins with an extensive synopsis of the main events of "Once upon a Time"—suggest that they are really two parts of a single, larger episode, designed to run for an hour and a half or so. Careful examination of the script tends to support this view. Not only do both episodes harmonize in terms of a common underground setting, a provocative set design, the centrally ambiguous role of the Butler, and the drama of an unyielding dissent at last overthrowing the power of an inflexible state-monopoly authority, but the mediatic resistances of the first are the logical complement of the mediatic rebellions of the second. This may explain why the first episode is not only the purest theater of the series but also the purest television, wherein a series of pitched battles rages between No. 6 and No. 2 (superbly played by the inimitable Leo McKern) in the confines of a hallucinatory playground, a school, a boxing match, and even a fencing match. The visual motifs and icons of a range of media narratives, everywhere from the school drama to the high school graduation ceremony, the job interview to the car chase, and the courtroom drama to the World War II movie, are all stripped down to the basalt bedrock of supercharged, electrifying dialogues, often involving the simple repetition of numbers or nonsensical words. Meanwhile, the usual Portmeirion scenery we have come to expect is replaced by an eerie, blank darkness and unusually crisp, blinding lighting effects, as if the stage and its objects were floating in a dazzling void; our visual sensors are thus redirected away from the scenery and toward the suddenly visible shot editing and cutting techniques themselves, counterpointed by the literal and figurative machinery of the sound track, which we see the Butler turn on and off in synch with the action. This reflexive twist on what might be called the set of the television set begins to disclose its specific content during the seesaw scene, when the contrasting vertical shots of No. 2 and No. 6 slowly accelerate in tandem with the rising verbal antagonism between the two. The result is a displacement of what we have termed the video cut, namely, the accelerated zoom used previously in the series, with its latent reference to the physical motion of the camera through three-dimensional space, by the extreme close-ups of No. 2 and No. 6 in motion around the screen. The movement of objects through time turns into the instantaneous juxtaposition of moving objects in space, the embryonic forerunner of the hegemonic windowing aesthetic of the early 1990s global consumer culture. Conversely, the video frame we identified earlier as the clacking wooden spinnets of the interrogation scene in "Arrival" is rehearsed once again in the courtroom scene, wherein No. 6 counters the machinations of No. 2's solemn Judge by invoking that central political innovation of the 1960s rebellions, the globally mediatized nonviolent civil disobedience campaign, and is subsequently dragged off to "jail" (actually a mobile home, complete with a dining area and kitchenette).

This sets up one of the greatest confrontations of the series, wherein No. 2 says, "You're dead," and No. 6 responds by offering him a knife taken from one of the kitchen drawers, saying, "Go ahead, kill me." No. 2 cannot refuse this gambit and approaches No. 6 hesitantly, knife raised, but, of course, he cannot bring himself to kill, simply because No. 6 does not attack him or offer any kind of physical resistance. This is not only the significant inversion of an earlier scene, the fencing match where No. 2 tries to goad No. 6 into killing him, and No. 6 lunges wildly but merely wounds him, but also recalls to mind Genet's famous flourish at the end of his magnificent play *The Blacks*, where the Judge bursts out, "But let's get things straight: one corpse, two, a battalion, a drove of corpses, we'll pile them high if that's what we need to avenge ourselves. But no corpse at all—why, that could kill us."[2] To paraphrase Adorno, every inhuman order founded on the logic of sacrifice requires the routinized dehumanization of that which is to be sacrificed: mostly notoriously, as the numbers tattooed on the inmates of the death camps, but of course McGoohan has the prisoners of quite another empire in mind. The true perversity of the jail is that it is the only self-evident piece of the consumer culture in the Embryo Room; it is literally the prison within the prison, just as the Embryo Room is itself a prison within the larger prison of the Village. Consequently, No. 6's breakout will rely not on that deus ex machina of the Bond series, a superior brand of technology, but on the strategic fault line between the multinational consumer culture of the Village and its state monopoly technologies of repression. That is, the utopian promise of the consumer culture will turn against the late capitalist institutions in which it is housed. The crucial moment here is the scene where No. 2 pretends to be a German interrogator in a World War II prison camp and No. 6 refuses to play along, which recalls a similar moment in Thomas Pynchon's novel *Gravity's Rainbow,* when the conclusion of the war suddenly opens up that space of the consumer culture in which Slothrop can miraculously escape from the multiple traps and conspiracies-within-conspiracies set all around him. This is not, as the Right has so often charged, the blind identification of the Establishment with fascism but the New Left cognition of fascism as the distorted and doomed prototype of a hegemonic American state monopoly capitalism.

It is this essential cognition that underpins No. 6's shocking reply to No. 2's incessant questioning as to why No. 6 resigned: the simple, powerful, unanswerable "Why don't *you* resign?" This is far more than a simple inversion of rhetorical positions. This is the moment when resistance mutates, viruslike, into revolution. It is not merely that No. 2 cannot imagine himself as an autonomous human being, capable of making decisions without the crutch of an immense power bureaucracy at his side, nor is it that No. 6 really does care not just about himself but about everyone, and therefore offers the scandalous gift of a socialist equality precisely where No. 2 can envision only the neoliberal alternatives of a poisoned mastery (the freedom *of* the marketplace) or utter submission (freedom *for* the marketplace), though these are true enough. The point is that No. 2 incarnates, at that moment, the class position of the overlords of the global village, the CEOs of the multinational corporations, and the rentier elites of global finance capital, who are prisoners of the very system they claim to own. Capital revenges itself upon the bourgeoisie by making them just as contingent and incidental to the overall mode of production as the workers they are forced, by the very logic of the ruthless and unbounded global marketplace they administer, to exploit. Despite their relatively privileged position, they and their fortunes are in truth no less vulnerable to market downturns and the juggernaut of global accumulation than the average wageworker. This is nicely symbolized by the clock running out on No. 2, who despite all his power and influence is, like anyone else in the total system, subject to the judgment of labor-time, that is to say, the performance principle; he was given one week by No. 1 to break No. 6 and discovers that not only has he failed his assignment, but even worse, he does not really want to succeed anymore. In a clever inversion of the numbers battle of the courtroom, McGoohan counts off the last sixty seconds, while the increasingly desperate No. 2 comes totally unglued and begs for clemency. In response to his pleas, No. 6 brusquely replies, "Ask on. Ask *yourself.*" The death scene is also noteworthy for its unusual shot technique, the handheld close-up of McKern's face and the sound track of a thudding heartbeat and a ticking clock, while a voiceover intones in No. 2's ears, "Die, 6, die, die, die . . ." Not two, but *six,* which suggests that either he has completely lost his own sense of identity and that the mysterious No. 1 is ordering No. 2's death before he has time to join No. 6's rebellion, or perhaps that No. 2 is haunted by his own internalized No. 6 or conscience, and thus falls on his own sword before his conscience gets the better of him.[3]

Who, then, *is* the mysterious No. 1, the arch villain of the entire series and the malevolent force of evil responsible for dreaming up the diabolical prison of the Village and overseeing its operation? The answer lies in the nether gulfs of "Fall Out," whose two-word title is the ultimate thermonuclear pun in a series studded with cold war puns. It opens with a bizarre scene in which No. 6 confronts a tailor's dummy of himself with a crude mask of his own face on it, wearing his original clothes and flanked by rustling coat hangers. This is actually a clever retake of a scene in the "Dance of the Dead," where No. 6 is invited to the carnival and finds that his costume is nothing other than his own personal attire—dark clothes and leather shoes as opposed to his Village uniform, the characteristic single white-edge-on-black fabric plus sneakers. At one point the maid, an agent of No. 2, comes in and asks, in reference to the clothes, "What does that mean?" No. 6 responds, "That I am still . . . *myself.*" The maid's response is halfway between repressive nonchalance and envious petulance: "Lucky you." The first scene of "Fall Out" radicalizes this motif of an alienated subjectivity by deploying a handheld, jostling camera angle and running low, rolling kettledrums in the background, thus thoroughly disorienting our visual and aural sensibilities. When No. 6 finally reaches for his clothes, the hit Beatles single "All You Need Is Love," serenades No. 6, the Butler, and the Supervisor as they pass through a rocky passage lined with juke boxes in recessed partitions (a clever reference to the culture of extended musical reproduction). The Butler then opens a door, revealing a massive underground vault, the true political and metaphorical powerbase of the Village, crawling with mysterious technicians, black-goggled troops with automatic rifles and white helmets, computers and surveillance equipment. It is overseen by a strange, hooded assembly, which we later learn is a kind of parliament, outfitted with theatrical masks (half black, half white) and white hoods and gloves that completely cover every inch of their bodies. The parliamentarians are identified not by name but by tags describing their departmental zone of authority (these include "welfare," "pacificists," "activists," "identification," "therapy," "reactionists" and—touché!—"nationalists"). Off to one side, we also see the central design motif of the Control Room, the video carousel, only with twin machine gunners at each revolving end instead of the earlier videocamera teams.

We see, in short, anything and everything but the Bond stereotype of the megalomaniac arch criminal in a control room planning to wreak havoc, out of greed or malice, on the world. The reason, of course, is that this particular assembly *is* the cold war world system, in its most naked and concrete form: an assembly that preaches nothing but democracy but practices nothing but coercion, that upholds the doctrine of unlimited technical progress in order to maintain an asphyxiating status quo, that oversees everything and is watched over only by No. 6's seemingly powerless gaze (and, by extension, that of our own), and whose collective decisions are actually decided in advance by No. 1—represented here by a giant mechanical eye implanted in what appears to be some sort of enormous conning tower. Nor does No. 1 even use words or other obvious commands but issues orders to the President, the leader of the assembly, via two intriguing symbols, a curious high-pitched siren and a flashing green strobe light. This is actually a rewrite of the brainwashing sequence in the earliest part of "Once upon a Time," when No. 2 uses a pulsating lamp to hypnotize No. 6, and the Supervisor's voice suddenly reverberates, against a background of psychedelic noise: "Five . . . five . . . five . . . five . . ." The number system and the specific image (the videoscreen by which No. 2 is monitoring No. 6) are replaced with a twittering, high-pitched electronic reverb vaguely reminiscent of Morse code and the opening and closing of the mechanical eye.

The numberless President, clad in suitably juridical robes and wig, then calls for order and explains that the assembly has been called in a moment of "democratic crisis" to decide what to do with three specific rebels, or more precisely, three forms of rebellion: the countercultural youth, No. 48 (played by Alexis Kanner, reprising a similar role from "Living in Harmony"), the mainstream revolt of the ex–No. 2 from "Once upon a Time" (Leo McKern), and of course that as yet unclassifiable threat to the status quo represented by McGoohan himself. No. 48 arrives in a strange elevator, a cross between a giant piston and a circular platform that can be lowered into the depths and that discharges a regular cloud of vapor with a sound halfway between a steam engine and an aerosol can. Evidently bolted to the steel column against his will, he immediately starts singing an African American gospel song, "Dem Bones Gonna Rise Again," the mere words of which cause the assembly to plunge into disorder. Finally, to restore order, he is released and allowed to venture onto the stage, while the President waxes forth about the fecklessness of youth. No sooner is he free, of course, than he runs wildly across the set, reciting the same song, at one point even shouting the lyrics into a microphone while ducking the guards and plunging the entire assembly into chaos.

When No. 48 at last is cornered, No. 6 intervenes to save him, saying, "Young man . . . don't knock yourself out." No. 48, unsure of whether No. 6 really is the rebel he seems to be, tests him with the response: "Gimme the rest." No. 6 replies gravely, "Young . . . *man.*" This respectful familiarity elicits the immediate hostility of the President, who is forced, however, by No. 1 to negotiate directly with No. 48. The resulting dialogue between the two is a brilliant pastiche of a Beat culture on the cusp of turning beatnik, with the President batting key phrases such as "Got the message," "Got the light," and "Got the word" back and forth with No. 48 in an attempt to prove his hipness (and aided by some remarkably fast cutting). Of course, the President is interested only in forcing No. 48 to confess to the authorities, which the youth steadfastly refuses to do. Also significant is the call-and-response role of the assembly, which joins in the dialogue at various points. Visually, these moments are always tied to close-up shots of a specific desk tag: When the assembly chants "Take . . . take . . . take . . ." and beats on the desks with both hands to the beat, the tag in the center of our view reads "Education." When No. 48 is lip-synching a recording of "Dem Bones" by the Four Tops, the tag reads "Recreation," and when a member of the assembly reads the charges against No. 48, the tag reads, appropriately enough, "Anarchists."

But where No. 48's rebellion seems to hinge on the latent possibilities of the countercultural music scene, the revolt of the ex–No. 2 is more directly linked with those of video or, more precisely, those of a certain kind of Shakespearian political theater mediated via the specific video clip. When McKern awakes from his slumber, a videoclip of McKern's role in "The Chimes of Big Ben" is shown, along with a sound track of his laughter, which provokes the assembly to laughter in turn. They are clearly laughing at him, not with him. Later he takes the stand and recounts his glory days as a government functionary of some sort (we will assume an MP), and then his subsequent abduction to the Village. "What is deplorable," he observes, "is that I resisted for so short a time. A fine tribute to your methods." Sadistically, the assembly then replays the MP's mediatized "death" at the end of "Once upon a Time," causing his barely contained hostility toward the Village to boil over into outright rebellion: He walks over and stares directly at No. 1's mechanical eye, despite warnings from the President not to do so, finally tearing his Village lapel pin from his coat and summoning up the courage to spit directly in No. 1's electronic face. No. 1 hastily orders the guards to carry the MP off to the same holding cell as No. 48.

Imagine our surprise when, after all this, we hear the President turn around and *praise* No. 6's successful rebellion in fulsome terms, even going so far as to offer the Prisoner a choice: He may either stay and lead the Village, or leave a free subject and go wherever he wishes (a canny retake of our previous aporia, the Long March through the institutions versus the street resistance, now cast as a decisive, existential—and of course utterly false— choice). McGoohan, who has been watching the performances of the first two rebels from the throne of honor like a hawk (at one point the President says, "I take it you approve of the proceedings, Sir?" and No. 6 parries: "I . . . *note* them"), is not so easily fooled. We have already learned that the reach of the Village is global and that they are hardly likely to offer their most tenacious dissident a post of real authority. To be sure, unlike the other two rebels, he is not interested in simply scandalizing the authorities, nor does he appear to have his own power agenda. In fact, it's not clear that he has any agenda at all, which seems to be the main worry of the Village:

PRESIDENT: You are free to go.

NO. 6: *(Skeptical.)* Free to go.

PRESIDENT: Anywhere.

NO. 6: Why?

PRESIDENT: You have been such an example to us.

NO. 6: Why?

PRESIDENT: You have convinced us of our mistakes.

NO. 6: *(More serious.)* Why?

PRESIDENT: You are pure, you know the way, show us.

NO. 6: *(Relentless.)* Why?

PRESIDENT: Your revolt is good and honest and you are the only individual. We need you.

NO. 6: I see.

PRESIDENT: You do. You see all.

NO. 6: *(Skeptical.) I'm* an individual?

PRESIDENT: You are on your own.

NO. 6: I fail to see.

PRESIDENT: *(Leaving the rostrum and striding onto the floor.)* All about you is *yours*. We concede. We offer, we plead for you to lead us.

NO. 6: Or go.

PRESIDENT: Go if you wish.

NO. 6: I, I don't know.

PRESIDENT: Take the stand, address us.

NO. 6: *(Lightly.)* Should I?

PRESIDENT: You must. You *are* the greatest. Make a statement, a true statement which could only be yours but for us, remember us, don't forget us, keep us in mind. Sir, we are all yours.

All yours, indeed. The transcript does not do justice to the wonderful interplay here between Kenneth Griffith's oily President, oozing malignancy and paranoia, and McGoohan's skeptical, quicksilver No. 6. McGoohan deploys the simplest of words, the interrogative "why," as the most cutting critical instrument imaginable (the same word plays a similar function in the conclusion of "The General," only on the level of typed rather than spoken material) and thus extracting the maximum of information with a minimum of effort. His suspicions are later confirmed when he takes the stand to give his speech, only to discover, to his chagrin, that whenever he opens his mouth the parliament drowns him out with applause, shouting, "Aye aye aye," or words to that effect. Repeated recourse to the gavel has no effect. Finally he simply shouts out his words, uselessly, while the assembly effectively censors whatever it is that he has to say. This scene does more than just raise miscommunication to an art form: In retrospect, we know full well he would have said exactly what he has been saying all along—that he will not be manipulated, bullied, or controlled in any way, shape, or form by the Village and that he will not play their game, ever. As if to give us the broadest possible hint, the camera cuts to a close-up of the parliament, allowing us to decipher the desk tag in the center as "Entertainment." This suggests McGoohan is recuperating the archaic form of the direct political address or soapbox speech from the standpoint of a video politics that will turn the extended reproduction of the consumer culture against itself, very much as the New Left outflanked the official censorship of both superpowers by means of a whole new set of rhizomic cultural spaces, alternative media, and innovative modes of dissemination.

None of this is immediately obvious, of course, when McGoohan takes the strange circular elevator down to No. 1's inner sanctum, passing helmeted, heavily armed guards and entering a room with the Young Man (still humming "Dem Bones") and the MP (still laughing hysterically) both locked inside plexiglass cylinders marked Orbit 48 and Orbit 2. This striking image of what Jameson would term a trope of recontainment, of the countercultural youth and the Shakespearian fool literally bottled up inside their own monads, is completed by steam hissing from various vents in the background and technicians working on control panels. One other cylinder, which is unmarked, opens up, presumably for No. 6. But just when we expect the worst, the clarion horn call of the Village's outdoor broadcast system resounds, informing us that someone is saving the day. It is none other than the Butler, who bows before No. 6 and directs him to the stairs leading up to No. 1's inner sanctum. After the door glides open, the camera pans slowly across a set of globes resting on a central table, all turned to clearly meaningful positions. One reveals the Pacific Ocean bounded by the United States and Latin America, another is showing an area from the Middle East over Southeast Asia to Indochina, the next shows North America again, the next the east coast of North America, the Atlantic, and Western Europe, and the last shows North America again. (Singularly missing are Russia and China, suggesting that McGoohan knew exactly where the Village had its global headquarters.) No. 1 is standing at a set of controls, hooded and masked, and watching a videoscreen that first displays the live image of the approaching No. 6 and then No. 6's speech to No. 2 at the beginning of "Arrival" ("I will not be pushed, filed, stamped," etc.), while some sort of high-pitched sonar or radar apparatus chirps in the background. These seemingly clear-cut references to global geopolitics and a top secret military technology of some sort are loosed from their moorings, however, when No. 1 turns and hands a miniature crystal ball to No. 6. He takes it and looks within, seeing the usual image by which all the previous episodes ended—bars slamming shut across a fast zoom of No. 6's face, all set against an aerial shot of the Village. Stranger still, the sound track loops back on the very beginning of the "Arrival" clip: "I . . . I . . . I . . ." and slowly accelerates this single word, raising the pitch higher and higher, while the prison shot wells up over and over again within the crystal. No. 6's response is to let the crystal drop and shatter on the floor, a gesture not entirely unknown to other significant works of British postmodernism.[4] But what follows breaks all the rules, even those set by McGoohan's earlier episodes. The tape loop continues to accelerate until it is little more than a whining bleat against a rising jumble of orchestral noise, until No. 6, grinning like a skull, removes No. 1's white-and-black mask to reveal—the mask of an ape, which mugs wildly for the suddenly unstable, shifting camera until No. 6 pulls that mask off, too. And the true identity of No. 1, the source of all No. 6's torment and misery? None other than

McGoohan himself—who laughs maniacally, lunging toward the camera, setting off a brief chase sequence around the table with the globes. After some of the tightest, fastest camera shots of the series, McGoohan literally chases *himself* up an escape hatch and seals it, and then returns to the control panel, this time not to maintain the status quo but to jumpstart the Revolution.

This is the absolutely dazzling culmination of a long, long line of identity critiques, ranging from No. 12 in "Schizoid Man," No. 6's exact duplicate (wherein No. 12 gets some wonderful lines such as, "Where'd they get you, at one of those people's copying services, or are you one of those double agents we keeping hearing about so much these days?"), to a deliberate blurring of the lines in "Free for All" between No. 2 and No. 6, to the no-holds-barred identity struggle mapped out in "Once upon a Time." This particular scene solves two particular mysteries for us. For one thing, the assembly's chant, which drowned out No. 6's address, was in all likelihood the same as the tape loop: "I I I," the deliberate repetition of the opening word of McGoohan's speech ("I feel that . . ."). Repression in late capitalism does not typically involve the absolute expropriation of the subject typical of liberal or monopoly capitalism (the nationalism that violently excludes other nationalities, the sexism that expropriates women's household labor on behalf of masculinized national corporations and power bureaucracies, the racism by which the colonies and colonized are held in subjection to the colonists, and so forth) but what might be termed its relative immiseration on the multinational marketplace of identity: thus the celebrated media superstar whose very existence depends on the implicit devaluation of noncelebrities; the CNBC style of telejournalism, which reduces the global economy to the chatter of wealthy white male stockholders retailing the retailing of retailing on behalf of even wealthier (and whiter) male stockholders; or the business culture of the giant multinationals or multis, which is open to any cultural group just as long as they swear fealty to the commodity form. Second, the Village's Mephistophelean offer to No. 6—to lead the Village, or to go—needs to be taken quite literally indeed. The true mastermind behind the Village and all its power structures is not really a unitary government or even a set of conspirators. Rather, it is the principle of unrestricted competition unleashed by global capitalism, that is to say the desire to be the global number one in whatever marketplace is at hand. The rebellion against the market must thus operate on two levels: first, the subjective one of a psychological or internal liberation from the dictates of the market forces, and second, the collective emancipation of subjects joining together in a freely chosen solidarity on the very terrain of the marketplace.

All this is staged with exemplary clarity by the subsequent uprising, where McGoohan finally plays his hand and completes the transformation of what began as an individual escape attempt into the collective overthrow of the Village, not from without, but by means of the accumulated social forces stored up from within. Taking a fire extinguisher from the wall, he begins to descend silently into the Orbit Room, until the Butler gazes up and sees him. Lo and behold, the Butler, heretofore the loyal agent of the Village, joins the rebellion by indicating with his glance precisely where the hooded, uniformed technicians are. McGoohan swings into action, blinding and knocking down the technicians, and tossing the fire extinguisher to the Butler, who helps him finish them off. They quickly free the Young Man and the MP. McGoohan returns to the control panel and starts some sort of countdown, plunging the President and the assembly into panic and chaos, as they realize they are no longer in control of the situation. After the rebels ambush the guards in the passageway, we encounter the most visually startling and politically powerful sequence of the entire series: While the four rebels shoot their way out to the mobile home espied earlier in "Once upon a Time" in a vicious firefight with the guards, the Beatles' "All You Need Is Love" pours from the sound track against the clatter of machine guns, explosions, sirens, and chaos. The panic of the authorities turns general, as the command to evacuate the Village resounds. Incongruous frogmen in wetsuits flee the carnage on equally incongruous children's bicycles, and the Villagers scramble madly, driving and heliporting their way to safety, just as the four rebels drive to freedom in a truck, hauling the mobile home. Behind them, the final countdown reveals No. 1's domicile, which we had previously thought was a conning tower or bunker of some sort, to be a gigantic booster rocket (McGoohan intersperses some footage from the Apollo space program here), which thunders majestically into the sky and whose backwash melts Rover down into burnt slag.

Here at last the thunder of the opening tag, the thunder of the open road, and the rolling thunder of the battlefields of Vietnam all converge in the nova express of the 1968 earthquakes, shaking, pitching and yawing the edifice of state monopoly capitalism to its globalizing core. One would be hard-pressed to top this mediatic hijacking of the rocket, that central media icon of the scientific-technological might of the cold war superstates, by the New Left alliance of the counterculture, revitalized Social Democratic and Left parties, McGoohan's superstar culture workers, and that last space symbolized by the Butler. Still, McGoohan has one more surprise in store for us, relayed by the very last sequence of the series. We see the Young Man return to hitchhiking the highways, while the MP reenters the Parliament building to resume his former duties. But McGoohan and the Butler are immediately confronted by a suspicious London police officer, who demands some sort of explanation for the mobile home. Cleverly, McGoohan shoots the scene from a distance, using no dialogue, and we see him pantomime some patently bogus explanation to the stolid officer and then point to the Parliament building, as if to say, the MP will explain everything, before turning and rushing off with the Butler in the nick of time. The pair dash not to a taxi but to that great symbol of European public sector socialism, the double-decker bus. When they arrive at No. 6's home, the Butler, silent to the very end, enters the building while McGoohan drives away in his customized Lotus, and the scene shifts to a simple urban panorama, with McGoohan racing off into London traffic while the word *prisoner* is displayed, in Village font, prominently at the bottom of the screen.

Aside from the implicit social critique here (late capitalism surely remains the prison from which we must all escape), the specific association of the Butler with the urban space of London, that prototypical global city, and McGoohan with the ambient flow of traffic (a multinational assemblage of cars) suggests that our New Left alliance includes a crucial fourth term: a class of people who are spoken to but have no voice of their own; who perform the innumerable tasks of the Village bureaucracy but make none of the decisions; who may seem to be utterly brainwashed and subservient but who will, if given the opportunity, finally strike out against the system that they know from long and bitter experience oppresses them. This, of course, can be nothing less than that strange new thing, the transnational proletariat (something subtly underlined by the fact that the Butler drove the truck that carried McGoohan, the MP, and the Young Man to freedom; while the three celebrated their escape, the Butler had to remain at the wheel), which symbolically moves into the privileged urban space formerly held by McGoohan's media professionals. This casts a new light on the final moment, where McKern's MP enters the Parliament building under the watchful gaze of a policeman, while thunder roils in the background; presumably the MP is at last representing the Butler, who has never before had a say in the running of things. This allows us to decipher the very last shot of the series, which is also the very first of the series: McGoohan roaring down an empty highway while thunder echoes in the background. This is no longer the atomic thunder of the cold war but rather the informatic heat lightning of the nascent European Union, whose embryonic political conflicts and class struggles are just beginning to flicker on the horizon—the storm, in short, of the video future.

Krzysztof Kieslowski's Eurovideo 4

Interviewer: If you were to turn the camera on yourself, what would you say? The first words of your story?
Kieslowski: I turn the camera on myself in all my films. Not all the time, perhaps, but often. But I do it in a way so nobody can see it. And although I want you . . . *[corrects himself]* us to be successful in our work, I won't reveal it.
—Krzysztof Wierzbicki, *Krzysztof Kieslowski: I'm So-So*

Amid all the luminary achievements of the late-twentieth-century Eastern European media culture, ranging from Jan Svankmajer's animation classics to Heiner Müller's fire-breathing plays, and from Stanislaw Lem's cybernetic fables to Andrei Tarkovsky's sweeping historical epics, nothing quite prepares the unsuspecting viewer for the intricate subtlety, dazzling ironies, and unobtrusive genius of Krzysztof Kieslowski. To be sure, Polish artists and intellectuals have a centuries-old history of saying one thing in order to do another and think still a third, for all the usual colonial (and, starting with the debt crisis of the 1970s, neocolonial) reasons. Yet if Kieslowski's mature works seem too dark, too austere, too allegorically Polish ever to be reconciled with the cellphone speculations and high-tech consumerism of the European Union, this is only because they are also too exactingly European to ever be shoehorned into the categories of national cinema. Shuttling between the antipodes of the Eastern bloc propaganda film and the Hollywood blockbuster like diplomatic telegrams between cold war embassies, his greatest works fluidly recombine Western-style production techniques and visual framing with Eastern-style scripting and narrative exposition, thereby creating some of the first genuinely multinational aesthetic documents of the European Union.

Kieslowski also sheds a revealing light on Eastern Europe's unexpected twist on the classic postcolonial dilemma of nation-state formation. Unlike the EC countries, which had thirty years to prepare for the EU, the Eastern bloc countries experienced the equivalent of decades of social ferment (wild street protests, democratization, economic crisis, neoliberalization, dire austerity and impoverishment, and finally resistance to neoliberalism and the creation of social democratic institutions) in a matter of a few years. Put another way, the enabling feature of Polish neonationalism was EU multi-nationalism, which is why it is the least surprising thing in the world to discover that (1) the post–Communist Left parties of Eastern Europe are often the most strident partisans of the European Union, and (2) so many of these parties were immediately voted into power, in spite of the horrific legacy of Stalinism, Brezhnevism, and its local variants.

Historically speaking, one can argue that the formal economic switchover of trading links, export markets, and managerial models away from the Soviet Union and toward the EU between 1989 and 1992 was simply the last act of a much broader and deeper redirection in the global flow of symbolic, scientific, and cultural capital, that is, the turn away from the USSR and the United States and toward the European Union and East Asia. By the early 1980s, the resistance to the one-party state had spread from the intellectuals, students, and a few class-conscious workers to a wide variety of grassroots organizations and civic institutions. By the middle of the decade, the authorities did not even bother to jam radio and TV broadcasts from the West or to control imports of VCRs and videocassettes.[1] As a popular saying goes, the Berlin Wall didn't fall; it was *pushed*.

Conversely, the malaise, despair, and gloom in the 1990s that followed in the wake of the Velvet Revolutions were more than just the inevitable hangover of a massive social transformation. The wave of bankruptcies, capital flight, factory closures, and Depression era levels of unemployment that ravaged the post-Communist countries was bad enough. But what hit below the belt was the realization that this economic crisis was the flip side of a no less brutal and far-reaching cultural devaluation: the abrupt cancellation of decades of accumulated social, intellectual, and aesthetic capital by Eastern European artists, intellectuals, and ordinary citizens, who quickly discovered that the unfettered rule of the market could be every bit as cruel and destructive as the unfettered rule of cadre elites. As a famous Russian joke goes, five years of capitalism really did achieve a miracle: They made fifty years of Communism look good.

In this decidedly unpromising situation, Kieslowski displayed remarkable powers of continuity, by making one extraordinary film after another under the auspices of Swiss and French media firms. Eastern European cinema has a long and exemplary tradition of outwitting the harsh necessities of censorship, cultural subalternity vis-à-vis Hollywood, and arbitrary state power, by means of glorious sound tracks, magnificent scripts, and inventive visual puzzles or conundrums. Yet in the late 1980s Kieslowski would go even further, integrating all these things into a powerful aesthetics of Eurovideo capable of pulling the multimedia rug out from underneath the Hollywood blockbuster. The result was the ten-part TV series *The Decalogue* (1988), unquestionably one of the three greatest television productions of the twentieth century along with McGoohan's *The Prisoner* and Anno's *Evangelion.* Not content to stop there, Kieslowski would continue to revise and refine his visual palette in *The Double Life of Veronique* (1991), before scaling the breathtaking summit of the Three Colors trilogy (*Blue* in 1993, *White* in 1993, and *Red* in 1994). Despite officially retiring for health reasons, Kieslowski continued to sketch plans for another trilogy until his death in 1996. One of his scripts, written with his longtime associate Krzysztof Piesiewicz, was later turned into a film by Tom Tykwer, director of the hugely entertaining *Run, Lola, Run.*

Why did Kieslowski succeed where so many others fell by the wayside? And how did a relatively obscure Polish director at the margins of the EU innovate so many of the basic categories of European video well in advance of the much more heavily capitalized French, Italian, and Spanish competition? Part of the answer lies in the institutional peculiarities of Eastern European film and the unique window of historical opportunity that opened up between the moment of the auteurs of the 1950s and 1960s—the specifically national cinemas of Bergman, Truffaut, and Fellini—and the late developing consumer cultures of the Eastern bloc. One of the major contradictions of the state autarkic regimes in their late or Brezhnevite phase was that they invested heavily in training, science, and education, but could not effectively utilize the human capital thereby created. Heiner Müller zeroed in on this contradiction by noting ascerbically that the main economic activity of the Eastern regimes was always the production of state enemies. (In other words, the system produced vast numbers of literate, well-educated workers who could not fail to notice the yawning gap between the ideal of a people's democracy and the despotism of the one-party state.)

As it turns out, Kieslowski was unwitting beneficiary of two aspects of state autarkic development. First, he attended the legendary Lodz school of cinema, a hothouse center of underground innovation that recruited, trained, and launched a host of brilliant film directors in the 1960s, in much the same way that the Beijing Film Academy incubated the Fifth Generation filmmakers of China between 1978 and 1982. The Lodz students were given practically unlimited access to screenings of all the great modernist film classics, even those forbidden to the general public, something tremendously important in the era before VCRs and satellite TV. Second, the Polish system of decentralized film studios run by media professionals rather than Party hacks meant that daring experimental films could be produced and shown to other filmmakers and film students, though not necessarily screened in theaters or distributed to the public.

Starting out as a maker of quirky documentaries, Kieslowski gradually worked his way up to television productions and feature films. He was also a key albeit understated participant of what Janusz Kijowski christened the "cinema of moral anxiety" (the Polish term has the connotation of a collective sense of unrest, rather than purely psychological or private angst) prevalent in Polish film from 1974 to 1980. Probably the greatest discovery of this movement was that the most efficient way of subverting the censorship boards of the one-party state was to make films more realistic (and more socialist!) than the compulsory doctrine of socialist realism itself. The result was a series of gritty, reality-based films such as Andrzej Wajda's *Man of Marble* (1976) and *Man of Iron* (1980), which employed a range of semidocumentary and New Wave techniques to narrate the rise of the Solidarity movement. These films proved enormously popular with audiences, and there is no doubt *Man of Marble* catalyzed the resistance to the Gierek regime of the 1970s in much the same way that Costa-Gavras's magnificent *Z* crystallized the opposition to the brutal Greek military junta of the late 1960s. In the end, when Solidarity trade union activists began to turn cinematic protests into the real thing, the one-party state cracked down. Martial law was declared, strikes were crushed, dissidents and union leaders were arrested en masse, and for a brief period political chaos and economic shortages meant that almost all media workers (including Kieslowski) were out of a job.

Although the situation gradually normalized in the months following the imposition of martial law, the deep psychological scars left by the experience saturate Kieslowski's first major work, *Blind Chance,* which was in many ways the final epitaph on the "cinema of moral anxiety." Made in 1981 but not officially released until 1987, the film sketches out three possible futures of an ordinary youth named Witek. In the first version of events, he catches a train, runs into an honest, decent Communist Party veteran who fought against Stalinism, and ends up joining the Party in a bid to change the system from within. In the second, he misses the same train, meets a Gandhiesque pro-democracy activist, and ends up joining Solidarity. In the third, he misses the train but avoids politics altogether, settling down to pursue a career and raise a family. The conclusion shows this last protagonist, now happily married, aboard a jetliner on a routine tourist flight to the West. To our shock, the jetliner explodes in midair, killing everyone on board.

On one level, this would appear to be a fairly straightforward variant of the existential thriller, wherein the greatest sin of all is not so much choosing the wrong side but not having the courage to take sides in the first place (with the LOT jetliner as the postmodern reprise of the doomed *Patna* in Conrad's *Lord Jim*). This cannot explain, however, the curious shot technique of the disaster, which combines an ultraclose shot of the protagonist in the doomed plane and a long-distance zoom, which shows the plane slowly going down in flames. This is clearly a lateral reappropriation of that leading 1970s mass-cultural phenomenon, the big-budget disaster film. Nor does the existential explanation mesh with the sheer narrative density of the script, which employs an astonishing range of vividly drawn minor characters, each with a particular role to play in motivating the story. (We even run into them again and again in the various endings, in varying circumstances.)

This suggests Kieslowski had already started to push beyond the narrative limits of the existentialist film, the political thriller, and the documentary cinema alike, something confirmed by his next major work, *No End.* The story is deceptively simple. A progressive lawyer, Antek, charged with defending a worker active in the Solidarity movement, has a heart attack and dies, leaving behind a wife and child. His ghost "haunts" his wife, Urszula, who becomes more and more distraught and eventually commits suicide. Despite its flaws, this 1984 film represents a watershed in Kieslowski's oeuvre for three reasons. First, he met scriptwriter Krzysztof Piesiewicz and composer Zbigniew Preisner while shooting the film. Both would become key creative partners or counterplayers, to borrow Erik Erikson's suggestive term, in all of Kieslowski's subsequent works. Second, his screenplays shift dramatically away from male protagonists and the generally voyeuristic tropes associated with such (most obvious in the filmmaking protagonist of his 1979 *Camera Buff*) and toward powerful, complex female characters who exert a degree of control over the politics of the image. Third, his editing techniques begin to absorb, via some strange historical osmosis, the multinational forms pioneered by the Hong Kong and horror films of the 1970s. The result is a streamlining and compression of his shot selection and a corresponding emphasis on extracting the maximum intensities of color and sound out of otherwise routine scenes. Although Kieslowski was quite critical of the result, insisting that the parts did not quite add up to a whole,[2] the response from the audience was remarkable. As he later told Danusia Stok:

> *No End* wasn't shown for half a year. Then, when it was, it was terribly received in
> Poland. I've never had such unpleasantness over any other film as I had over this
> one. It was received terribly by the authorities, it was received terribly by the oppo-

sition [Solidarity], and it was received terribly by the Church. Meaning, by the three powers that be in Poland. We really got a thrashing over it. Only one element didn't give us a thrashing, and that was the audience. Never in my life have I received as many letters or phone calls about a film from people I didn't know as I did after *No End*. And all of them, in fact—I didn't get a single bad letter or call—said that I'd spoken the truth about martial law.[3]

Kieslowski's uncanny admixture of courtroom drama, psychological thriller, ghost story, and gothic romance story had struck a sensitive nerve indeed. In fairness to the critics, there was nothing directly comparable to *No End* in the Eastern European cinema of the day. Jan Svankmajer's animated classics come close, of course, but at that point the field of animation was still regarded as a marginal genre unworthy of serious critical attention on either side of the Berlin Wall. Possibly the closest Western European analogue to *No End* was J. J. Beineix's 1981 *Diva,* which drew upon the French New Wave, the cold war blockbuster, and the punk film (thanks to the show-stealing Dominique Pinon) to create the breakthrough postmodern European film. But where Beineix's crackerjack thriller had instant access to stylish scenery, hypersaturated visuals, and the latest cultural commodities, Kieslowski had no such easy recourse in the context of Eastern Europe's underdeveloped consumer and media culture. In the harsh austerity of 1980s Poland, the Diva would be just another hard currency émigré, while in France, the character of Urszula would be just another bored housewife. Kieslowski's ingenious response was to transform this narrative impossibility into a kind of thematic material in its own right, something most apparent in the startling narrative erasure of the deceased lawyer. At the beginning of the film, Antek functions as the existential observer or testifying witness, very much in the mold of the external voice-over of the private eye in film noir or the internal monologue of the existential thriller. But midway through the story, precisely where we might expect a series of flashbacks to illuminate Antek's heroic past, Kieslowski scandalously edits him out of the story and shifts the focus almost exclusively onto Urszula.

This was a shocking provocation on two levels. First, Kieslowski deliberately cast Jerzy Radziwilowicz as the deceased lawyer. Polish audiences would immediately recognize him as the morally exemplary hero of Andrzej Wajda's legendary *Man of Marble* and *Man of Iron,* films that rely heavily on flashbacks and retrospectives to create heroic parables of the Solidarity movement. The effect is to criticize the 1970s protest film on its own grounds, by zeroing in on the key weakness of the genre: its patriarchal gender politics. (Wajda's films basically reduce the women to mere helpmeets of heroic males.) Even the best-intentioned countericon to the Party orthodoxy remained all too orthodox and iconic. The second shock was presenting the audience with a complex, sexually emancipated, and economically independent female character. Urszula, as it turns out, is a translator, a self-employed culture worker with limited access to foreign languages, culture, and hard currency. Not only does she own and drive a car, something of a prestige object in mid-1980s Poland. She even has the gumption to seek out some sort of psychological therapy for her grief from a hypnotist—yet another scandal in a culture that condemned any mention of mental illness, stress, or psychotherapy as Western decadence. Even her stylized "suicide" (it's not quite that, for reasons we'll explore a bit later) doesn't follow the usual rules of melodrama. One would expect tearful scenes, cars being driven off cliffs, people jumping into rivers, and so forth. Instead, she methodically packs her child off to the grandmother, dresses in black, seals off the room, and tapes her mouth shut while gas fills the room. Nor do we see the happy couple finally united in death, in the manner of the bittersweet conclusion of Kusturica's dazzling tragicomedy, *Underground.* Their blurred forms walk away from us through a translucent window without even holding hands.

The fundamental narrative scandal of *No End,* then, and the reason that audiences loved it while critics hated it was that it portrayed the tragedy of a Western European protagonist trapped inside an Eastern European story line. For Polish audiences, the effect was roughly comparable to watching *Jules and Jim* crash headlong into the plot machinery of *Man of Marble.* What stamps the film as a transitional work, on the other hand, is the fact that Kieslowski did not have the narrative means to move beyond this point. The suicide sequence, for example, is simply too obviously allegorical of the plight of Polish filmmakers and other culture workers who were forced by the state censors to "play dead" in their own studios, publishing houses, and theaters, much as Urszula seals herself off in her own private space. Put another way, *No End* lacks a visual vocabulary capable of fully utilizing the multinational contradictions of its script. This is most apparent in the central visual leitmotif of the film: close shots of the ghostly or fleeting touch of hands. Annette Insdorf's comprehensive filmography of Kieslowski's work has this to say on the subject:

> Hands are central to *No End,* beginning with the ghost's abstracted fingers: this image introduces hands that have no agency—an impotence like that of Urszula's fingers in close-up playing frustratedly with her stockinged toes until the hose tears. The shadow of Antek's hand passes over his son's sleeping body and then touches gently the back of the boy's neck.

The delicately understated expression of Urszula's loss is first expressed in a close-up of her hands: she automatically makes two glasses of coffee, suddenly stops, and throws one out. The same glass shape returns in the session with the hypnotist: she sees Antek moving his finger on the rim of the empty glass, making a hypnotic sound of his own. She subsequently holds a glass of coffee in her kitchen: in close-up we watch the glass slip slowly down and finally crash on the floor.

Hands that are unable to touch or hold inform Kieslowski's larger theme: *No End* takes to its ultimate limit the notion of man's inability to do anything. We feel that Antek is not made for these times. On the other hand, the concrete presence of this ghost conveys the director's metaphysical belief in how the dead continue inside the living.[4]

After a promising beginning, the analysis stops exactly where it should start. Hands communicate, above all, the aesthetic register of *tactility*, something that Insdorf hurriedly seals off in the vacuum chamber of a suspiciously nontactile and patriarchal metaphysics (the hand, in short, as the symbolic currency of the body, in other words, the phallus). This glosses over the deeply subversive connotations of tactility in Eastern European media culture.[5] By the mid-1980s, public images of hands had lost whatever remaining connotations of honest manual labor they still had at the time of the Prague Spring and were identified almost exclusively with the mailed fist of the one-party state. This is why one of the first and most joyful acts of the Velvet Revolutions was the demolition of the single most obvious corporeal register of the one-party state, the neo-Stalinist statues littering public squares. In retrospect, the demolition process had begun decades earlier, as Eastern bloc artists refunctioned, outflanked, and undermined the military phallic symbols of the state, everywhere from the ferocious corporealities of Heiner Müller's plays to the restless tactilities of Jan Svankmajer's animation classics.

A careful rereading shows that *No End* deploys a sophisticated double strategy, wherein the hands of political authority (both the hands of the state, and the hands of the official opposition) are explicitly devalued, in favor of new types of corporeality and tactility. Antek's hands at the beginning of the movie are completely upstaged by Urszula's near the end. Similarly, the glasses, books, and steering wheels that Urszula's hands invest with meaning gradually accede to bodies—the body of a British stranger, whose hands remind her of Antek's; her own body, in the intriguing masturbation scene, where she *imagines* Antek's hands on her body, only to accidentally awaken her son, who is apparently going through his Oedipal phase; and, finally, that most interesting new body of all, the bundles of American dollars that reappear at crucial junctures throughout the film. This is a double-edged satire of the Polish government's position that its critics were whores of Western capitalism, as well as a rebuff of the moral pretensions of the extreme pro-market wing of Solidarity, who later became the shock troops of Eastern Europe's disastrous experiment in neoliberalism. This suggests, in turn, that the white tape across her mouth at the end of the film is more than just the reflexive signifier of artists forbidden to speak or films forbidden to touch on real subjects. It strongly hints that Urszula's Western subjectivity has *also* been rendered voiceless, for reasons that Kieslowski cannot yet define or specify. This is supported by the visual contrast of the white tape against Urszula's stark black clothing, which eerily echoes one of the central tropes of Patrick McGoohan's *The Prisoner:* the sequence where Rover, the giant white weather balloon, englobes and silences the black-clad No. 6. Although there's no record that Kieslowski ever saw McGoohan's work, there are good historical reasons to think that each might have arrived at the same aesthetic solution independently: Both were fiercely committed artists, one from semiperipheral Ireland and the other from semiperipheral Poland; both were pushing beyond the narrative boundaries of their respective genres (the spy thriller and Solidarity epic, respectively); and both were located at the right time and right place to document the moment when their respective societies were about to boil over (for McGoohan, the radical surge of 1968; for Kieslowski, the radical surge of 1989).

The Decalogue

It is somehow utterly characteristic of Kieslowski that, faced with the patent impossibility of making an apolitical film in an intensely politicized environment, and the no less impossible task of producing a political film in a climate of virulent repression, he pulled off the double-jointed miracle otherwise known as *The Decalogue.* This ten-part series was commissioned by Polish television in 1987 and aired in 1988, on the very eve of the Velvet Revolutions. Although each 60-minute episode is loosely based on one of the Ten Commandments, the series has more to do with the digital gospel of the nascent European Union than anything in the Church canon. In fact, *Decalogue* marks a genuine aesthetic revolution, the point at which Kieslowski dynamited the prison-house of national cinema and seized hold of the video tropes of the information age. The crucial innovation here was the introduction of an entirely new character trope, the border-crossing double or Euro-doppelganger. Curiously, the Euro-doppelganger does not come to us prepackaged in any recognizable mass-cultural form, like the detective fictions and Freudian binaries of the late nineteenth century, the paranoid narratives of the cold war spy thriller or Bond blockbuster, or even the dialectics of the gaze documented by the postwar existentialisms and film noir. This is because Kieslowski's doppelgangers are always *outside* the immediate action. Like the dream-sent emissaries of other worlds in Stanislaw Lem's science fiction parables (or, for that matter, the dream technologies of the vanished Krell in *Forbidden Planet*), they incarnate the objective limit point or outer horizon of the media culture and its interpretive machinery.

This aesthetic of interpretation stands in striking contrast to the closest Hollywood equivalent to Kieslowski, the expatriate Eastern European filmmakers of the 1970s. One thinks of the conclusion of Milos Forman's *One Flew over the Cuckoo's Nest* (1975), for example, wherein the Chief symbolically cancels out McMurphy's "false double," that is, the lobotomized shell of the latter, before carrying out the prison breakout, which McMurphy could only (sacrificially) anticipate, or the film noir of Polish émigré Roman Polanski's *Chinatown* (1974), where an unspeakable, incestuous doubling haunts the prototypical Los Angeles land speculation like one of Henry James's sexually charged ghosts. Tarkovsky's *Solaris* (1972) provides an intriguing intermediate case, wherein the multiple clones of Khari (the deceased wife) are both the psychological manifestations of Kelvin's individual wish-fulfillments, as well as direct "broadcasts" from the semisentient Solaris Ocean, that is, projections of a clearly Soviet unconscious. (Although Tarkovsky did not emigrate to Europe until the early 1980s, his notorious conflicts with the Soviet censors and film establishment meant that he was very much an exile-in-waiting.)

One of the most intriguing analogues of the Euro-doppelganger is the theme of the twin brothers or doubled brothers-in-arms relayed by John Woo's resplendent Hong Kong blockbuster trilogy: the brothers of *A Better Tomorrow* (1986), the cop and hitman of *The Killer* (1989), and the supercop and undercover agent of *Hard-boiled* (1992). Woo's greatest achievement was the synthesis of video forms out of the kinetic energies of the U.S. action blockbuster, the sound track of the 1980s music video, and the editing techniques of the Hong Kong martial arts films. In effect, Hong Kong turned its economic subalternity vis-à-vis Japan and the United States and its political subalternity vis-à-vis mainland China and Great Britain into a double-barreled opportunity, by means of a compensatory speculation in the realm of cultural capital. Hong Kong's vibrant and commercially successful film biz was simply the latest in a long line of successful export industries, ranging from footwear and textiles to consumer electronics.

Polish cinema in the era of autarkic accumulation did not, of course, have an indigenous export-platform industrialism at its fingertips. Kieslowski's ingenious response was to reappropriate *someone else's* export-platform industrialism—that of East Germany (in the form of the dialogue and script-writing innovations of Heiner Müller's Eurotheater) as well as the mediatic capital of West Germany (in the form of crucial financial and production support provided by Freie Sender Berlin). Put another way, where Woo transformed a range of Chinese, American, and Japanese materials into the transnational Pacific Rim thriller, Kieslowski refunctioned an equally broad range of European mediatic materials into the space of Eurovideo.

This is already an issue in the opening sequence of "Decalogue 1," which moves from a long shot of a frozen pond, to a close-up of the Euro-doppelganger (played here by Artur Barcis) seated by a fire, paced by Preisner's austere, haunting musical score. Barcis's gaunt countenance will reappear at crucial moments throughout the series, with the important exception of "Decalogue 7" and "Decalogue 10," two episodes where the role of the doppelganger undergoes a profound mutation (a mutation that, as one might expect from a director of Kieslowski's caliber, is by no means accidental). In "Decalogue 1," Barcis stares into the camera like some telecommunicatory Barnabas (the youthful messenger in Kafka's novel *The Castle*). The next shot is that of Aunt Irena, staring in shock through a storefront window at a news video on TV, cycling through slow-motion stills of Pawel running with his classmates. The final shot is that of a cobbled, Svankmajeresque surface, suggesting pebbles on a frozen beach. The camera tilts back, and we realize it is the cement facing of a tenement block, while pigeons fly into the sky overhead. (Pigeons, it should be noted, are another favorite John Woo trope.) This striking conjunction of a doppelganger who watches the watchers and a series of video surfaces mediated by glass windows and TV screens is part and parcel of an extraordinary polarization of visual material. In a nutshell, Kieslowski counterpoints intricate, detailed close-ups against a range of brilliantly framed long shots, while avoiding, excising, or masking midrange or panoramic shots. We almost never see the full extent of hallways, roads, or vistas, and where these do exist, they are condensed by low-level lighting, artful frames, and other camera techniques. During the auto accident scene of *No End,* for example, the medium-range shot of the victim being pulled from the wrecked car is visually unremarkable. Here, by contrast, the scene of the body being pulled from the frozen pond is an electrifying long-distance shot, set against the flashing lights of the rescue squad, and the close shots of the horrified faces of the onlooking crowd. (The body of the accident victim in "Decalogue 3," framed by the gleaming corridors of the casualty ward and the white sheets of the examining table, is another example of the same technique.) The result is a drastic compression of cinematic forms and the corresponding emergence of video surfaces.

Two of the most significant of these surfaces are the translucent "green screens" of Krzysztof's two home computers and the rough, shaggy fur of the stray dog that Pawel, Krzysztof's precocious young son, discovers frozen to death in the snow and ice outside his apartment. Whereas the algebraic equations and messages on the green screens are clearly meant to evoke the home computer aesthetic and high-tech rationalism of the 1980s, the characters' faces and bodies are almost always framed by sweaters, coats, and other clothing. (The doppelganger, for example, is practically encased in a thick, fur-lined parka, Aunt Irena always wears some sort of headgear, and Pawel's shirts and sweaters are usually the only object in our field of vision that is bright and colorful.) At the breakfast table, Pawel asks his father about the meaning of death, resulting in the following exchange:

PAWEL: So what's left?

KRZYSZTOF: What a person has achieved, the memory of that person. The memory's important. The memory that someone moved in a certain way, or that they were kind. You remember their face, their smile, that a tooth was missing. . . . It's too early, what do you expect of me so early in the morning? *(Close shot of milk swirling in morning tea or coffee.)*

PAWEL: The milk's sour.

KRZYSZTOF: *(Nodding.)* It's sour. *(Pause.)*

PAWEL: "For the peace of her soul." You didn't mention a soul.

KRZYSZTOF: It's a form of words of farewell. There is no soul.

PAWEL: Auntie says there is.

KRZYSZTOF: Some find it easier to live thinking that.

PAWEL: And you?

KRZYSZTOF: Me? Frankly, I don't know. Why? What's happened?

PAWEL: Nothing . . . only . . . *(Pauses, grows more and more upset.)* I was so happy when I got the right answer . . . and the pigeon came for the crumbs, too. *(Fighting back tears.)* But then I saw the dead dog, and I thought: so what? What's it matter if I worked out when Miss Piggy would catch Kermit?

KRZYSZTOF: Which dog?

PAWEL: *(Calming down.)* The one with yellow eyes. The one who scavenged around the trash cans, you know? *(Reflects for a moment.)* Perhaps he's better off now, huh?

This is extraordinary scriptwriting, on a par with anything celebrated in the auteur canon or enshrined in the annals of Hollywood. Using the simplest sentences, Kieslowski constructs a web of extraordinarily subtle and complex ideas, which are never redundant or extraneous to the story line, but which are never allowed to degenerate into abstract moralizing or tendentious metaphysics either. To some degree this was due to the presence of cowriter Krzysztof Piesiewicz, whose prior vocation as a lawyer gave him a keen sense of the politics and aesthetics of testimony. One could also point to television's brevity as a medium, as well as the accelerated shooting schedule of TV series, which forced Kieslowski to reduce the elements of narrative exposition to their absolute minimum by condensing a given shot selection, visual motif, or dialogue into the smallest configurable space.

One of the great examples of this is the single most prominent visual signifier of "Decalogue 1," ice, ranging from the frozen pond to the frozen bottle of milk, and from the frozen dog to the harmless ice on which the schoolchildren are playing. At the end of the episode, this subtle motif takes on a heartrending emotional resonance. The distraught father, who has just knocked over a row of votive candles in the darkened church, wipes his fevered brow with a small, circular piece of ice fished out of the cistern in the frosty church. Meanwhile, the overturned candles drip hot wax onto a religious icon, painting ironic "tears" on the icon's cheeks. Still another is the theme of intelligent computers or cyborgs, ranging from the wired appliances of the apartment that Pawel shows off to his aunt, to Krzysztof's university lecture on the possibility of programming intelligence into a computer.[6] In the context of the fatal accident on the pond, this might be taken to be a straightforward denunciation of the hubris of technocrats. Kieslowski, however, is not really interested in playing rationalism off against theology. (He even shows the father testing the ice himself during the night, to make sure it is safe.) Rather, he's interested in the aesthetics of *play:* Pawel plays with the pigeons, asks questions about the frozen dog, helps his father play a round of speed chess at a tournament, solves equations involving Miss Piggy and Kermit, and even provides an apt comment when the computers malfunction and turn themselves on. (The cursor says, "Ready," and when his father turns them off, Pawel asks innocently, "But what if it really wanted something?")

Nor is religion really the issue in the scene where Pawel visits Aunt Irena and asks what faith is. Not only is this the one moment where she takes off her hat, giving us a sense of rare intimacy. We also glimpse three open windows in the background—an unusual medium-range shot of an adjoining apartment house, subtly mirroring the three photographs of the pope laid out on the table. Both signifiers turn out to be empty spaces rather than positive signifiers:

> PAWEL: *(Referring to the pictures of the pope.)* Do you think he understands the meaning of life?
>
> IRENA: I think so.
>
> PAWEL: Dad told me that we are living in order to make life easier for those who will come after us. But it doesn't always work out.
>
> IRENA: Not always. Your father's right. It's just, if you can do something for others, to help, to be there, even if it's only a little thing, you know you are needed, and life becomes brighter somehow. There are big and small things. Today you liked the dumplings, so that made me happy. One is alive, and it is a present, a gift.
>
> PAWEL: Dad's your brother, isn't he?
>
> IRENA: You know he is. *(Significant pause. She rests her head on her arm.)* You'd like to know why we are so different, your father and I. *(Pawel nods.)*
>
> IRENA: We were brought up in a Catholic family. Your father noticed, even earlier than you, that many things could be measured. Later, he concluded that measurement could be applied to everything. Perhaps he doesn't always believe it, but he wouldn't admit it. Your dad's way of life may seem more reasonable, but it doesn't rule out God. Even for your dad. Understand?
>
> PAWEL: *(With refreshing honesty.)* Not really.
>
> IRENA: God is very simple if you have faith.
>
> PAWEL: Do you believe in God?
>
> IRENA: Yes.
>
> PAWEL: *(Unimpressed.)* So who *is* he?
>
> IRENA: *(She embraces him.)* What do you feel now?
>
> PAWEL: *(Murmuring.)* I love you.
>
> IRENA: Exactly. That's where he is.

Given that Pawel asked his father about the meaning of death and questioned his aunt about the meaning of life, this suggests that the real issue is the paradox of mortality: the fact that what is alive is meaningful only in relation to what is dead, whereas death, in turn, has meaning only to the living. Indeed, the entire episode is full of living beings who perish, as well as dead things, for example, computers and cartoon characters, which spring unexpectedly to life.

What this explanation omits, of course, is the doppelganger, who seems to occupy a vantage point somehow beyond life and death alike, a position

associated not with the objective fact of mortality per se but with the subjective experience of bearing witness to such, that is to say, temporality. This
comes very close to Adorno's notion of transience or the self-reflection of
subjects grasping their own inner historicity.[7] This may help to explain the
significance of the moment when Irena asks about Pawel's mother, who is
apparently somewhere abroad and who sent him a letter detailing what she
was doing each and every hour. All of the main characters are marked by quite
specific pairs of visual motifs and temporal registers: Krzysztof is associated
with the green computer screen (global space) and with foreign languages
(global time); Irena, with windows (urban space) and the photographs of the
pope (urban time); and the absent mother with foreign travel or exile (overseas space) and a daily schedule (work time). Pawel himself is most strongly
associated with the mediatic space of the news report (this is also hinted at
during his father's university lecture, where he peers through what is either
a videocamera or slide projector) and the fatal ice skates (play time).

This suggests that the real tragedy of the story is the annulment or betrayal of the utopian promise of mediatic space and leisure time. The first
hint of this is the eerie sight of blue ink welling up, sudden and irresistible
as blood, through the white sheets of paper on which Krzysztof is penciling
in calculations and jottings. When the latter washes off the ink in the porcelain sink, he suddenly stares at his own reflection in the mirror, overcome
by a strange foreboding. As he begins the search for his son, the camera
angles become more and more feverish and hectic, employing increasingly
sophisticated editing and contrast techniques. For instance, when he visits
a female friend who was supposed to give Pawel English lessons, the teacher,
who was ill with the flu and had sent Pawel away, invites Krzysztof inside,
ironically mistaking his nervous tension for an evidently welcome romantic
overture. He then bends from left to right across our field of vision, fooling
us into thinking he's entering the room. At the last second we realize he was
simply reaching to pull the door shut. It moves right to left, a visual effect
that is exactly like having a door unexpectedly shut in our face.

Such editing techniques are matched by the simultaneous compression
of the close-up shot and the slim, spare sound track. Previously fully lit faces
are suddenly darkened, cast in shadow, or framed by jagged slivers of intense
backlighting. Thus, when Krzysztof is walking around the grounds of the
apartment complex, the camera shifts to a low-angle shot, looking upwards
at Krzysztof from close to the ground—that is to say, from the missing Pawel's
point of view. Acoustically, we hear Krzysztof radio for his son on a hobby-
ist walkie-talkie, against the raucous chop of a helicopter in the distance. The

only response is random static and the voices of the rescue squad. The result is an aesthetics of splintering, the direct negation of the "crisis mode" sequences in countless police and rescue melodramas, where handheld shots, disorienting camera movement, and extremely intense lighting and sound effects are supposed to signify a state of emergency.

What prevents this splintering effect from becoming all too capricious (as in the case of Jean-Luc Godard's uneven *Weekend,* a film best described as a Monty Python sketch in search of a comedy writer), or deadeningly objective (as in the stereotypical flashbacks of the soap opera or police drama) is Kieslowski's rigorous sense of visual symmetry. This is most apparent in the use of extended visual citations or reflexive samples, which cite or quote previously seen material in new ways. Thus an earlier scene, where a little girl knocks on the door shortly after the incident of the spilled ink and asks for Pawel, forms the crucial background to a much later scene, where a girl by the pond tells Krzysztof that Jacek (one of Pawel's friends who had just been whisked away by his family) knows what happened to his son. Similarly, when Krzysztof chases after the family, a quick series of tense, off-kilter handheld shots shows them exiting our field of vision at the pond, at the elevator, and later at the hallway of their flat, generating a kind of horizontal vertigo that perfectly offsets the vertically oriented shots of the father we saw previously. In this hallway scene, where Jacek cries out that he and Pawel were playing on the ice together, Jacek's face is framed horizontally by his mother and vertically by the door, while the sound track is polarized between the mother's hysterical screams and Krzysztof's stunned silence. Finally she tears him away, literally and figuratively plunging Pawel's father (and viewers) into darkness.

If "Decalogue 1" had ended here, it would be all too easy to slap a moral or allegorical coda onto the story, to feel outraged at the shocking selfishness of Jacek's parents, who are so relieved that their own son survived that they simply turn their backs on Krzysztof. Kieslowski quickly nullifies this interpretation, however, by manufacturing two specific visual tropes that abolish the lingering vestiges of the rescue melodrama and the soap opera alike. The first is the uniquely Kieslowskian reinvention of the video frame pioneered by the Hong Kong films of the 1970s, the slow-motion, semicircular pan, wherein we watch a close shot of someone who is watching (or being watched by) someone else, their face slowly rotating left or right. This is the scene where Krzysztof is seated in the apartment, still in shock, when he suddenly becomes aware of the computer staring blindly right back at him, his face highlighted by the eerie green backlight of the computer screen.[8] The second is Kieslowski's version of the horror film cut, the video freeze-frames of Pawel and his schoolmates cycling across the TV screen. Instead of the full image we see at the very beginning of "Decalogue 1," we glimpse only partial, abstracted close-ups of such or what amounts to a video aesthetic created out of the extended reprocessing of telejournalistic images.

These two tropes, which we'll provisionally call the video pan and the video still, will form the narrative antipodes or axial termini around which the rest of the series will organize its aesthetic content. The price paid for this advance is, of course, the definitive abolition of the existential film and its associated mediations (film noir, the adventure-thriller, the private eye, etc.), and it is surely no accident that "Decalogue 1" is the only episode where the Euro-doppelganger stares at the audience for lengthy periods of time, an all too existential gesture that Kieslowski quietly drops from later episodes. As a result, the doppelganger "falls into history," as it were, thereby losing its status as an objective witness or alien observer, but gaining the subjective power to intervene directly in the story line. This subjective turn is matched by an equally far-reaching objective transformation, wherein the ionized subcomponents of the existential thriller, the detective drama, and the TV melodrama all begin to fluoresce with a genuinely multinational content.

In "Decalogue 2," for example, this multinational content emerges out of a dense network of framed bodies and corporeal signifiers, ranging from scenic posters of mountain climbers to the black-and-white photograph of the Consultant's vanished family, and from the disembodied voices on telephones and answering machines to the recorded materials of stereo systems and radios. Even the bodies of the patients in the hospital ward have their counterpart in the Consultant's carefully tended cacti, pet birds, and bubbling aquarium. Traces of visual and aural bodies circulate unceasingly throughout the entire episode, everywhere from the deceased animal a worker finds at the beginning of the story, to the ironic introduction of the two main characters. (Dorota, played to perfection by the inimitable Krystyna Janda, introduces herself: "I live above. Do you remember me?" The Consultant responds, "Yes. You ran over my dog two years ago." Later, when he refuses to yield any information about her critically ill husband, she snaps, "Pity I didn't run over *you*.")

But whereas Aunt Irena in "Decalogue 1" was associated with medium shots of windows and storefronts, Dorota is associated with two explicit symbols of global consumerism: a state-of-the-art Japanese stereo system and the West German Beetle she drives. Meanwhile Andrzej, Dorota's critically ill husband, is associated not with visual registers per se but with acoustic and tactile ones, thus the ruby depths of the jellied preserves Dorota leaves at Andrzej's bedside, for example, or Andrzej's fevered hallucinations of slow, dripping leaks across rusted surfaces and peeling paint. This may have something to do with the fact that Dorota is a musician, a self-possessed, Western-oriented young professional who has no time for self-pity or re-criminations. During a later meeting with the Consultant, she presses him by saying, "The Americans [American doctors] tell their patients."

What Dorota wants from the Consultant, however, is not really informa-tion about her husband but a strange kind of absolution—not for the past but for the future. She is pregnant, thanks to another man, and doesn't want to keep the child if her husband is going to live. The Consultant will con-vince her, for reasons of his own, that he is doomed. At one point she asks:

> DOROTA: Do you believe in God?
> DOCTOR: I have a God; there's only enough of him for me.
> DOROTA: A private God? Then ask him for absolution.

This is not a theological or metaphysical motif but a material and Euro-pean one, something hinted at by the black-and-white photograph he turned away from our field of vision at the beginning of Dorota's visit. After she leaves, he reverses it, revealing a woman and two young children, whose identity will remain a mystery for some time.

Retroactive suspense is the central leitmotif of "Decalogue 2." The dead animal at the beginning of the episode, for example, is not revealed to be a rabbit until late in the story; the Consultant's fragmentary family history to his housekeeper, Barbara, is left unfinished until the end of the episode, and so forth. Conversely, the key visual symbols of the episode are never static or fixed, but constantly acquire fresh layers of meaning. Thus the wall post-ers first hint at some sort of exotic mountainscape, with connotations of for-eign exile, but later turn out to symbolize Dorota's husband, who is a moun-tain climber; the leaves of the house plant Dorota rips apart in a moment of anguish return later as a medicinal tincture for her husband; and the cup of tea or coffee she tips onto the floor (Kieslowski employs a magnificent, slow-motion shot of the cup shattering into a million pieces) turns out to herald not the definitive rupture with her husband but the break with her lover.

This complexity extends to the role of the doppelganger in "Decalogue 2," represented here as a medical intern or orderly who is present at two key moments. The first is a scene where the Consultant works up Andrzej's medical tests in the laboratory and asks a colleague for his opinion. The lat-ter hesitates, then says the disease is clearly progressing. The second is the moment where Dorota tells her unconscious husband she loves him; the doppelganger watches through a glass door. All this would seem to be innocent enough, were it not for two additional events that cast quite a different light on the characters involved. First, we learn that the Consultant's mysterious photo is a shot of his wife and children, killed in a World War II bombing raid. His motivation—restitution for the past—at last becomes clear. But Dorota's motive is not at all obvious. Even after the scene at her husband's bedside, she barges in on the Consultant, demanding a definitive diagnosis of whether Andrzej will live or die. This suggests the doppelganger's presence registered her *ambivalence* toward her husband, rather than any one-dimensional register of guilt or affection. If this is so, then why is the Consultant visited by the doppelganger as well? What on earth could he possibly feel ambivalent about?

The answer is suggested by the long, slow pan from Dorota at her window to a long-distance zoom on the Consultant in his apartment, backlit by the most peculiar red light. This is followed by a fast pan onto Andrzej, who is reawakening into the land of the living. The first thing he sees is a fly struggling heroically to free itself from the sticky trap of the fruit preserves. Our initial disgust at this unsanitary intruder fades as we realize this tiny creature wants to live as badly as we do. (Eventually it flies off under its own power, just like Andrzej.) The themes of animal bodies and human corporeality merge into a shining amalgam of collective compassion, the direct negation of the personal tragedy or private catastrophe. The logical and irresistible conclusion is that the Consultant *knew* that the lab results were ambiguous at best. It's quite possible he even reversed the order of the slides, in order to keep the truth of Andrzej's recovery to himself.

This artful ambiguity is also, however, what stamps this episode as an essentially transitional work, a skillful reappropriation of the conventional hospital melodrama rather than anything fundamentally new. One of the main reasons here is the underdevelopment of Dorota's character, who is clearly meant to be the professionalized, late 1980s version of Urszula. Unfortunately, we learn almost nothing of her professional career or workplace aspirations, and as a result, Janda's superb performance cannot quite paper over the scission between Dorota's evident self-possession and tenacity and her indecision about her pregnancy. As a result, the Consultant takes on the role of theological or existential arbiter, between the dictates of conscience versus those of convenience. The depth and richness of Kieslowski's subsequent female characters, on the other hand, is based on their capacity to be their *own* arbiters, that is to say, emotionally complex, self-sufficient professionals, whose dilemmas, crises, and struggles for self-definition will form a microcosm of the birth pangs of the European Union.

This European turn is broadly hinted at by the audacious opening sequence of "Decalogue 3," where two new visual registers make their first appearance: the shimmering, crystalline nightscape of a downtown Warsaw not yet overwhelmed with commercial logos and neon signs, and close shots of Ewa in her car, watching holiday partygoers through the windshield. Whereas the former is tinted a harsh, wintry blue, the latter is backlit with gorgeously diffuse low-level reds, reflected and refracted every which way, and seconded by Ewa's signature red scarf. The other main character of the episode, Janusz (Ewa's former lover, who returned to his wife and family), is dressed as Santa Claus, and it is no accident that the camera zooms in on his luxurious false beard, neatly adding the third visual and tactile register of a cottony or snowy white. Surprisingly, this register is *not* associated with the family or domestic sphere but with social spaces of circulation, such as the hospital, the drunk tank, the train station, mass transit systems, and even Janusz's taxi. As if to hammer the point home, when Janusz turns to say Merry Christmas to a neighbor, the latter turns out to be Krzysztof, the father from "Decalogue 1"—if not quite the ghost of Christmas past, then surely the avatar of a canceled-out or negated family sphere.

The other significant narrative space that is canceled out quite early in "Decalogue 3" is that of the Church. The Christmas Mass scene, in particular, is a secular miracle of shot composition straight out of the John Woo playbook. Kieslowski employs glowing chandeliers and the ominous vertical shadows of pillars to frame a video pan around Janusz, who realizes that Ewa is somewhere in the audience, watching him. Nothing in Woo's films, however, quite compares with the moment when Ewa phones Janusz and gets him to meet her outside. Janusz's wife, unaware of who is calling, is framed from the back and side, while Janusz himself is completely silhouetted by the bright light behind him. (Appropriately, he tells her a "white lie," to the effect that someone reported that their car is being stolen.) Once outside, he suddenly glimpses Ewa's tantalizing reflection in the glass door, lighting up a cigarette. Where Woo excels in rapid shot editing and the dynamic compression of space, thereby anticipating the visual revolution of the 1990s 3D video game, Kieslowski specializes in framing and the dynamic expansion of space, thus foreshadowing the aesthetics of streaming video.

No streaming video, however, could do justice to the plot, which revolves around Ewa's claim that her husband, Edward, has disappeared and her subsequent attempts to inveigle Janusz into something that is not quite an affair but very far from a friendship, either. Whereas the story line moved inexorably toward tragedy in "Decalogue 1" and toward redemption in "Decalogue 2," D3 keeps us perched on the edge of our seats with the spectacle of characters playing games within games, for stakes somehow beyond both these categories. When the two characters visit a local hospital, for example, they confront a bloodied, shockingly graphic corpse, and Ewa's aghast response causes Janusz to instinctively throw his arms around her. As it turns out, the body wasn't her husband at all, and when Janusz begins to pull back, she lashes out:

> EWA: I wish it *was* him. Or you. How often I've pictured your faces crushed by truck wheels. Once I dreamed about you. Your neck was broken. Your tongue lolled out. I looked at you and laughed. I wonder who this one hurt, who is going to rejoice? *(Janusz slowly turns away.)*

This shocking ambivalence, perched midway between a raging fury and a consuming guilt, is just the opening gambit of a full-scale struggle of wills between the two that rages throughout the night. Later he counterattacks by deliberately speeding past a police car, setting off a chase sequence through wintry roads and an underground tunnel. Kieslowski splices in an impressive close-up of a flashing police siren, pulsing blue on the right and red on left. (Even the cars, by the way, follow the tripartite color scheme of the episode: The police car is blue, Janusz's taxi is white, and Ewa's car is red.) Ewa uses her quick wits to prevent them from being arrested, claiming, plausibly enough, that the car had been stolen but they had just found it on the embankment. After the police depart, Janusz ups the ante by engaging in a terrifying game of chicken. He accelerates straight at an oncoming streetcar, avoiding a collision at the last possible second. A brief shot shows the streetcar driver to be none other than Artur Barcis's mysterious doppelganger.

Not only does Ewa pass the test, never once wavering or breaking down, but she will respond in kind, by mobilizing the interior of her apartment precisely where Janusz mobilized his car. After phoning the hospital with a bogus report of her husband collapsing on a nearby street corner, she mysteriously hangs up her husband's coat and hat in a prominent location, and she even puts a razor blade and an extra toothbrush in the bathroom. During the following dialogue, she is filmed against a darkened background, while Janusz is beautifully framed by the red, blue, and violet refractions of Christmas lights in the upper right background:

> JANUSZ: I didn't make that phone call three years ago, honestly. It was important to me. You were important. The truth is that I loved you and I was willing to . . .

change everything. When we were getting dressed, he stood with his back
turned. You never once looked at me. I took your hand. You snatched it back.
Then he said that when we were dressed you could choose whether to stay or
to leave with him. You followed him without a word.

EWA: Yes, that's how it was. *(He nods.)* But Edward made one more condition. I
could follow him, provided we two never met again.

JANUSZ: Mmh, you said you didn't intend us to meet again, and I agreed.

EWA: Give me your hand. Unloved . . . misunderstood . . . you are right. My fault.
But you fell on your feet. You're as you were, aren't you? *(With increasing
hostility.)* You strove to make things work again. You are kind, caring. *(He grits
his teeth, forcibly pulls his hand away.)* Take your hand. It stinks of gasoline.

The next sequence is Kieslowski at his finest. Rather than allowing the
emotional energy to dissipate, he heightens the tension when Janusz gets up
and opens a door, giving us the impression he's leaving, when in fact he's
just entering the bathroom to *wash his hands* (whether of her, of this night,
or of life itself is unclear). Once in the bathroom, he sees the razor and begins to remove the blade, and we suspect the worst. Instead of the spilling
of blood, however, we see the spilling of Ewa's tears. (She cries out, not entirely truthfully, "Did you ever think what happened after we left the hotel?
How I feel when there's a romance film on TV and he stares at *me* instead
of watching the screen? I've not slept with him once, not once.") Fortunately
the blade is dull, but the eerie close-up of the metal surface sliding against
Janusz's skin is enough to make the flesh crawl. This gesture will be mirrored
somewhat later in an equally excruciating moment, where Ewa closes the
bathroom door and drags the harmless blade across her own wrist. This
undertone of mutual self-destruction brackets the scene where they kiss
Orthodox style (once on either cheek) as a gesture of amity. Just as their lips
start to touch for a third and obviously romantic kiss, the doorbell rings.
Their rescuers are the neighborhood children, out singing carols.

Quite another ritual of self-destruction is on display when the pair search
the drunk tank, where the attendant, an anti-Semitic thug with a shaven head,
hears Edward's last name (Garus) and sneers at Ewa, "A Jew." The authoritarian connotation is heightened when he proceeds to hose down the drunks
in a metal cage, sprawled naked and half-conscious on the tiled floor (reminiscent not just of Auschwitz but also of the Communist government's tac-
tic of deploying water hoses against demonstrators). Through close shots
of the wire mesh of the case, a framing device that anticipates many of the
scenes of "Decalogue 4," we see one inmate clinging desperately to the
branches of a Christmas tree under the icy stream. Finally Janusz loses his

temper and wrests the hose away from the attendant. The Christmas tree returns with a vengeance in the next sequence, when they accelerate down the road and Ewa suddenly seizes the steering wheel. They screech to a halt, knocking the gorgeously lit Christmas tree on the embankment over onto the roof of the car, splaying red lights every which way—undoubtedly the capstone metaphor of the episode.

Kieslowski has one more surprise in store for us, however. The concluding sequence opens in a deserted, early morning train station. We see a single Christmas tree twinkling gaily amid a sea of cheerless concrete, watch an automatic camera tracking nonexistent passersby, and glimpse the banks of security TV monitors through the window of the station office, two canny references to the video still. Suddenly Kieslowski interpolates a wildly careering shot of a skateboarder thundering in front of us. Off hops the rider, a cheerful young woman straight out of a 1980s music video, who just happens to be the station attendant on duty. ("If I don't move around, I fall asleep," she explains guilelessly.) Ewa hands her a black-and-white photograph of Edward, and although the young woman doesn't recognize him as a passenger, Janusz immediately notices something odd: The woman in the photo isn't Ewa. At last, Ewa reveals the truth: Edward has lived in Krakow for three years with a new wife; Ewa was play-acting all along.

> EWA: I told a pack of lies tonight.
>
> JANUSZ: Why?
>
> EWA: I'm not sure. Do you know the game, if a man comes around the corner, it means luck, but a woman means bad luck?
>
> JANUSZ: I know it.
>
> EWA: I played it today. I thought that if I could get through the night with you until seven in the morning . . .
>
> JANUSZ: What?
>
> EWA: Then everything would be fine.
>
> JANUSZ: And if you failed? *(She drops a tiny white pill from her hand on the ground.)*
>
> EWA: I thought of everything. I live alone. It's difficult to be alone on a night like this. People . . .
>
> JANUSZ: People shut themselves in, draw the curtains.
>
> EWA: When I was driving to church, I saw a boy. He'd escaped from the hospital in his pajamas. *(Brief, partially obscured long-range shot of train station; we glimpse two guards on patrol and an unidentifiable figure dressed in white. It is unclear whether they are chasing the figure.)* They caught him.

Her final words bury the hatchet, in more ways than one. "I know it wasn't you who made that telephone call." This is not merely the fitting conclusion of the episode, the ultimate gesture of abnegation in a plot teeming with abnegations. Astonishing as it sounds, this is also Kieslowski's severance notice to the one-party state. It should be remembered that Janusz is a taxi driver, the sort of independent entrepreneur or professional only grudgingly tolerated (and often crudely repressed) by the cadre state. Ewa is not, however, a symbol of state authority in her own right, a role assumed by the incidental characters, who directly incarnate the logic of their respective social spaces. (The police are properly credential-conscious, the warden is properly brutal, the train attendant is properly mobile, etc.) Half unwilling participant, half self-conscious provocateur, Ewa occupies a position adjacent to but somehow beyond the reach of the state and the family sphere alike: the shadowy space, in short, of the nongovernmental or independent mass media. Instead of recycling a Dickensian Christmas fable or indulging in an antigovernment screed, Kieslowski cleverly transforms every single index of political repression under the one-party state—tapped phones, surveillance cameras, spies at Church meetings, police sweeps, and secret denunciations—into the mediatic spaces of the hospital, the taxi service, the telecommunications network, and the train station.

The politics of mediatization are also the crucial issue in "Decalogue 4," only not in the sense of adults regressing to the state of adolescents or a threatened family sphere but rather the storm and stress of adolescents growing into adulthood. The opening hints at this nicely by contrasting the faces of the two main characters—Anka and her father, Michal—through half-drawn blinds. Anka, shrouded in darkness and framed in gorgeous backlighting, gazes wistfully through one set of blinds at her father, who is partly obscured behind another set of blinds, his face fully lit by warm, rounded yellows. In fact, "Decalogue 4" marks an important breakthrough for Kieslowski, the point at which the visual forms innovated by "Decalogue 1" and "Decalogue 3" blossom into their content, namely, the politics of a nascent Euroconsumerism. Our first clue is the strange letter Anka finds underneath her father's passport, inscribed: "To be opened after my death."

Whereas medicalized and biological bodies circulated throughout "Decalogue 2" and spaces of traffic and circulation were the issue in "Decalogue 3," envelopes (external packaging) and scripts (internal logos or symbols) are the modus of exchange in "Decalogue 4." In addition to being a receptacle of meaning, the envelope is also a powerful visual trope in its own right. This is acknowledged by a gorgeously framed interior shot preceding the moment when Anka's boyfriend phones her. Two open doors and various furnishings are arranged in the background, forming an intricate latticework of intersecting rectangular frames, subtly counterpointing Michal (leaning on the couch) against Anka (stretching sensuously against the blue and white paint of the bathroom) in the background. This is a powerful anticipation of the streaming aesthetic of the late 1990s, where boxes of multiple media stream messages on a single page, thereby collapsing several layers of information into a single screen. This suggests that, in a curious kind of way, Anka's image corresponds to the absent space of consumer technology (the imported stereo, TV, VCR, or computer) we would otherwise expect to be displayed in the room.

This is confirmed by the next sequence at the airport, which is also the first time we see an explicit shot of a corporate logo or graphic icon in the entire series—in this case, the bright red LOT symbol of Poland's national air carrier. Kieslowski then zeroes in on the whole question of *viewing:* Anka visits a matronly eye doctor, saying she couldn't see the airliner taking off in the distance! The ophthalmologist is, if not quite Kieslowski's own personal doppelganger, undoubtedly one of the quirkiest and most enjoyable bit characters in a series overflowing with superb bit characters. After quizzing Anka about theater school entrance exams (apparently her own son is trying to enter the school), the doctor points out the letters *f-a-t-h-e-r* on the eye chart. Anka immediately recognizes the English word. The doctor tartly notes, "I check intelligence at the same time."

The second explicit reference to logos and icons occurs in the scene where Anka finds the letter and sits down at a desk, pondering whether to open it or not, framed by a giant white lamp globe. These two motifs—the off-white trapezoids of script-bearing letters and envelopes, and luminous, light-bearing bubbles—are the direct descendants of a similar scene in "Decalogue 1," when Pawel dialed the meteorological bureau. Two lamps framed Pawel, one glowing white above, and the other forming a bright sliver on the left, the whole forming an unwitting rebus of that other great meteorological symbol, *The Prisoner*'s carnivorous weather balloon. This is not to say Kieslowski consciously quoted from McGoohan's work (as a rule, Kieslowski shies away from all such quotations). Instead, it underlines the fact that both worked with the same mass-cultural material. This is nothing less than the streamlined consumer goods and bubble shapes of the 1960s consumer culture, an aesthetic still widely prevalent in 1980s Poland, and one that will reappear at key moments for the rest of the series.

The consumer culture is also an issue in Preisner's haunting sound track,

most notably during the scene where Anka tries to open the letter in a wintry park by an icy river. In the background, Barcis's doppelganger materializes on a small boat, vigorously paddling across the rapid current. Just as
Anka is about to cut open the letter, she freezes, realizing he is watching: He
is ashore and carrying the boat on his back, the craft forming a trapezoidal
white shape behind him. Just as his urgent glance is echoed in Anka's look
of guilt, so too is the shape of the boat echoed by the much smaller trapezoid
of the envelope in her hand. The theme music to the entire scene is orches-
trated with a piano, violin, and horns, yielding a curiously hollow, piercing
sound that focuses on a single, sparse tone, moves a half step down, and then
returns to the original tone before moving up one full step and then another.
What prevents this from being the sort of standard I–III chord transition
typical of mainstream North American pop music is the bass line, which
subtly outlines the interval of a fifth behind the melody: What seems to be a
I–III transition is an eerie, unsettling minor third–major fifth transition.

The result is a set of major tones that rattle around inside a minor transition like a skeleton in the closet. As it turns out, this has the most striking
resonance with the work of quite another European cultural producer of the
1980s, Ireland's U2. U2's greatest achievement was to transform the acoustic
materials of the 1980s—electronic beeps, whines, chirps, and whistles—into
an autonomous musical content. This was accomplished by the extended repetition of a single jagged chord structure, shorn of the overproduced bass
effects, strings, or horns that cluttered mainstream 1970s and 1980s rock
music. The result was an extraordinary sonic polarization, capable of generating a maximum of coloratura with an absolute minimum of melodic
materials. This perfectly complemented the admixture of Irish and gospel
registers of Bono's lead vocals, the direct antecedent of the lyrical MCs of
the late 1980s, who were called upon to intermediate between the heavy bass
line and high-pitched samples and scratches of hip-hop music.

The state-of-the-art sound track in "Decalogue 4" is matched by state-
of-the-art scriptwriting, which deftly weaves an extraordinary array of sub-
sidiary cultural forms into the narrative fabric. The eye doctor episode is
merely one of these. One could also point to the family friend who recur-
rently shows up to procure various unlikely items (sketches, hair tonic, etc.),
the cameo appearance of the Consultant from "Decalogue 2" during a tense
elevator sequence, or, indeed, the theatrical-romantic subtext of Anka's
boyfriend, a fellow student at her drama school. During one class, for example, she has trouble focusing on the lines of a romantic drama, despite (or,
more likely, precisely because of) the fact that her partner in the scene is her

boyfriend. Symptomatically, she steps into her role only when the professor, an older man, unexpectedly takes over the boyfriend's role. The same narrative complexity is evident in the set design, wherein the airport, the apartment cellar, the elevator, Anka's bedroom, and even the apartment block's walkway are all transformed into profoundly theatrical or performative spaces, brimming with video tropes.

The very first of these tropes appears shortly after Anka discovers the faded black-and-white photograph of her mother, when she sits down at her desk to write something on her mother's paper and envelopes. She is exquisitely framed by a McGoohanesque bubble lamp on her left and the horizontal red and white stripes of an American flag tacked brazenly to the wall behind her—the scandalous conjunction of a neonational surface with a multinational consumerism. Later, we *hear* a video trope, the whine of jet aircraft, in the scene when Anka confronts her father at the airport and recites what we have been led to believe is her mother's letter:

> ANKA: *(Reciting in a provocative tone.)* My darling daughter, I don't know how you will look when you read this. *(Whine of jet increases along with emotional tension.)* You must be grown up and Michal no longer alive. You're tiny now. I've seen you only once. They don't bring you to me because I am about to die. I have something important to tell you. Michal is not your father. *(Whine of jet begins to decrease.)* It is not important who your father is. A silly moment and much suffering. I am sure Michal will love you as his own and you will be happy with him. I try to imagine you in the future, reading this letter. Your hair is dark, isn't it? Your hands are slender, your neck is soft. I'd like so much to . . . signed Mother. (He slaps her, once.)

What provokes him is not so much the actual content of the letter as the sexualized swagger (beret slung back, head inclined, every inch the Western European fashion model) she adopts during her recitation. All this, of course, is just the opening gambit of an intriguing game of mirror performances or reciprocal self-identifications, that is to say, Anka's self-identification with someone who is not quite her father, and Michal's identification with someone who is not quite his daughter. This is highlighted by the conversation in the cellar, where Michal shows Anka the envelopes, letters, and a black-and-white photograph showing her mother and three men (one of whom is her real father). Kieslowski employs a combination of extreme close-ups and masterful low-level lighting here, framing the two characters between two candles in the foreground and the grille of a wire mesh in the background. Anka's face, still in her signature beret and red scarf, is directly open to the camera, with a light shining in from the far left. Michal, on the other hand, is partially hidden by an occluding mesh. This is a direct reprise of the title sequence of "Decalogue 4," only with the key qualification that Anka is clearly asking *herself* questions, using Michal as a kind of proxy or psychological counterplayer:

> ANKA: When did you realize?
>
> MICHAL: I never knew for sure, but I always suspected.
>
> ANKA: You deceived me.
>
> MICHAL: It never seemed to matter. You were always my daughter.
>
> ANKA: But you should have told me.
>
> MICHAL: I planned to give you the letter when you were ten. At ten it turned out that you were too small. So I planned to give it to you at fifteen. At fifteen it turned out that you were too big. So I put it into the envelope.
>
> ANKA: As simple as that.
>
> MICHAL: I thought that nothing would change between us. *(She stares at him.)*
>
> ANKA: A lie—
>
> MICHAL: —is a lie.
>
> ANKA: Look, two candles. This one is mine; this one is yours. Whose goes out first has the right to ask a question. Agreed?
>
> MICHAL: Agreed.

She loses the bet, but of course it doesn't matter. He is silent, knowing full well that there are questions she has to ask anyway, even if it means framing them as *his* questions! She guessed, of course, that he deliberately left the letter from her mother out in the open, wanting her to open it herself. At one point she asks him if he ever read it. Mildly, he says no, because it was addressed to *you.* This nonpluses her, and she grabs his hand during the following sequence:

> ANKA: At school they keep telling us to think: Why say that? What hidden meaning? Aren't you interested in the hidden meaning? *(He tries to retrieve his hand, but she hangs on.)* It's that for some years I sensed the contents of the letter. When I first went to bed with a man, I somehow felt unfaithful. It was you. I am constantly searching for someone. Yet when I'm touched, I think of your hands. Close to a man, I'm not with him at all. *(He presses his hand against her mouth to quiet her.)* How should I address you now?
>
> MICHAL: I don't know.

He knows perfectly well he'll always be her father. But he also realizes that this is not something he can simply tell her. She's reached that stage of early adulthood when she has to come to such realizations herself. This moment also marks the birth of an entirely new video trope, displayed during the transition scene where Anka casts herself on her bed in tears. She is framed by the familiar giant white lamp globe in the foreground to the right, with a small lamp globe to the left. In addition to the significant presence of a telephone and a stereo system, there is also a mobile hanging from the ceiling (a motif that will return in "Decalogue 6"). Behind her bed is a German-language poster for Winston Salem, a vista of snow-capped mountains and heroic explorers, which reads, "Grosser Geschmack eines freien Landes" (literally, "the great taste of a free country," with the connotation of wild or untamed country). This is an amazing triple pun, at once the ingenious quotation of the mountain-climbing posters of "Decalogue 2," the coldest slap in the face of the one-party state imaginable (even the palpably false advertising of the West is somehow truer than the state propaganda of the East), as well as an authentic symbol of those prosperous Central European export economies against which the Eastern European countries defined themselves.

The turning point is reached when Michal sits down to read the letter, demonstrating that he has been listening to her after all. At that point one family secret pours out after another—the fact that he apparently fled from her, three years ago, after he caught her in bed with a boyfriend, the fact that she was pregnant and had an abortion but never dared to tell him, etc. Finally, she asks the question she really wanted to ask all along, when she confronts him (that is, herself) with her own desire to be desired, her own autonomy as an adult woman: "I'm not your daughter and I'm grown up now. Do you want to?" In a wonderfully sweet moment, he recuses himself from the witness stand, as it were, quietly consoling her:

> ANKA: I want you to answer one more question.
> MICHAL: Only one.
> ANKA: Why did you want me to read the letter?
> MICHAL: Because I wished for the impossible.
> ANKA: You didn't know that it was impossible?
> MICHAL: No. That's why I hit you today, for the first time in my life. Because you opened the letter, because I wanted you to, because of your mother, because she told you something she didn't tell me. Because I love you and you are not my daughter. Because everything could have been different. Because the past will never return.
> ANKA: Because of the times you caressed my back when I cried . . . Candy King . . . Gingerbread Page." *(Together they hum the tune to Marzipan Princess.)*

The children's song reconciles the irreconcilable, by preserving the memory of the childhood happiness that is irrevocably lost in the passage to adulthood, while acknowledging that only adults can properly appreciate the happiness and joy of others.

Nothing quite prepares viewers for the shock, however, of the concluding sequence, where Anka wakes up and finally accepts her new role as an adult. This is the first time her bedroom is visible in full daylight, enabling us to see that the heroic explorer-figure in the scenic poster is paddling a kayak—shades of the doppelganger! Significantly, the giant lamp globe on the left is no longer radiating the deathly white so strongly reminiscent of Rover. It gleams with a beatific, wholesome blue—an unmistakable reference to planet Earth and a utopian aesthetics of globalization. With this in mind, she glimpses Michal from an open window and runs after him, finally admitting that she never actually opened the letter—she simply copied her mother's handwriting, writing (and of course reciting) what she imagined her mother *would* have said. Right on cue, the doppelganger walks by, still carrying the same upended boat. Anka stares at him, goggle-eyed, her shock hardly less than ours.

Wisely, they decide to let the past be the past, by burning the letter together. It vanishes quickly, leaving only a fluttering remainder that Anka unfolds and reads: "My darling daughter. . . . I would like to tell you something very important. Michal . . . Michal isn't . . . It's burnt." During this final bit of dialogue, Kieslowski unexpectedly deploys a video pan that focuses on the objects in Anka's bedroom. We see a close shot of the face of the kayaker on the wall poster, then the red covers and pillows, forming a striking contrast to the wall, then a fluffy teddy bear (a utopian tactility, also a significant symbol in "Decalogue 7"), and next the white lamp globe on the table. This last is shot in an extreme close-up that practically blots out our field of vision, Rover-style. Finally, the camera pans onto the black-and-white photo of her mother and her boyfriends, sandwiched between the lamp globe on the right and the red telephone on the left. (A blue table completes the obligatory tricolore.) Just as the German poster sublated the red stripes of the American flag into red-lettered script, here the faded snapshot, nestled securely between the symbols of a vibrant telecommunications network and a homogenizing multinational consumerism, hints at a new and specifically political genealogy. The European Union has many fathers, indeed!

We have already seen how the first four episodes of *The Decalogue* bridge the divide between Eastern European and Western European cinematic forms, by integrating the dissident thriller, the Solidarity drama, the hospital soap opera, and even the holiday romance film into a genuinely pan-European mediatic space. During the next six episodes of the series, Kieslowski will wire this space with an extraordinary array of visual, aural, and scripting mediations, thereby raising *The Decalogue* to the level of one of the greatest video productions of the twentieth century. Where McGoohan refunctioned the cold war allegories of the 1960s, and where the Hong Kong and horror films reappropriated the progressive internationalisms and neonationalisms of the 1970s, Kieslowski will reconvert the multinationalisms of the late 1980s and early 1990s (global neoliberalism and its local resistances) into the materials of Eurovideo. It is somehow fitting that the first moment of this process, the finely balanced crime thriller and courtroom drama of "Decalogue 5," should cast a sidelong glance back at *No End* and the moral verities of the Solidarity era, in the form of the interior monologue of Piotr Balicki, an aspiring young lawyer preparing for his final examination:

> PIOTR: *(Thinking to himself.)* The law should not imitate nature; the law should improve nature. People invented the law to govern their relationships. The law determined who we are and how we live. We either observe it or break it. People are free; their freedom is limited only by the freedom of others. Punishment means revenge, in particular when it aims to harm, but it does not prevent crime. For whom does the law avenge? In the name of the innocent? Do the innocent make the rules?
>
> DOORMAN: *(Aloud.)* Piotr Balicki. Go in, please.

The references to the doorman, the law, and juridical procedure are just the first of several pointed references to Kafka's elliptical, Expressionistic parables, ranging from the mention of Castle Square to gloomy, washed-out shots of downtown Warsaw, shot through heavy green filters that expunge almost all of the color from our field of vision. Intriguingly, the only objects that manage to stand out in the claustrophobic murk are articles of red clothing, worn by the artist at the town square, the young girl he is drawing, and an attractive young deliverywoman at a vegetable kiosk, who is eyed lustfully by a cab driver. In fact, images of young women play a key role in defining the spatial boundaries of the story, everywhere from the little girl at the square to the cashier at the movie theater, and from the two girls at the corner café to the clerk at the photography shop. The ultimate referent for all these images is, of course, the mysterious black-and-white photo carried around by Jacek, the antihero of the story, which he asks the clerk to have enlarged. (As if to hammer the point home, when the photography clerk sees his metal baton and coiled rope, she asks innocently if he happens to be a picture hanger—a truly grisly multimedia pun, given what happens later in the episode.)

What prevents "Decalogue 5" from becoming just another death row thriller or crime drama, on the other hand, is the finely tuned symmetry between the visual registers of the courtroom drama and those of the horror film, as if Kafka's juridical labyrinths were retrofitted with snapshots of Dostoevsky's lower depths. In particular, Piotr's ascent into the ranks of the legal profession turns out to be the flip side of the downwards spiral of Jacek, a psychotic youth who commits a series of random acts of mayhem, culminating in the brutal murder of a cab driver. (Piotr is Jacek's public defender during the subsequent trial.) By carefully avoiding courtroom speeches, lengthy monologues, or the scopophilic registers of the Hitchcock thriller, Kieslowski highlights the fundamental equivalence of two killings: the meticulously planned butchering of the cab driver, and the no less horrifying extermination of Jacek by the criminal justice system. The result is somewhere between the horror film and the detective narrative, such that the absolute or unrestricted subjectivity of the murderer, which transforms everyone else into a dead object, turns out to be the flip side of the murderous absolutism of the state, which reduces everyone to administered (undead) subjects.

"Decalogue 5" does, however, make one significant nod in the direction of the detective narrative, in the form of the documentary shots of the cab driver on his daily rounds. One of the first shots of the cabbie shows him washing down his car, a provocative moment in an episode overflowing with impure surfaces of all kinds, ranging from dirt-encrusted windows to grimy cafés, and from swampy fields to dank prison cells. Like the sacrificial victim trotted out in the prologue of every whodunit, the cabbie seems at first to be a somewhat unsympathetic character, whose tendency to harass, capriciously abandon, or otherwise insult his customers earns him first our mild reproach and later (once we learn of his grim fate) a strange kind of sympathy. It is striking that the closest analogue of the cabbie in the auteur canon, the Fool in Fellini's *La Strada,* deploys the symbolic categories of

Kleist's marionette theater in order to denounce the overbearing American-ism of Zampano.[1] But instead of hauling out the tried-and-true toolkit of theatrical modernism, Kieslowski unexpectedly launches a lightning guer-rilla raid on the archives of American postmodernism.

What makes the murder scene in "Decalogue 5" so excruciating, even for contemporary viewers jaded by the latest video techniques, is its canny in-version of the visual categories of the 1970s horror film. Leatherface, Freddy Krueger, Jason, and Michael all wore masks or bore masklike visages, in what amounts to the mass mediatic update of the executioner's hood, while the faces of their screaming or panic-stricken victims were shot in extreme, disjointed close-ups. Here, however, it is the victims who are draped in hoods (first the cabbie, and later Jacek, blindfolded in the execution chamber), while Jacek's face is highlighted by a series of extreme close-ups—none more powerful than the moment when a land surveyor stops the unwitting cabbie and his future killer on the highway, another incisive Kafka reference. The surveyor turns out to be Artur Barcis's Euro-doppelganger, who stares piercingly at Jacek while shaking his head, ever so slightly, as if conscious of what the youth is planning to do. Jacek, in the back seat, can't bear to meet his gaze directly and tries to shrink out of sight in the half-darkness of the cab. In the background we hear the anxious, high-pitched electronic whine of an automotive turn signal.

This is more than simply the ironical anticipation of the wrong turn we know, on some level, Jacek is about to take. In fact, the entire murder scene is explicitly framed by the compartmentalized space of the high-tech or postmodern automobile. When the cabbie is slowly strangled, the car seat is highlighted behind him; when he flails desperately at the car horn, Jacek attacks him from the side with the baton; and the final blow with the stone, which silences the cabbie forever, is linked to the destruction of the car ra-dio, which Jacek tears out in a fit of sudden fury (it is playing a seemingly harmless children's song).[2] What seems to be missing from this brief glimpse of a high technology charged with a ferocious corporeal violence is, of course, a properly postmodern identity politics. With typical subtlety, Kieslowski has already provided us with an essential clue, in the form of an earlier scene in a public pissoir, where a young man dressed in upscale Western clothing, fashionable outdoor vest, and expensive shoes smiles unexpectedly at Jacek. The latter lashes out, knocking the stranger down in a scene strongly sug-gestive of an episode of gay bashing. This puts a decidedly gender-bending spin on Jacek's final revelation that his treasured photograph is a shot of his deceased sister, not to mention his otherwise inexplicable request to be buried in his mother's grave plot.[3]

This suggests, in turn, that the signifying machinery of the murder sequence is somehow related to the juridical machinery of the execution sequence, only not in the sense of Kafka's notorious *Penal Colony* (bodies directly savaged by fascist or colonial violence). The contradiction hinges on the antinomy of capital punishment first identified by Benjamin, who noted that the carrying out of the death penalty might be moral, but never its justification, something that has an especially painful and bitter resonance for Eastern European countries who suffered through the successive scourges of fascism, Stalinism, Brezhnevism, and the latest of all neoliberalism. As an old saying goes, someone who kills one person is a murderer; someone who kills ten people is a psychopath; someone who kills one hundred people is unimaginably evil; but someone who kills a million people is either a general or an IMF banker. That Jacek killed a fellow human being is horrifying enough, but the executioners compound the interest on the original crime, as it were, by what amounts to an act of war. Not the least of the achievements of "Decalogue 5" is its unshakable commitment to nonviolence, which neither scapegoats those who break the law nor demonizes those who enforce it, but simply asks us to think through what the law at its most utopian and redemptive—the moment when it becomes justice—might truly be:

> PIOTR: Now it's all over, I would like to ask you . . . would an older, famous lawyer have made any difference to the case?
>
> JUDGE: None at all.
>
> PIOTR: My speech . . . perhaps if I had put things differently . . .
>
> JUDGE: Your speech was the best against capital punishment I've heard in years. The verdict was inevitable. You were faultless, either as a lawyer or as a human being. Difficult circumstances, but I'm glad I've met you. *(Piotr is silent, then thanks him and turns to leave, but the judge continues.)* One could, perhaps, wish for a better judge in this case, because I am responsible for what will happen. Does that comfort you?
>
> PIOTR: No. Perhaps it doesn't really matter . . . but on that day, when he wound the cord around his hand . . . I was there.
>
> JUDGE: Where?
>
> PIOTR: In the same café, a year ago, after passing my examination. I might have done something.
>
> JUDGE: You are too sensitive for this profession.
>
> PIOTR: Too late now.
>
> JUDGE: Now you are a year older.

A year older and, presumably, a year wiser. To simply contravene the law would be as barbaric as forsaking the concept of justice altogether. Even the methodical, painstaking division of labor by which the execution is carried out contains within itself a respect for abstract procedures that may someday blossom into a respect for living human beings.

It is somehow fitting that "Decalogue 5" concludes by canceling out the death row melodrama on its own aesthetic grounds. In a scene reminiscent of Heiner Müller's *Germania Death in Berlin* (a play best described as a bullet train through the Stygian depths of German prehistory), the execution chamber accelerates from utter silence to absolute pandemonium in mere seconds. Jacek cries out horribly, with the guards surging around him like the lynch mob they indeed have become, while the assistant ratchets up the noose in a frenzy. After the trapdoor falls, there is a truly spine-tingling reverse shot from underneath the floorboards, where we see Jacek's lifeless feet, framed by the open trapdoor, swinging gently in front of the upturned face of the assistant. (The assistant's head is twisted at an excruciating angle, reminiscent of some woodblock carving of a medieval executioner.) Instead of salving our conscience with a hackneyed moral coda or indulging in melodramatic platitudes involving the victim's family or Jacek's relatives, Kieslowski unexpectedly cuts to a pastoral scene in the countryside. Piotr is seated in his car, his head framed by a rolled-down car window and lush tree branches. Shaking with anger and grief, he recites over and over again, "I abhor it! I abhor it!" with properly Conradian fervor. Meanwhile, a mysterious object (we are never shown quite what) shines brightly from a distant field, which could be anything from the glint of a high-tech factory in a greenfield site to the inextinguishable beacon of a more humane future, depending on your taste in allegory.

Kieslowski's protest did not go in vain. In one of the most heartening examples of life imitating art, one of the very first acts of the post-Communist governments was to revoke the power of the state to kill. By the year 2000, almost every European country had either formally abolished or ceased practicing the death penalty, a dire contrast to the judicial barbarism sweeping over the United States.[4]

Decalogue 6

It is a familiar scene in any semiperipheral country in the world economy: A customer wants to cash a (most likely foreign) money order at the post office. In "Decalogue 6," however, the country is Poland on the eve of the Velvet Revolutions; the postal clerk is a nineteen-year-old man named Tomek; the customer is an attractive woman, Maria, who is the object of Tomek's secret affection; and the director is Krzysztof Kieslowski, who has something other than a semiperipheral aesthetics in mind. Following in the footsteps of Ousmane Sembène's postcolonial classic, *The Money Order,* which denounced the economics of neocolonialism and Third World debt bondage, "Decalogue 6" mobilizes the neonational form of the money order on behalf of a genuinely multinational content. This is the subtle interplay between Magda's reflection in the teller window and Tomek's eyes, which gaze at her through the circular teller window. (She is framed, in turn, by an outside window behind her.) The scene is cut short by an ominous crash of glass on a darkened floor, denoting both Tomek's illegal entrance through a window into some sort of storage space, as well as marking a decisive turn in the visual logic of the entire series. In Kieslowski's previous works, broken glass or smashed crockery alluded to impending catastrophes or fateful decisions. Here, the glass shards twinkle alluringly, refracting blue backlight like piles of uncut gems, something seconded by the sight of Tomek skulking about like a jewel thief. It is not the imported Western luxury good or some other symbolic wealth fetish that is the issue here, however, but rather the stealthy emergence of a new kind of visual content: the video color spectrum. Whereas the initial episodes of *The Decalogue* restricted their respective visual palettes to just a few basic colors (the green, white, and yellow overtones of the first episode; the alternating blue, white, and red hues of the second; or the absence of color in the third), "Decalogue 6" will exult in a veritable riot of color from beginning to end.

This dramatic expansion of chromatic content, running the full gamut from vibrant greens and blues to pulsating reds and yellows, will be matched by a no less striking expansion of shot techniques, which reconfigure the video pan and the video still into the building blocks of a nascent windowing aesthetics. Significantly, while the video pan will retain most of its original features, most notably in the glorious full circular pan midway through the story (the moment when Maria finally agrees to meet with Tomek), the video still undergoes a far more radical mutation. This is most evident in the subtle interplay between the long-distance shots of Maria's apartment and the close shots of Tomek's hiding place, which powerfully transform the zoom shots perfected by Hitchcock's *Rear Window* in two ways. First, nothing about Maria's numerous love affairs or Tomek's infatuation is hidden from the viewer. There is no secret, dismembered corporeality, jaw-dropping clue, or any other variation on a cinematic scopophilia. Second, the modernist trope of sheer kinetic energy or acceleration through space is displaced by the trope of movement through visual fields of information. Thus each successive shot of Maria's apartment is slightly closer than the previous one and reveals new layers of visual details, each of which is tied to the story line. Put more concretely still, an aesthetic of multiple levels of viewing or simultaneous, overlapping windows, each of which is meant to access and be accessible to all the others, takes the place of Hitchcock's cinematic voyeurism (the policing or existentializing gaze, searching for clues or hidden meanings). What is at issue here is one of the most overlooked aspects of video culture: the transformation of intermittent visual surfaces such as movies, photographs, and TV sets into digitally computed surfaces, which are viewed at close range by viewers for extended periods of time, both in the workplace and at home. Such surfaces feature a genuinely multinational aesthetics of texturing, determined objectively by the state of graphics and display technology, available screen resolution, and other hardware, and subjectively by the graphical codes, animation programming, and icons indigenous to the specific matrix of visual technology in question.

Both themes are prominently displayed in an early sequence, where we see that Maria's apartment is divided into a kitchen space on the left and a bedroom on the right, separated by a curious hanging screen or textile fabric imprinted with some sort of neo-Expressionist design. Meanwhile her bed is flanked by two mysterious objects: a silvery, refractive lamp globe on the left, and a curious pattern of dots on the right, suggesting a crude digital pattern printed on transparent plastic. Hidden away in his secret niche, Tomek trains the beam of his flashlight across several dormant computer screens, random electronic equipment, a microscope, and finally a magazine cover showing the planet Earth, before he finds the telescope he was looking for all along. These two spaces of mediatic consumption and production are linked by an explicitly global technology: that of the telephone. Indeed, their first contact ends with a shot of him framed by the telescope, while she is framed by what we now see is a transparent globe on the left, which refracts a subtle microcosm of the bedroom onto our field of vision (a motif that will reappear in Kieslowski's *Double Life of Veronique*). We have already seen how the demolition of a crystal ball plays a crucial role during the mind-bending finale of *The Prisoner*. Here, Kieslowski seals the reference by a brief shot of Tomek's landlady, who is watching a variety show on TV.

The action shifts at this point to a variety of explicitly commercial spaces, beginning with a grocery, where Tomek is framed by rows and rows of reflective and refractive glass surfaces of all kinds, a replication of images mirrored by his decision to become a milk deliverer (glass bottles of milk are one of *Decalogue*'s most prolific symbols). It is at this point that he begins to intervene in her life on a variety of levels, everywhere from secretly intercepting her mail to calling in a bogus report of a dangerous leak to the gas utility, in order to interrupt her during a lovemaking session with one of her boyfriends. The first time he knocks on her door in his guise as the milkman, his silhouette is framed by a set of bright red translucent window blocks in the background, creating a visually arresting block of color that is offset by a thin band of color reflected from her door: the gendered inversion, as it were, of the zoom shot of Maria and her microcosmic lamp globe. At one point, sensing an opportunity, Tomek plants another bogus money order in her mailbox. Still suspecting nothing, she demands to see the manager, who rudely brushes aside her questions, tears up the note, and goes so far as to accuse her of being a swindler—another wonderful citation of the money order narrative. When Maria storms off, Tomek at last summons up the courage to confront her directly:

MARIA: *(Walking furiously.)* What do you want?

TOMEK: *(Keeping pace.)* I want to tell you there was no money.

MARIA: What about the notices?

TOMEK: I sent them.

MARIA: Why?

TOMEK: I wanted to see you.

MARIA: You wanted to see me? *(She continues walking. He stops, wrestles with himself, finally shouts.)* You were crying yesterday.

MARIA: *(Stopping.)* How do you know?

TOMEK: I peeped on you. I saw you through the window.

MARIA: *(Roughly pushing him.)* Get lost, busybody. *(He slouches off, devastated.)*

The next time he spies on her, we are at last able to discern the mysterious object to Maria's right. It is not a sheet of plastic but rather a children's mobile decorated with flat, multicolored discs. The mobile is not only a significant symbol of a mass mediatic subjectivity in several episodes of *The Prisoner* (especially "Once upon a Time") but it also plays a key role in Anka's room in "Decalogue 4." This leads to a genuine breakthrough, where she looks out her window and raises her phone in a gesture telling *him* to call *her.* When he does so, she promptly double-crosses him, revealing his identity to one of her boyfriends. When the boyfriend goes outside and begins making a scene in front of the entire apartment block, Tomek has no choice but to appear, whereupon he is pummeled to the ground. Not content with this victory, the next morning she surprises him on his milk run, opening her door suddenly to bowl him over. Refusing to speak, he walks over to the painted glass window, which suffuses the scene with sensuous red light. Suddenly intrigued, she asks:

MARIA: Why are you peeping at me?

TOMEK: Because I love you. I love you. It's true.

MARIA: *(Baffled.)* And what do you want?

TOMEK: *(Mildly.)* I don't know.

MARIA: Do you want to kiss me?

TOMEK: No.

MARIA: Perhaps you want to make love to me?

TOMEK: No.

MARIA: So what do you want?

TOMEK: Nothing.

MARIA: Nothing?

TOMEK: Nothing. *(He turns to go. Stops, thinks, and then asks her out to a café. We learn later she has agreed. The next shot is an exquisite circular pan of him trolling his milk truck behind him, framed by the bright green colors of spring. He almost runs into Artur Barcis's doppelganger, who stands dressed all in white, with a large white satchel and a brown luggage case.)*

Here the privatized registers of the voyeur and the existential gaze suddenly give way to semipublic performances, played out everywhere, from the green sward of the apartment block to the hallway, and from grocery shops and cafés to the line in front of the post office. To paraphrase Judith Butler, a video performativity upstages its cinematic predecessor. What intrigues Maria is not anything Tomek says but his positively Beckettesque silence. (He even wears black clothing, as if in mourning.) This silence is the flip side of an undreamt-of abyss of aesthetic speculation, something nicely underlined by Slavoj Žižek's comment that Maria is really the desiring subject who lacks an object (when Tomek says, "I love you," she replies, "There's no such thing"), whereas Tomek serves as a kind of objective currency of desire, caught up in the throes of a catastrophic devaluation.[5] This allegorical reading of "Decalogue 6" as the clash between a feminized desire to consume (read: Western European consumerism) and a masculinized desire to speculate (read: post-autarkic Visegrad Europe) is fairly convincing in regards to the first two-thirds of the episode, but runs into acute difficulties toward the conclusion.

The reason is that Kieslowski, with typical subtlety and discretion, moves beyond neonationalism as a narrative form. This first becomes apparent during the café scene, where we learn in rapid succession that (1) Tomek is an orphan (not connected with the traditional family sphere); (2) his friend, the original peeping Tom, is with a UN force in Syria (neatly canceling out any link to cold war geopolitics), and (3) his hobby is studying Bulgarian, English, and Portuguese (thereby bracketing the Iberian and Eastern European peripheries of the future Eurostate). She responds with her own memory of a thin boy she once favored, who left for Austria and Australia. Blushing, Tomek hands over the letters he collected. This ritual exchange of geopolitical coordinates is sealed by the moment when she takes his hand and symbolically dangles a wooden carving (a curious cross between a teardrop and a child's spinning top) on his palm.

This is followed by one of the most original seduction sequences ever filmed. First, Tomek's landlady discovers the telescope, symbolically assuming Tomek's role as voyeur. Next, Maria takes Tomek back to her apartment, caresses him, and gradually induces him to masturbate her. Unable to bear the strain, he ejaculates prematurely, whereupon she remarks brutally, "That's all there is to love. Wash in the bathroom. There's a towel." Here at last the mediatic machinery Kieslowski has patiently been constructing comes to life with a jolt. Tomek unexpectedly jumps to his feet and rushes outside, only to bump into Barcis's doppelganger, who is still standing in the apartment courtyard in precisely the same pose and carrying the same luggage as before. Not only is the joyous video pan that accompanied their first meeting extinguished here by an icily objective long-distance shot, but Tomek's own position as voyeur will be literally and figuratively annihilated when he subsequently locks himself into his bathroom and slashes his wrists.

One of the major symbolic compensations for this catastrophe is the emergence of Maria as a viewer (rather than a viewed object) in her own right. This was already hinted at during the seduction scene, when she was framed against a series of lush, glowing surfaces. Later, she gestures prominently with the phone, indicating he should call her and even writes an impromptu message, "I'm sorry, please come back," on the back of one of her paintings or prints, holding it up against the window. With typical subtlety, Kieslowski leavens this otherwise heartbreaking moment with just the right touch of black comedy: One of Maria's lovers, the same one who beat up Tomek, suddenly rings at the door at the worst possible moment. Naturally she refuses to see him, but not before Kieslowski sneaks in a terrific fishbowl shot of the lover through the peephole, the unmistakable negation of the microcosmic lamp globe in Maria's room.

In fact, this will be the first of a whole series of inversions, wherein subjects become objects and objects become subjects, and where the voyeuristic energies formerly attached to the realm of the private sphere are transferred onto an externalized public space. Thus when Maria goes to speak to Tomek's landlady, the landlady treats her with a kind of noncompliant courtesy, yielding almost no information aside from Tomek's name, as if Maria were some state agent or snooping official. Somewhat later, when Maria opens her door, hoping to see Tomek on his milk rounds, the deliveryperson turns out to be the landlady, filling in for her lodger and as tight-lipped as ever. Tomek's absence at the post office is highlighted by a noteworthy shot of Maria standing next to her mailbox, framed by a few prominent red dots painted on the windowpane behind her, the sorrowful echo of the glorious torrent of red hues that provided the backdrop to their hallway conversations. This formal symmetry extends even to the phone call that announces his return: He is not really contacting her (he does not speak), but merely acknowledging her calls. She ends up speaking for both of them: "I've looked for you everywhere. I've looked for you in several hospitals, to tell you . . . you were right. Do you hear me? You were right. I don't know what to say to you. I don't know how." Once again, Kieslowski provides just the right comic note to offset the unbearable grimness of the scene. One of her lovers suddenly calls seconds later, and for a moment she suspects a prank. (It turns out the silent caller really was Tomek, whereupon she hangs up abruptly on the boyfriend.)

The real symbolic compensation for Tomek's absence, however, is not so much Maria's own voyeurism but that quite different visual register relayed by the splendid scenes of her peering out her own window with opera glasses, backlit in sensuous blues and whites. She is no longer the subject who is watching someone else, but a subject who is *scanning,* television-style, for someone or something worth watching in the first place. This is confirmed by the final scene at the post office, which is a precise inversion of the very first shot of "Decalogue 6": Not only does the circular slot of the teller window frame *her* eyes instead of his, but a prominent white bandage around his wrist replaces the white paper slip of the money order. After he says, simply, "I'm not peeping on you anymore," she stares at him with a curiously abstract, ambivalent expression, best described as a kind of distant nearness, with the most uncanny resemblance to the gaze of the doppelganger.

This is not the erasure of desire but its transfiguration into something new and mysterious: a desire somehow linked to consumerism, but not yet mediated by the stupendous flood of televisual surfaces and video tropes characteristic of Kieslowski's *Three Colors* trilogy. In retrospect, it is Tomek's competitor, the telltale boyfriend, who finally gives the game away. The latter's role is clearly an allegory of the commercial interruption: the knock of the door-to-door salesperson, the ring of the telemarketer, the annoying TV ad, etc. This suggests that the final shot is meant to negate two registers at once: the visual register of the glass window, and the tactility of the rounded, plastic bubbles of the 1960s consumer culture. Both are henceforth integrated into the new social space of *customer service,* that is, the service sector of the multinational workplace.

Decalogue 7 and 8

We have already noted Kieslowski's penchant for arranging his material in formal pairs, everywhere from the character trope of the doppelganger to the appositions of window reflections and refractions, and there is a sense in which "Decalogue 7" and "Decalogue 8," in some ways the most provincial episodes of *The Decalogue,* are best understood as two parallel attempts at defining a single problem: the passage of the national past into a multinational future. Both episodes turn the codes of a specifically generational politics against what Jameson famously termed an allegorical Third World nationalism, but which amounts in the Polish context to the autarkic cadre state, as well as the official opposition movements ranged against such. Thus in "Decalogue 7," the first postwar generation (Majka's mother, a school-teacher, and her father, a skilled craftworker who makes musical instruments) battles the disaffected generation of the 1960s (Majka, who dreams of emigrating to Canada, as well as Wojtek, her former lover, who has chosen to stay in Poland in a kind of internal exile), with the fate of the postmodern generation (Majka's daughter Anya) hanging in the balance. In "Decalogue 8," Elzbieta, a Polish Jew who escaped from Nazi-occupied Warsaw as a young girl and grew up in the United States, returns to Poland in the 1980s to confront her own past as well as the ambiguous role of Zofia, a university professor who is also an unusual human rights activist.

The first notable shot of "Decalogue 7" is a semicircular pan of Majka at the office window, her head framed by the back of the clerk's head to the left, with telltale Eurocard, Visa, and MasterCard logos imprinted on the office glass. This striking reference to the multinational credit market is later counterpointed by a close shot of Anya, reminiscent of the close shots of Danny Lloyd in Stanley Kubrick's film *The Shining.* Like Danny, Anya has recurrent nightmares that foreshadow real events to come. Kieslowski shies away from the ghost story, however, in favor of the all too human trauma of parental jealousy (the grandmother, Ewa, rudely shoves Majka aside to comfort the child and pours scorn on her ability to be a mother). Later, when

Majka decides to run away with Anya, Kieslowski will make one other explicit reference to *The Shining,* during the scene where she rolls a ball down the carpet to distract a theater concierge. (In Kubrick's film, a ghost does this to entice Danny into Room 312.) Inside the theater, a group of children are participating in a children's theatrical, and Majka chooses an opportune moment to grab Anya from the stage flies and carry her off—a clever inversion of classic folktales that tell of witches abducting innocent children, as well as a subtle nod in the direction of Eastern Europe's thriving theater culture. Whereas Danny exhibits an uncanny grasp of the ghostly traces of mediatic images, Anya displays an equivalent affinity to all sorts of tactilities, ranging from the gestures of physical affection so apparent between her and her mother and grandmother, and so painfully absent between everyone else, to the abstract patterns Anya traces with her fingers in the window of the tramcar, and even to the way her hand clings desperately to Wojtek's hand when she falls asleep. It is therefore fitting that Majka and Wojtek should rehash their painful past in a room filled with teddy bears, the mute reminders of a vanished childhood tactility and human warmth:

> *They watch Anya fall asleep on the teddy bears.*
> MAJKA: Do you still think of me? *(She unconsciously reaches for him.)*
> WOJTEK: No. *(Just as unconsciously, he pulls away.)* I suffered a lot for it, but not anymore. *(Sits down.)* Do they know?
> MAJKA: No. *(She smiles.)* I took her from the theater. Mother almost fell down the steps.
> WOJTEK: Why speak like that about her?
> MAJKA: You should be pleased. *(Becomes serious.)* For some time now . . . I think I hate her.
> WOJTEK: As always: with you it's either/or. No half measures.
> MAJKA: No, and I've taken Anya, and I'm not giving her back. I've thought about it for three or four years. I'm no longer the sweet little girl who fell in love with her young teacher because he didn't talk like the others. *(He flinches.)*
> WOJTEK: You've still plenty ahead. You haven't stolen, you haven't killed.
> MAJKA: *(Bitterly.)* Can you steal something that's yours?

Majka's apparent heartlessness turns out to be the product of quite heartless circumstances. We learn that her mother was the headmistress of the school that employed Wojtek as a teacher when Majka became pregnant at the age of sixteen. The scandal was hushed up at the price of a double (and suspiciously gendered) sacrifice: He gave up a promising writing career, and she gave up her motherhood. It is here, where we initially expect an impassioned confession or a melodramatic shouting match to break out, that Kieslowski discreetly interposes two variants of the video still: Majka's passport and the birth certificate that proves she is Anya's mother. This motif will be completed somewhat later, when Wojtek flees from Majka and Anya in another video pan, this one framed by the white and yellow sheets hanging out on the clothesline to dry. At the same time, the explosive conflict we have been expecting is displaced elsewhere, onto the crackling telephone dialogue between Ewa and Majka and, more ominously, between Majka and Anya. When Anya wakes up, she sleepily mutters one of the great lines of "Decalogue 7": "You've both stolen yourselves from me." She stubbornly refuses to call Majka "mother," despite Majka's cajoling. When Wojtek goes out, allegedly to procure a van (but really to inform Majka's parents), she instinctively flees with the child, who clutches a teddy bear for dear life. Somewhat later, Wojtek will find the same teddy bear, discarded on a riverbank. Symbolically, he begins to wade into the river, framed by the modernized superstructure of a modern steel-and-masonry bridge and the overgrown banks and wooden pilings of the river.

Both motifs—an abandoned childhood tactility, and a surcharged aesthetics of framing—culminate in the scene at the train station. Here Kieslowski rewrites the three individual futures of *Blind Chance* into three generations of identity politics: The first (Ewa) remains within the orbit of the nation-state, the second (Majka) flees to the West, while the third (Anya) oscillates unhappily somewhere in between. Significantly, this is also the first moment that Kieslowski undercuts the gender identity of the heretofore male doppelganger. This is the matronly station attendant, whom we later glimpse reading Flaubert's *Madame Bovary* and who knows just what to ask Majka:

> ATTENDANT: A guy? Are you running away from a guy?
>
> MAJKA: *(Despairingly.)* Everything.
>
> ATTENDANT: Come inside. It's warm. You can sleep.

This is an extraordinary evocation of a new kind of postmodern solidarity, the moment where a Second Wave feminism emerges in the Europeriphery and begins to fight against the entrenched forms of symbolic and physical violence perpetrated against women. Although the attendant is ultimately unsuccessful in her attempt to hide Majka from her parents, it's significant that Kieslowski already had the insight to gender-bend the figure of the doppelganger, neatly anticipating the powerful female protagonists of his later films. The episode concludes with Majka's solitary escape onto the moving train, as Ewa gathers Anya up in her arms. This is commemorated by a heartrending *double* video pan, one focused on Majka's face, sliding into obscurity behind the train window, and the other focused on Ewa and Anya, sliding past Majka's point of view. At the last second, Anya wriggles free from Ewa's arms and runs, too late, toward the disappearing train, the expression of astonishment on her young face already freezing into the stigmata of trauma, with Preisner's spare, sorrowful score echoing in the background.

If the fundamental issue of "Decalogue 7" is the universal experience of exile, then "Decalogue 8" offers the logical corollary to this theme: the possibility, however fleeting or fragmentary, of a multinational solidarity between fellow exiles. We first run into Elzbieta as the American translator of Zofia's works, who is a guest of honor at Zofia's university seminar. During a classroom discussion of ethics, Zofia realizes she's gotten more than she bargained for when Elzbieta unexpectedly describes an event from her past: When she was a six-year-old Jewish girl in Warsaw in 1943, she was denied refuge from the Nazis by members of the Polish underground, for reasons she never found out. (Zofia was, it seems, one of those members.) Just when the tension seems unbearable, Kieslowski provides his usual note of comic relief: A mentally disturbed person stumbles into the classroom, bobbing and weaving, until an African student yells, "Go out!" in English, until the visitor is ushered away. This reference to a multinational student body and mass homelessness is not accidental. When Elzbieta continues with her story, the camera pans onto Barcis's doppelganger, present here as a student in the audience. To our surprise, when Zofia finally confronts Elzbieta after the class, she is the furthest thing from reproachful:

> ZOFIA: *(Amazed.)* It's you. You're alive. I've wondered all my life. Whenever I see someone toying with a gold chain, I wonder . . . Lord . . . You are alive.
>
> ELZBIETA: I was hidden by other people, relatives of the man who brought me to you. I lived with them for about two years. They're with me in America now. . . . Well, he is dead.
>
> ZOFIA: *(Calmly.)* And you traveled so far to watch my face when you told the story.
>
> ELZBIETA: I intended to talk to you when you were in America. I tried to write several times. I planned to come. But for your words about the child . . . I would never . . .
>
> ZOFIA: Yes, I understand.
>
> ELZBIETA: There is a theory that a rescuer has one character, those rescued have another character.
>
> ZOFIA: Yes, such characteristics may exist.
>
> ELZBIETA: You have them.

ZOFIA: Me?

ELZBIETA: Your activities, even after me, are well known. Thanks to you, several people of my world are still alive. It's interesting that a student easily spotted the false note in that apparently Catholic reasoning.

ZOFIA: There's an ashtray over there.

ELZBIETA: You don't smoke.

ZOFIA: *(A twinkle in her eyes.)* But I observe.

This seemingly ordinary dialogue trespasses against two sacrosanct Polish national myths simultaneously. In the first place, Pilsudki's Poland was virulently anti-Semitic, and the Resistance did almost nothing to save the Jewish community from extermination, something that is still a sore point in Poland to this day. But as Elzbieta points out, Zofia saved *several* Jews from death, suggesting she was not the average partisan. The other great neo-national myth punctured here is that of the Solidarity priest or religious activist: Rather than a dogmatic believer, Zofia is the intriguing prototype of the Žižekian activist, with one foot in the university system and the other in a postmodern identity politics.

This is confirmed by Zofia's offer to have dinner with her, which turns out to be a ploy to drive Elzbieta to the meeting place she remembered from so long ago, a place she is both horrified by and yet very much drawn to. After a curiously childlike game of hide-and-go-seek in the shadowy courtyard, they catch up with each other and Elzbieta recalls:

ELZBIETA: A terrible place. I went to my old flat. When my custodian, my father's friend, didn't know what to do next, it was here I decided I'd never be so afraid again.

ZOFIA: Why didn't you come here for forty years? Didn't you want to see this place?

ELZBIETA: No. It's humiliating.

ZOFIA: Accepting help?

ELZBIETA: Yeah. People don't like witnesses of their humiliation, even bricks and mortar. We research, analyze, describe, but can we resolve unfairness? Why do some rescue others, why others can only be rescued? Do you know?

ZOFIA: No.

Zofia knows quite well that Elzbieta's real question is not why some individuals were saved but why some people manage to stand up and fight against injustice in the first place. But like any good teacher, she also knows that this is not the right time to bring the issue up. Later, at Zofia's apartment (exquisitely framed with household objects hanging on the walls to the right, and a luminous yellow lamp with a curved white spindle in the center, like a half-opened eye—the conscience-stricken version of our old friend, the bubble lamp), she will gently turn these questions back onto Elzbieta herself, by revealing that shortly before her arrival in 1943, her partisan group received a tip that the visit was a setup by the Gestapo. The information later proved to be false, but at the time they sent the young Elzbieta Loranc away, a decision Zofia continued to fret about for decades. "You're right," says Zofia gravely, "there's nothing more important than the life of a child," both forestalling the immediate response, which is that no one could possibly blame her for doing what she did, given that multiple lives were at stake, while also acknowledging that every single human life is irreplaceable. Kieslowski punctuates this Benjaminic insight, that there can be no truly good moral choices amidst the bad totality, with a close shot of her hand clasping Elzbieta's, the moving echo of the opening shot of "Decalogue 8" (a child's hand held in an adult's).

Put another way, Zofia's ethical calling is based neither on juridical abstractions nor on moralizing reproaches, however honorable these might be in other circumstances, but rather on the pragmatic task of defending human dignity on this earth, through a kind of committed or Sartrean teaching of the value of human life.[6] This respect for human life cannot be separated from a respect for the cultural documents by which human beings endow themselves with dignity and subjectivity: thus Elzbieta's gold chain, Zofia's own never-quite-settled painting, the double-jointed gymnast Zofia runs into in the park (a subject who is his own puzzle picture, as it were), or the special collection of a stamp-collecting neighbor (the father of the brothers in "Decalogue 10") who briefly stops by. As Zofia explains to Elzbieta: "He shows me his stamps the way people show photographs of their grandchildren or children."

It is somehow fitting that a narrative that centers on the impossibility of ever really stitching together the past with the present should conclude with Elzbieta's visit to the tailor who saved her but who is no longer willing or able to talk about the past. Kieslowski sets up the scene with a long shot of a darkened traffic tunnel that opens up to a glorious panorama of the city, an expanse that feels like pure freedom after an eternity of close, constricting shots. Ironically, the tailor himself, squirreled away in his shop, absolutely refuses to say anything about the past, saying only he would be very happy to make Elzbieta a dress, showing her some fashion plates of blonde models from a rather old set of German-language magazines. Even here, Kieslowski manages to work a small miracle: When Elzbieta offers to send the tailor some up-to-date magazines, he somehow finds it within himself not to decline, clearly the only gesture of acknowledgment he is capable of making. "What a strange country!" murmurs Elzbieta to Zofia somewhat later, at last beginning to appreciate the miracle of the smallest of all things, the miracle of everyday solidarity.

Decalogue 9

If "Decalogue 7" and "Decalogue 8" are the swan songs of neonational gender ideologies and historical mythologies, then the last two episodes of *The Decalogue* sound the clarion call of the multinationalisms of the future. One of the most striking aspects of "Decalogue 9" is the sheer panache, confidence, and stylistic sophistication by which the materials of the romance melodrama, the espionage thriller, and the Hollywood blockbuster are pressed into the service of a Velvet gender revolution. The storyline is simple: Roman, a well-paid surgeon who has been repeatedly unfaithful to his wife, Hanka, has just been informed by a clinician that he is incurably impotent. One of the first scenes is an extreme close shot of their well-appointed apartment, framed by a desk in the extreme foreground, an empty glass to the left, and a telephone on the right (the rewriting of the lamp globe and mobile of Maria's apartment into signifiers of extended visual and acoustic reproduction). The camera swivels in a kind of reverse video pan, tracking Hanka across the apartment, keeping the glass and phone in our view at all times. This is followed by a scene where Roman almost crashes his luxury car. Screeching to a halt, he punches at the dashboard in rage and despair, while Barcis's doppelganger pedals slowly by on a bicycle hitched to a cart (the bicycle will become an important symbol later on).

These initial references to video forms and a trans-European transportation network culminate in a gorgeous outdoor sequence, wherein Roman paces in the pouring rain against the backdrops of misted windows, blue lighting, and Preisner's haunting sound track, his symbolic placelessness highlighted by the airport stickers festooning his luggage, until Hanka's ghostly reflection suddenly wells up in the window. After persuading him to come in from the rain, they ascend in the elevator, in a static shot that intersperses moments of stark blue lighting with moments of complete darkness, rather like a slow-motion strobe effect, a technique that will reappear at key moments of Kieslowski's later classic, *Blue*. The couple's subsequent bedroom talk is similarly highlighted by means of a series of extreme close-ups, probably the closest in the entire series, framed by his hand nestled against her shoulder. This sudden compression of the visual field is conjoined to an explicit inversion of the traditional patriarchal gender roles: When Roman tells Hanka that she probably should find a lover to satisfy herself, she demures and says she loves him anyway. The scene ends with a tender shot of her masturbating herself against him. The freely given caress displaces the cadre state phallus, in a moment of grace that testifies to Kieslowski's extraordinary ability to reconcile the most intimate (not to mention potentially vulgar and obscene) materialities of the body with the deepest kind of compassion and collective spirituality.

The next day this spirituality is put to the test, when Roman notices a suspicious stranger walking near his car. This is none other than Mariusz, Hanka's lover, who is studying physics at a local university. Driving into the city center, Roman will later stop to assist a stranded motorist at a traffic concourse, consisting of two mysterious rows of rounded concrete pillars outfitted with smooth white domes, vaguely reminiscent of twin squadrons of flying saucers. This is a set of bubble tropes straight out of the lexicon of *The Prisoner,* pointing to an intriguing politicization of the space of the automobile. Back at his job as a surgeon, he talks to an attractive girl brimming with Lolita-esque vitality, who is trying to decide whether or not to have an operation to strengthen her heart, something necessary if she is to pursue a singing career. (This girl, by the way, is the direct model for the title character in Kieslowski's 1991 *Double Life of Veronique.*) After informing him she sings Bach, Mahler, and Van den Budenmayer (Zbigniew Preisner's own playful pseudonym), she says: "Mother wants me to have everything, but all I want is . . ." (here she pinches her fingers in the symbol for a thimbleful) "*that* much." This is followed by a shot of her walking sexily down the hospital corridor, the palpable irony being, of course, that Roman still eyes women as voyeuristically as he always did, but is physically incapable of seducing anyone.

The appearance of the girl marks a turning point in Kieslowski's work, wherein the trope of the dematerialized or free-floating Euroconsumerism first glimpsed in "Decalogue 6" begins to generate its own specialized cultural mediations. The very first of these is undoubtedly the Walkman the girl listens to in the hallway; Roman himself will provide another, in the form of the record of Van den Budenmayer that he plays in order to find out what exactly his patient was talking about. The austere, high-pitched tonality of Preisner's score neatly complements the blanked-out, glassy surface of Roman's watch during this scene, hinting at the stoppage of time itself, until his wife opens the door behind him, thereby setting the jealousy plot in motion again. This machinery of cultural reproduction, which will be echoed in the close shots of a keymaking machine (Roman duplicates his wife's keys, in order to spy on her), then becomes a full-fledged machinery of dissemination, when we see Roman soldering a wire into the innards of a telephone and then listening in on the line with an earplug. This is more than just the rewriting of the cold war trope of political surveillance and high-tech spy agencies into a kind of acoustic voyeurism, on the order of the (literally and figuratively) wired conclusion of Orson Welles's *Touch of Evil*. Rather, by foregrounding this scene with an intermediary shot of the deskbound glass and phone, those icons of visual and telecommunicatory transparency, Kieslowski pole-vaults over the entire corpus of the cold war media culture at a single bound, reinventing the state-of-the-art 1980s hacker drama innovated by *Wargames* and *Neuromancer* in an Eastern European turn.

This is confirmed during a later conversation Roman has with the girl, when the aesthetic space of the Walkman turns out to be associated with a performative content. While she sings a couple of bars of Van den Budenmayer, the camera lingers on her intriguing hand gesture, which traces out the notes only to fall gently to her knees. This striking moment of a free-floating, utopian tactility somehow emancipated from the narrowly privatized registers of the voyeur and the medical ones of the hospital drama alike is then linked to two new visual signifiers: the external scenes through the car window, where we glimpse modern glass office towers and other structures, and the internal shot of the glove compartment, which reveals one of Mariusz's physics notebooks, conclusive evidence of Hanka's affair. The antipodes of objective market competition and subjective sexual competition—what might be termed the twin poles of professional envy and private jealousy—will merge again in a radiant shot of Hanka sleeping on the bed. Roman's gaze pans slowly across her, taking in a book next to her, sporting a neo-Expressionistic design stamped with a flaring red logo of some sort, before zeroing in on a bag with an English-language commercial logo, which he quickly rifles through to get a critical phone number.

What interests Kieslowski, then, is not so much the specific objects of Euroconsumerism (the VCRs, camcorders, stereo equipment, upscale fashion clothing, and luxury cars already filtering through the upper echelons of Polish society during the late 1980s) but the informatic content of such. Rather than simply quoting the latest high-tech commodities or citing the latest video shot techniques with no regard for their relevance to the story line, Kieslowski constructs a complex, interlocking web of framing and mirroring techniques, opacities and transparencies, color spectrums and lighting schemes, designed to reappropriate the materials of a largely Western media culture, rather than being themselves expropriated by such. Thus the scenes where Roman bicycles furiously across roadways and embankments, the sun glaring down between two highway overpasses as he splashes into a shallow river, negate the mountain bike commercial and the sports event of the racing marathon. Hanka, who works as an airport ticket agent for KLM, is framed first by an enormous calendar spread on the wall behind her, and later by a detailed model of a jet airplane stamped with the KLM logo in the foreground (the spaces of mass tourism and air travel, respectively). At the same time, it becomes apparent that Hanka is losing interest in her affair, growing increasingly despondent over her deception. After one tryst with Mariusz, she leans her head wearily against the car horn, which beeps monotonously, the car lights flashing. Later that night, Roman and Hanka have the following conversation, brimming with unspoken double entendres and framed by a full-length body mirror on the right side of the screen and a doorway on the left:

> ROMAN: I can't sleep. Tell me, you were very good at physics. How does it go? When a body is immersed in a liquid, its loss in weight . . . I forget how it goes.
>
> HANKA: *(Not quite understanding the dig at her lover.)* Its apparent loss in weight is equal to the weight of liquid displaced. Something like that.
>
> ROMAN: Like that. *(Extended silence, his brow furrows.)*
>
> HANKA: You had a bad day? *(Starts caressing him.)*
>
> ROMAN: *(In a clipped tone.)* Yes.
>
> HANKA: Surgery? You lost a patient?
>
> ROMAN: *(Even more clipped.)* Yes. *(Refers to her touch.)* Don't do it.
>
> HANKA: Who was it?
>
> ROMAN: *(Angrily.)* Don't touch me.

Though we are never told directly, we suspect the patient was the aspiring young singer. The next scene offers another wondrous close-up, this one centered on the telephone in the foreground, while a cartoon plays across a TV set in the background. Hanka is using the TV as camouflage while she telephones Mariusz to arrange a meeting. (Unbeknownst to her, Roman is listening in on his wiretap, and he decides to spy on them from a closet.) This meeting is shot entirely from Roman's point of view in the closet, using a narrow vertical field shepherded by leaves of darkness to the left and right. As it turns out, Hanka simply wanted to tell Mariusz the affair was over. After silencing his protests and ushering him out, she realizes someone is in the closet. (The camera backpedals beautifully from her suddenly alert gaze, just as we would if *we* were caught spying on someone.) Enraged, hurt, and humiliated, she screams at Roman to come out, not realizing that he is experiencing something much worse: After years of betraying her, he is finally learning what it is like to be betrayed. We never actually see the door between them open, but as he slumps to the floor, holding his head in his hands, Kieslowski intervenes with his characteristic providential touch: The doorbell rings. Mariusz is back, this time with an offer to marry Hanka. She closes the door on him, but not before we feel a moment of sneaking sympathy for Mariusz, who is at least honest about his feelings. Roman has in the meantime fled from the closet. After searching wildly through the apartment, Hanka finds him collapsed over a sink:

> HANKA: *(Takes him in her arms.)* Hold me tight. Hold me.
>
> ROMAN: I can't. *(He really can't; his limbs are powerless.)*
>
> HANKA: *(Embraces him more tightly.)* Hold me. Please. *(In tears.)* You won't leave me just because I jumped into bed. I know you, but I didn't think . . . I didn't realize you would be so hurt.
>
> ROMAN: *(Dully.)* I've no right to be jealous. I can't expect it of you.
>
> HANKA: You can. And you were right about things being discussed to the limit. Now I'll always tell the truth, so you needn't hide behind wardrobes.
>
> ROMAN: I made a duplicate key.
>
> HANKA: We'll never again have to. . . . We should have had a child. We should adopt one, you were right.
>
> ROMAN: *(Stirs.)* We must take a break apart.
>
> HANKA: While you're gone, I'll ask a lawyer about adoption.
>
> ROMAN: You go away. I don't want that physicist . . . *(He finally embraces her; the door closes tactfully on our point of view.)*

This is followed by a set of close shots of bright plastic ski shoes, red and white bindings, and blue boots. Hanka is going off on a skiing vacation, after which the couple will presumably be reconciled. At this point, much to our surprise and welcome relief, we see the young girl again, who has now decided to have the operation and try her luck as a singer. ("I know I'm someone else," she says to Roman. "I want lots of people to hear me sing.") This hopeful moment is highlighted by an outdoor shot of a little girl playing on the street, framed by a narrow, vertical slot through the window—the negation of the voyeurism of the closet scene by a utopian public space.

At this point, though, contingency rears its ugly head. Roman sees Mariusz packing up his skis, discovers he's headed to the same resort as Hanka, and draws exactly the wrong conclusion from this. When Hanka runs into Mariusz at the resort, she brushes him aside, but quickly realizes that her husband might well suspect her of orchestrating all this. While she rushes back by bus, he writes what we later learn is a suicide note and goes out bicycling on the highway. Peddling furiously into the blinding sun, with Preisner's score surging in the background, Roman races past Barcis's doppelganger (still hauling the same cart) before plunging high off a freeway overpass into what he thinks is oblivion. Here, though, someone else fatefully intervenes, a character whose most consistent feature has been his studied neutrality in all the previous episodes. It is the doppelganger who saves him, by discovering his unconscious, twitching body and rushing off to get help. (To underline the point, a long-distance zoom shot of Barcis resolves onto the whirling spokes of the crashed bicycle.) Although Hanka finally arrives home and reads the note, the phone serves, for once, as an instrument of salvation rather than destruction. Speaking from strangely identical positions on the hospital bed and the apartment floor, framed in an immovable cast and a ski jacket, at the extremities of life and death, Roman and Hanka finally connect.

Decalogue 10

If "Decalogue 9" heralded the birth of truly European subjects, in the form of the border-crossing EU professionals who will crisscross the vast fabric of the *Three Colors* trilogy, then "Decalogue 10" is its objective cognate: the birth hour of the European marketplace, red in tooth and fiscal claw. Not only is "Decalogue 10" a prescient allegory of Maastricht monetarism. It is also the damning indictment of what Boris Kagarlitsky termed "market Stalinism"— the shotgun marketization of societies that were suddenly exposed to the gale-force winds of foreign competition, without the decades of careful preparation, EC subsidies, and restructuring available to post-autarkic economies such as Portugal and Spain. Far from bringing prosperity to all, the marketplace merely transformed an irresponsible, short-sighted nomenklatura into an equally irresponsible and short-sighted euroklatura, whose main entrepreneurial skill was an uncanny ability to plunder state assets at fire sale prices and funnel the proceeds into secret Swiss bank accounts.

The signal achievement of "Decalogue 10," however, is not merely to have accurately forecast the ravages of neoliberalisms to come but also to have anticipated the cultural, political, and social *resistances* to such. Two key innovations made this possible: first, the wholesale importation of a plot structure straight out of John Woo's Hong Kong thrillers, that is, the trope of brotherhood or some other form of domestic solidarity threatened by a society overrun by commercialism. Second, and no less important, the doppelganger will vanish completely, and its role as an objective arbiter or mediating observer will be replaced by the suave police detective. This latter is not, however, the same thing as the ubiquitous police agencies or postcolonial juridical categories of Woo's films. This is because Woo's greatest works are essentially tragedies that commemorate the traumatic violence of twentieth-century Chinese history in the medium of the postcolonial action thriller. "Decalogue 10," on the other hand, will deftly transcribe the theme of brotherhood onto the rather different registers of the black comedy. Two brothers, Artur (a free-spirited singer for a punk rock band) and Jerzy (a fastidious family man), inherit a seemingly ordinary stamp collection from their father, an event that turns their lives upside down.

Stamps, those reproducible series of images that intermediate vast networks of postal communication and written dissemination, have long been a staple of postmodern literature, everywhere from the utopian neonationalism of Soyinka's *The Lion and the Jewel* to the multinational Tristero network in Pynchon's *The Crying of Lot 49*. But what separates the stamp collection in "Decalogue 10" from these others is not its affiliation with a system of communication but its strange, ghostly existence as a bearer of speculative value in its own right—the rebranding of its potential exchange value into a multinational use value. The very first scene begins with the prototypical multinational form of the music video, relayed by a rough-and-ready handheld shot of Artur singing for a punk rock band at a rock concert. Artur's performance is counterpointed by the sight of his brother, Jerzy, signaling wildly to him from the audience. (The lyrics are a call to be utterly selfish, to dishonor the Church and family, punctuated by the hysterical cry, "Everything belongs to you.") The irony of the scene—Jerzy is trying to inform him about their father's death—is compounded by the band's name, City Death. This is more than just a sympathetic nod in the direction of the thriving underground musical scene of Eastern Europe, in the mold of Slovenia's Laibach. It is also a broad hint at the convergence of the punk rock music and horror film narratives of the 1970s that will transpire later in the episode.

A very different kind of convergence is at work during the burial scene, when an orator intones, "His family, his professional life, and perhaps his emotions were sacrificed for a noble passion," cleverly omitting the object of this passion. Meanwhile, Artur is listening distractedly to rock music on his Walkman, until Jerzy nudges him to be quiet. State funerals in the state-autarkic societies of the Eastern bloc were of course always the first act in the subsequent scramble for political succession, and here Kieslowski takes a page out of Heiner Müller's *Hamletmachine,* by reappropriating the form of the funeral in order to illustrate quite another impending power struggle. What is at issue is the arrival of the consumer culture itself:

ARTUR: *(Referring to the stamps.)* What can they be worth?

JERZY: Stamps are expensive now. 300,000 . . . 400,000 zlotys. Our misery, mother's wasted life . . . poor food, lack of money.

ARTUR: *(Not really listening.)* Yeah.

JERZY: *(Protesting.)* I even had to bring a suit to bury him in.

ARTUR: *(Thinks for a moment.)* Where does it come from, this urge to have something? You should know. You used to like things.

JERZY: No, I use things. I like comfort. I never understood the old man. *(Looks at his brother, nudges him.)* I haven't seen you for ages.

ARTUR: Mmh. More than two years.

At this point, Artur picks out a random series of stamps (a series from 1931, showing a German Zeppelin on an arctic journey) for Jerzy to give to his son as a present. The close-up shot shows three stamps, one red, one blue, and one green—the primary colors, it should be noted, of the TV set. Their first clue that something is not quite right is the appearance of an oily, devious debt collector, who tries to wheedle parts of the collection in exchange for canceling their father's debt. (Jerzy wisely refuses, of course.) But it is not until much later, when they try to sell the stamps at an exhibition, that the president of the local stamp collectors' club tells them the shocking truth: The collection was worth 250 million zloty, or about $250,000 in 1988 U.S. dollars—an unimaginable fortune in semiperipheral Poland. As the president pages through one series after another, telling them what each can buy (a Fiat; an apartment; two diesel engines, etc.), their eyes open wider and wider, and a low, rolling kettledrum sounds three times over, announcing the arrival of a properly Mephistophelean set of temptations, fetishisms, and obsessions. It's worth noting the great Czech animator Jan Svankmajer employs a similar technique in his live-action feature *Faust,* that ingenious fable of primitive accumulation in the Europeriphery set in mid-1990s Prague. Here, however, Kieslowski is mapping out the historical prelude to primitive accumulation, or a kind of gray accumulation halfway between state-autarky and multinational consumerism. "Your father, gentlemen, invested his life in this collection," concludes the president dryly, "and it would be a crime to dissipate somebody's life, even the life of a father one hardly knew."

The real crime, of course, is the gradual corruption of the two brothers, who begin to take on all the usual ills of commodity society: greed, selfishness, ruthlessness, and violence, as the people around them turn into exchangeable objects and the objects they own become more valuable than people. Thus when Jerzy goes home, he discovers a street hustler has talked his son into swapping his extremely valuable stamps for a slew of comparatively worthless stamps. Outraged by the swindle, he tracks down the hustler on the gray market (to the accompaniment of another drumroll), shakes him down, and learns that the stamps were sold to a corner shop. The shopkeeper feigns ignorance, and when Jerzy threatens to call the police, the most he will admit is that the stamps were purchased by an overseas buyer. Later, when Artur comes home from a gig, he sees the lights on in their father's apartment. Suspecting the worst, he creeps upstairs to surprise the thief, while a horror film sound track (barking dogs and a swirling, high-pitched tone) builds to a climax. But the visitor is just his brother, perched on the desk and poring through their father's diaries like some latter-day Faust. Together, they begin to discover the art of the deal. Their father was on the trail of a specific stamp in order to complete a full series, an "Austrian rose Mercury 1951," which was stolen at one point, bought at another point, and trafficked at a third, and which remains a unique series in Poland. Outside, they begin to worry about the security of the apartment and the possibility of thieves breaking in to steal the collection. Framed by the ranks of apartment blocks behind them and another ominous drumroll on the sound track, they begin to reflect on how quickly they've changed:

> JERZY: *(In wonderment.)* I forgot that I have problems. I quite forgot.
> ARTUR: I feel like in the old days, too; we kids ignored adults' problems. I have that old feeling again. We're here, and somehow nothing else matters.
> JERZY: *(Slowly.)* You forget. It's childish.
> ARTUR: But nice. *(They are silent for a moment.)* And perhaps none of it exists. If you don't want it, it ceases to exist.

Their corruption deepens when they cook up a scheme to get the zeppelin stamps back by entrapping the unscrupulous shopkeeper with a bogus stamp deal, using a hidden tape recorder. The scheme seems to work, and emboldened by this victory, they install a full-fledged security system, bar the windows, and even purchase a huge black guard dog. (This last is a deft reference to the occult thrillers of the 1970s, such as *The Omen*.) This is hardly the end of the matter, however. The shopkeeper asks to meet them, saying he has an angle on the fabled Mercury rose stamp, but needs their medical records first. As it turns out, the shopkeeper wants to swap the stamp for a donated kidney for his mortally ill sixteen-year-old daughter, and Jerzy happens to have the right blood type for the operation. After much soul-searching, they accept the deal, saying to themselves that in any case they are saving someone's life.

This extraordinary act of exchange, between an irreplaceable stamp and a no less irreplaceable human organ, is in fact the first in a series of exchanges between cultural bodies and bodies of culture. The first of these is a minor scene just before the operation, when Artur runs into a nurse at the hospital who recognizes him as the leader of the band City Death: "May I touch you?" she breathes in awe, or what amounts to the tactile reappropriation of the iridescent energies of the rock star poster. Intriguingly, the entire operation cuts back and forth between scenes from the operating room and scenes from the apartment: A shot of the surgeons washing their hands is contrasted with the image of a welding torch; surgical rubber gloves are associated with the guard dog, who is being petted by someone familiar to it (we assume Artur) wearing black gloves; bloodied bandages are counterpointed by a series of dazzling close-ups of various stamps, shot through a magnifying glass. It is only when Jerzy has recovered enough to walk under his own power that we learn the true meaning of these images: While the brothers were at the hospital, the apartment was robbed and the entire collection was carried off! Even worse, the guard dog clearly recognized the visitor, suggesting an inside job. Although Artur is the logical suspect, the police detective who arrives on the scene quickly determines that Jerzy was the one who disconnected the alarm. In short, mutual paranoia breaks out between the two, such that both brothers end up meeting privately with the detective to inform him of their suspicions of each other.

What is truly remarkable about this sequence, however, is Kieslowski's adamant refusal to classify any of the bodies involved in strictly national or neonational terms. This is shocking, for two reasons. First of all, the brothers' betrayal of each other turns out to have absolutely nothing to do with the entire repressive machinery of the one-party state, with its wiretaps, secret denunciations, surveillance, and censorship. The detective is no Party hack but a smooth, urbane professional, whose strangely neutral gaze, which records everything and judges nothing, is the logical successor of Barcis's doppelganger. The detective is also identified with a cutting-edge technology, the mobile phone in his police car, hinting at that Europeanwide telecommunication network that Nokia, Ericsson, and other innovative EU firms would create years later. This is very much the Central European equivalent of the conventional plot twist in the earliest Hong Kong action films, where the stateless, nationless hero always turns out to be an undercover Interpol agent. (Bruce Lee's role in *Enter the Dragon* is a somewhat later variation on the same theme.) Given that a nascent European civil society is the outer narrative limit of "Decalogue 10", one could argue that the fate of the brothers bespeaks a double expropriation of the Eastern European nation-state: Jerzy's donated kidney points in the direction of a high-tech, biological neo-colonialism, famously anticipated by the vat-grown body parts of Gibson's *Neuromancer;* while Artur's loss is more subtle, namely, his decision to shelve his singing career and to get a full-time job at a restaurant.

Kieslowski is not about to let the market forces have the final word, however. Instead of merely documenting the carnage of neoliberalism, the concluding sequence of "Decalogue 10" will draw upon the prodigious energies of the entire series to launch its own electrifying counterattack. Jerzy happens to be walking down the street when he sees some ordinary stamps displayed in a window. Fascinated, he stops at the counter and asks the clerk for a series (the clerk is Tomek, on loan from "Decalogue 6"). When he exits, we hear the same unearthly drumroll as before, only this time a sympathetic black magic is at work: He sees the oily debt collector, walking a huge black guard dog, the same as the one they own, talking in familiar terms with the hustler who swindled his son so long ago. On a nearby street, Artur happens to see the shopkeeper walking down the street with a third black guard dog, identical to the others. Against the backdrop of another drumroll, the shopkeeper walks right up to the debt collector and the hustler, and friendly greetings are exchanged all around. At a stroke, the brothers can see the gray bourgeoisie exactly for what they are: the Satanic agents of a multinational capitalism that delivers wealth to a select few while plundering, impoverishing, and ravaging the vast majority of the planet.

Reconciled at last, Artur and Jerzy look over the stamps from the post office: two exact series worth almost nothing, of course. Still, they have learned something extremely important from all this. For his part, Jerzy can now appreciate the pleasures of stamp collecting, this time as a plebeian activity accessible to all. What Artur has learned is revealed only when the credits start rolling, and we hear the same punk rock sound track as in the beginning. But this time Artur's lyrics have drastically changed. Indeed, they pulsate with an extraordinary new message:

> Darkness, lawlessness, and lying all the week
> You are the only hope, you are the only light in your tunnel
> Because all around you is within you
> Everything belongs to you!

This is the faint but unmistakable light of a new kind of solidarity, the phosphorescent ripple in the roseate dawn of the Eurostate, serving notice of a genuinely multinational solidarity that cannot be dictated from without but must be reconstructed from within. It will be the construction of this solidarity, that rainbow moment of grace forming an arc from May 1968 to Prague 2000, which unites the resistance to state-autarkic barbarians and the resistance to neoliberal barbarism, to which we must now turn.

Neon Genesis Evangelion 6

It seems to be East Asia's unique historical destiny to be the exception to late capitalism that nevertheless proves the rule. Caught between the hammer of U.S. corporate competition and the anvil of Communist insurrection, East Asia broke every rule in the neoliberal playbook to become one of the titans of the world economy. But the price of its success has been its ever-increasing entanglement in the world market it so fiercely (and effectively) resisted. Economic analysts such as Alice Amsden, Michael Gerlach, and Robert Wade have described in vivid detail how East Asia's canny developmental states and feisty corporate networks (Japan's keiretsu, South Korea's chaebol, and China's business groups) transformed war-blasted societies wrecked by imperialism, World War II, and bloody civil wars into thriving high-tech economies.[1] What has not yet been written, however, is the cultural side of this story: how some of the oldest cultures on the planet innovated some of the newest technology; how rigidly hierarchical societies developed astonishingly freewheeling business cultures; and most of all, how a mediatic explosion of anime films and karaoke clubs, Hong Kong epics and Nintendo video games erupted out of East Asia in the 1970s and 1980s like the incandescent plasma of some vast rift nebula, overturning all our star charts and cultural cosmologies.

East Asia offers far more, however, than just another belated variation on processes of mediatization and consumerism long taken for granted in the United States and the European Union. Above all, the region is a geopolitical scandal, whose very existence is proof that Wall Street reigns but no longer rules over the world economy.[2] As late as 1970, U.S. firms were broadly hegemonic in almost every economic sector one could name. By the 1990s, EU and East Asian firms caught up with and in certain cases even surpassed their U.S. competitors in industries ranging from automobiles to electronics, banking and telecommunications. While Wall Street has continued to wage the cold war with other means, deploying IMF and World Bank sado-monetarism in lieu of the direct military interventions of the past, the EU and Japan have quietly seized the high ground in the twenty-first-century world economy by bailing out their Eastern European and Southeast Asian semiperipheries, the EU via the European Investment Bank and Japan via the Japan Bank for International Cooperation.[3]

East Asian culture thus emerged at the site of a unique double contradiction. Not only did it have to answer for the historical erasure or displacement of the nation-state (a politically subaltern Japan, the two Koreas, the two Vietnams, and the three Chinas), but it also had to fend off the depredations of neoliberalism and neocolonialism without the heavy artillery of the EU's powerful social democratic states, thriving Euroculture, and common currency. Put another way, even though East Asia has a world-class production base equal to that of Central Europe, its geopolitical status is more like that of post-Soviet, semiperipheral Eastern Europe. But whereas Eastern Europe was forced to hitch its cart to the nascent Eurostate, East Asia is in the enviable position of having the financial, economic, and technological resources to bail *itself* out. The contradiction is probably most obvious in the long-running Japanese banking crisis, where the world's largest creditor nation, sitting on vast trade surpluses and a trillion euro mountain of rock-solid liquidity, took almost a decade to muster the political will to write off the bad debts of the 1980s bubble economy. In a nutshell, East Asia has the economic muscle of a superpower, but is just beginning to develop cultural and political superstructures characteristic of such.

As we shall see, these contradictions go to the heart of Hideaki Anno's *Neon Genesis Evangelion,* a weekly animated series that ran on Tokyo television from October 1995 until April 1996 and became a smash hit, inspiring two spin-off movies, countless fan clubs, and endless Web shrines, while raising Anno himself to the level of a superstar. It's important to note the field of anime (pronounced "ah-nee-may," the word comes from the French term for animation) did not emerge in Japan until the 1960s, when Americanization, the Ikeda economic boom, and rising levels of TV ownership spurred the creation of television shows based on Japanese "manga" or printed comic books. Even today, anime borrow extensively from the typographical and literary conventions of manga, in much the same way that Hollywood continues to borrow tropes and narrative conventions patented by the pulp science fiction and comic strip periodicals of the 1930s.

What distinguishes *Evangelion* from the run-of-the-mill mecha or giant robot cartoon is not simply its groundbreaking animation, sparkling editing, and world-class action sequences. Rather, Anno sublated the mecha as a form, transforming the latter into the basis for a new kind of multinational aesthetics, in much the same way that Patrick McGoohan's series *The Prisoner* created the basic vocabulary of video out of the 1960s spy thriller and 1950s theatrical modernism or indeed in the same way that Krzysztof Kieslowski's *Decalogue* transformed Western European auteur cinema and Eastern European theatrical and musical forms into the field of Eurovideo. By cutting and splicing narrative forms ranging from the Godzilla movies and the American science fiction blockbuster to John Woo's Hong Kong action thrillers, as well as artfully borrowing from the rich traditions of Japanese anime itself (especially Akira Toriyama's *Dragonball Z*), Anno created a thirteen-hour masterpiece with the narrative heft and density of a triple-decker Victorian novel, the epic sweep of a Hollywood blockbuster, and the breakneck visual energy of the 3D video game.[4]

Strange as it sounds, there is a curious sense in which *Evangelion*'s closest narrative predecessor is not a recent work of art but the serialized novel of Victorian Britain. Like the latter, the anime is a highly commercialized form of art, written for a metropolitan audience and tied to a sophisticated set of written and social conventions. The vast majority of anime are domestic comedies, a genre that, at its best, playfully mocks Japanese social conventions with slapstick humor, kinetic comic action sequences, and guerrilla street theater in much the same way that the U.S. sitcom satirizes the no less ritualistic social conventions of American consumerism. In Rumiko Takashi's uproarious *Ranma½* series, for example, the characters are magically cursed to change gender, shape, or form in certain conditions, resulting in episodes of truly priceless pandemonium. Just as the sheer length and prolixity of the Victorian novel was the unintentional result of a literary marketplace where authors were paid by the word, so too are many of the most characteristic features of manga and anime—exaggerated saucer-shaped eyes, the use of typographical symbols to connote surprise or shame, the creative use of framing and visual counterpoint, and of course wildly multicolored hair—merely the logical response of artists to the commercial limitations of the form, that is, the necessity to convey complex social situations using a medium that does not have live actors at its disposal.

What *Evangelion* did that was truly new, however, was to combine world-class mecha designs and action sequences with cinema-level scriptwriting and scorching emotional conflicts worthy of one of John Woo's Hong Kong blockbusters. The Achilles heel of the mecha was always its lack of character development, which was admittedly not a problem when the point was to portray giant robots crashing into each other. The characters of *Evangelion*, however, are the furthest thing imaginable from cardboard cutouts, and Anno will utterly demolish the stereotypes of the mecha jock and the kimono bimbo alike in favor of sensitive, complex male characters and a series of powerful and self-aware women without precedent in the history of anime. This is actually the culmination of a tendency that began in the mid-1980s, when anime such as *Dirty Pair* (1985) and *Bubble Gum Crisis* (1987) introduced strong female characters capable of taking on state-of-the-art action roles. Whereas *Dirty Pair* sparkled with irreverent dialogue and shotgun one-liners between police agents Yuri and Kei (pronounced "Kay"), *Bubble Gum* engaged in some fairly racy gender-bending of a cast of characters borrowed wholesale from Ridley Scott's *Blade Runner*. (For example, Priss, the leader of the Knight Sabers, is cast in the mold of the butch biker; Leon, the macho police officer, is not only pushed to the margins of the story by the all-girl Knight Sabers but also has an openly gay sidekick, Daley.)[5] That said, neither series departed significantly from the deeply patriarchal gender roles of 1980s Japan; *Bubble Gum*'s Nene, supposedly a computer hacker, still acts very much like a glorified OL, the Japanese neologism for "office lady" or low-level clerical staff.

By contrast, *Evangelion*'s female characters are powerful, self-motivated professionals who have no truck with medieval gender roles or the men who believe in them. As we shall see, this gender revolution is matched by a host of other micropolitical transformations, all tied to East Asia's irresistible rise to the economic coeval of the United States and the EU. Arguably, where Melville rewrote the Victorian seafaring swashbuckler into *Moby Dick*, that adventurous summit of a progressive nineteenth-century American nationalism, *Evangelion* rewrites the mecha narrative into the *Moby Dick* of the information age, with the crucial difference that whereas the allegorical crew of the Pequod quested for the White Whale, the no less allegorical inhabitants of Tokyo-3 battle a mysterious alien species (called "angels") from another dimension.

The reference to a third Tokyo is less futuristic than one might think. The reason is that Japan's capital city was leveled by the horrific Kanto earthquake in 1923, painstakingly rebuilt, and then incinerated by U.S. bombing raids in 1944 and 1945. There is a similar transcription of the past into the future in the basic story line of *Evangelion*, which takes place in the year 2015, fifteen years after an asteroid supposedly crashes into Antarctica, creating massive floods and sparking terrible wars, until the survivors band together to rebuild—an event christened the "Second Impact" (the English words are used). Such apocalyptic scenarios are a standard feature in the anime genre, where the atomic flash-photos of Hiroshima and Nagasaki are frequently cited next to baroque fantasies of sprawling supermetropolises and technological subsystems (these latter, in turn, regularly spawn demonic or cybernetic life-forms, as well as *Blade Runner*–style agencies designed to police or control those life-forms). Given that the Second Impact is a fairly transparent cover fiction for the destruction and territorial dismemberment of the Japanese Empire during World War II, one could be forgiven for immediately suspecting *Evangelion* to be just another deeply reactionary and politically obnoxious tale of mecha jocks *qua* kamikaze pilots who, in the infamous words of Rambo, finally get to win.

Nothing could be further from the truth. Anno quotes national culture not to praise it but to bury it, by systematically hacking into, hijacking, and disrupting almost every single protonational and neonational mediation available in the field of anime. In fact, *Evangelion* will provide the crucial bridge between the best anime productions of the 1980s and the 1990s, by setting the pacifist and theological registers of Hiroyuki Yamaga's sterling space drama, *Wings of Honneamise* (1987), in motion toward the progressive micropolitics and ecological insurgencies of Hayao Miyazaki's magnificent *Princess Mononoke* (1997). One of the little-known historical developments that made this possible was the rise of independent studios for Japanese TV and video markets in the 1980s. Both *Honneamise* and *Evangelion* were produced by Gainax Studio, and *Mononoke* was produced under the aegis of Ghibli Studio. These studios had relatively few ties to the existing production houses, entertainment conglomerates, or auteur traditions of national cinema, but powerful and enduring links to Japanese manga, U.S. science fiction, and early video culture. These studios become veritable hothouses of aesthetic innovation, transforming anime into a truly global art form in much the same way that small-scale producers powered the rise of early hip-hop music and home computer software in the United States, or the way that McGoohan and Kieslowski both assembled teams of extraordinarily talented scriptwriters, cinematographers, and actors for their respective video masterpieces.

The history of Gainax, Anno's own production firm, is especially revealing in this regard. The origins of the company go back to 1981, when Anno, Hiroyuki Yamaga, and Takami Akai were all film students at the same Osaka art college and decided to plunge, willy-nilly, into the world of anime. Their breakthrough project was the opening animation for Osaka's DAICON 4 science fiction convention in 1983, which bowled over the audience and earned them the commercial support they needed to produce *Honneamise*. (Gainax was officially founded in December 1984, in order to produce the film.) Anno worked as an animator on a number of anime projects, most notably the theatrical films of *Macross* and *Nausicaa: Valley of the Wind* as well as on *Honneamise* itself. His first stint as a director came in 1989 in the form of an above-average mecha called *Gunbuster: Aim for the Top!* Although fairly conventional in terms of its aliens vs. space soldiers plot, *Gunbuster* offered impressive visual designs, effective action sequences, and a young girl in the role of the heroic mecha pilot. The following year, Anno directed *Nadia: Secret of the Blue Waters,* a fast-paced, witty, and occasionally moving adventure serial loosely based on Jules Verne's *Twenty Thousand Leagues under the Sea.*[6] Not only was *Nadia* Gainax's first major commercial success, but many of its artists would make crucial contributions to *Evangelion,* most notably character designer Yoshiyuki Sadamoto (who worked on *Honneamise* and *Nadia*), and mechanical designer Ikuto Yamashita (whose previous credits included *Gunbuster* and *Nadia*).

Nothing in Anno's track record quite prepared viewers, though, for the supernova of *Evangelion.* One of the reasons is that Anno and his coworkers wrote the story as they went along, resulting in an unusually complex and subtle script. Indeed, it is not until we are midway through the series that we begin to realize that almost everything we assumed about the story line is drastically wrong: The Second Impact was no accident after all, the angels are not really the demonic creatures they seem to be, Nerv is not quite the heroic defender of humanity it advertises itself as being, etc. Most of all, Anno concluded the series with a mind-bending finale that sparked a genuine national scandal, very much as the final episode of *The Prisoner* instigated a near-riot at BBC headquarters almost three decades earlier. Visually speaking, the Gainax production team set new standards for animation, shot design, and editing, deftly integrating CGI (computer-generated imagery) with hand-drawn cel animation, while employing a wealth of framing techniques equal to anything in the canon of Kieslowski's *Decalogue* or *Three Colors* trilogy. In narrative terms, the series exhibits an almost nanometric formal precision. There are no extraneous details or gratuitous images. Each episode flows irresistibly into the next, and even the most minute visual, aural, and scripted details turn out to represent vast, glittering constellations, which coil and uncoil like shifting bands of neon DNA. Even the sound track, often the least developed element of the anime genre, is positively riveting, thanks to excellent voice acting and Shiroh Sagisu's inventive and stylish musical score. The action scenes frequently cite the horn-and-drum sequence of the helicopter battle in the 1967 Bond thriller *You Only Live Twice,* the first Bond movie to be set in Japan (which makes sense, considering that Blofeldt's underground base is very much the model for Nerv's geofront). More subtly, the song that accompanies the credits after each episode—Bart Howard's *Fly Me to the Moon*—not only is repeated in at least fifteen recognizably different 1990s musical styles over the course of the series, ranging from Japan-pop and techno to jungle. It also contains a clever karaoke reference: Most of the versions are sung by British pop singer Claire (she goes by her first name) while a few versions are done by various other voice actors of the series (such as the end of episodes 5 and 6 as well as 24, 25, and 26).

We get our first taste of this complexity in the opening credits, or tag, of the series. Whereas *The Prisoner*'s tag parodied the Bond thriller, and whereas the opening sequences of the *Decalogue* sampled and pastiched a variety of mediatic forms (the Solidarity thriller in "Decalogue 1," the Christmas movie in "Decalogue 3," the courtroom melodrama in "Decalogue 5," and the late 1970s music video in "Decalogue 10"), *Evangelion*'s tag will cycle through an intriguing mixture of science fiction, fantasy, and action-adventure motifs. We first see a tiny pulse of light at the center of the screen, which expands into a globular shockwave. Next, a red nebula materializes in the background, while a strange medieval glyph (vaguely reminiscent of a coiled dragon) gleams fitfully in the distance, to be replaced by the logo of the Gainax Studio. Finally, this latter dissolves into the familiar science fiction trope of a forwards zoom through neon-blue stars, while a glowing blue close-up of a magical diagram (the Systema Sepharoticum, penned in 1653 by a German priest named Athanasius Kirchner, and loosely based on the Kabbalah) scrolls downwards, before fading into a flickering blue fire, like the reflection of a flame in a pool of water. This mysterious array of cosmological and mystical images then fades to the title sequence proper, which displays the Japanese characters for *shinseiki*" (literally, "new century") against the English-language word *Evangelion* (from the Greek term for "gospel"). The title literally means "New Century Evangelion" or "Gospel for a New Century," but Gainax had an explicitly secular target in mind. The English title they chose was "Neon Genesis Evangelion." This is an explicit reference to one of the greatest lines of William Burroughs's *Nova Express* ("Explosive bio advance out of space to neon"), suggesting that the gospel of the information age is at stake.[7]

Needless to say, all this is a shocking contrast to all previous anime tags, which generally featured action footage, close-ups of the characters, and video tropes tied to recording devices or simple consumer electronics. The classic example is the opening tag of *Dirty Pair,* which concludes with the blinking red recording light of a futuristic videocamera. *Evangelion*'s tag proceeds to a video pan of Shinji Ikari, the youthful protagonist of the story, his hair blowing realistically in the wind, framed against the backdrop of a blue sky dotted with cumulus clouds. A shot of his lightless silhouette appears to the right. Later, this fades away, and his face is then framed by the shadowy silhouettes of two female bodies, which scroll vertically to either side of the screen (slow-motion replay reveals them to be two of the other mecha pilots, Asuka Langley and Rei Ayanami, to the left and right, respectively). Next, we see a luminous orange-yellow sky and a close-up of someone's outstretched hand, silhouetted against another shot of the intertwining branches of the Sephiroticum, scrolling upwards across the screen. The hand belongs to Misato Katsuragi, operations director of the Nerv organization, and we are treated here to a gorgeous multiple juxtaposition of Misato's face in the foreground, then her silhouette backlit by a dazzling sun, and then a close-up of Shinji's face to the upper right (one superimposed image cycles in just as another cycles out).

It requires a number of viewings to properly appreciate the extraordinary compositional subtlety of the sequence. Not only does every single moving object or frame offset an object or frame moving in a different direction but these frames are counterpointed by extraordinarily precise color combinations and shot pacing. Thus the glyph of the Sephiroticum moves down, while a later version moves up; the precisely balanced vertical silhouettes of Asuka (pronounced "ah-ska") and Rei (pronounced "ray") move up and down across the same screen, before acceding to the counterpoised horizontal silhouettes of Misato; shadows are framed against light sources, panes of light against shadows, etc. This aesthetics of framing or windowing is explicitly named by a medium shot of Rei standing behind a window, followed by an ultraclose shot of her eye (so realistically drawn that we glimpse the multiple refractions of light in her pupil). This extreme close-up of the eye, one of the most frequently cited tropes of the series, performs much the same function as the extreme close-ups of eyes in Kieslowski's *Blue*. Whereas the latter served as the index of Julie's video subjectivity, finally able to see itself in the eyes of another (Olivier), *Evangelion* sets this subjectivity in motion toward the giant robots who suddenly look up at us with almost human intelligence. The next shot of Shinji shows him piloting the mecha with his eyes closed, almost as if he were *listening* to the theme song of the series ("The Cruel Angel's Thesis," a surprisingly winning Japan-pop tune that manages to avoid most of the clichés of the genre by beginning and ending in a minor key and avoiding choruses.)

The last and most crucial innovations of the tag, however, are the brief cut-scenes of capitalized words or terms in English (*Test type, EVA-01, Angels, Tokyo-3,* and so forth). English neologisms are an enduring feature of Japanese consumer culture, and Japanese ads frequently cite wildly incongruous English catchphrases with the same carefree abandon that ads for luxury fashion goods quote French and Italian terms. Anno, however, will confront viewers with an ocean of non-Japanese scientific, technological, and conceptual terms, some drawn from the marketing and information culture of North America and others from the scientific and engineering culture of the European Union. The introductory titles for each episode, for example, alternate between Japanese and English, and the meanings often subtly differ (the Japanese title of "Evangelion 18" is "The Judgment of Life," whereas the English is simply "Ambivalence"). We also glimpse handmade pencil drawings or sketches of various characters, the mass mediatic equivalent of the artisan's signature, whose true significance will not be revealed until the very end of the series. For now, it's sufficient to note that the tag links Shinji directly to the subjective body of the mecha, while Misato, Asuka, and Ritsuko are linked to the objective registers of visual frames and corporeal tactilities appended to this body.

Intriguingly, our first glimpse of this body is not the Evangelions (hereafter referred to as "Evas") themselves, but the bodies of their mysterious antagonists, the angels. The first of these is a strangely abstract, gilled creature, embossed with a sigil vaguely reminiscent of a skull. Like some neo-Expressionistic Godzilla, the angel rises out of the sea to assail Tokyo-3, its carapace invulnerable to the UN's most advanced conventional weapons, including the apocalyptic fury of an N2 mine, a kind of superhydrogen bomb. But where the Godzilla movies tapped into the social history of the American monster film and the natural history of the komodo dragons indigenous to the South Pacific, respectively, *Evangelion* will draw upon two rather different sources of narrative material. The first is relayed by the airborne shot from a helicopter skimming the ocean's surface, gleaming with computer-enhanced reflections: the space of multinational or informatic forms. The second is the canceled-out space of neonational or monopoly-national forms, subtly rendered by the blocky, abandoned office towers of a largely submerged Tokyo-2 (and more obviously, by the UN's obsolescent military technology).[8]

The humming factories and modular office towers of Tokyo-3, by contrast, are tied to multinational categories of image production and consumption. Thus when Misato drives off to pick up Shinji, she has his classified security photo in her hand, counterpointing her *own* autographed color snapshot, which he holds in his hand (the first in a series of video stills). Probably the single most striking expression of this is the central viewing screen at the heart of Nerv's intercept center, its vast central view screen superimposing sliding yellow grids, green radarscopes, and orange 3D terrain maps. One perspective even frames the command center from *behind* this wall screen, contrasting the luminous maps in the foreground against the smooth, metallic surfaces of the conning towers to the left and right, and the central command station to the center. The effect is a teeming density of video images, which fill in the abstract data space first glimpsed by Fredric Jameson in the dizzying reaches of the Bonaventura Hotel with informatic content.

Nerv is the acronym for the elite scientific research unit of Tokyo-3 charged with defending humanity against the angels. It is also the first of several significant German puns in the series (the word means "nerve"). Headed by Gendou Ikari, Shinji's distant, mysterious father, Nerv is nominally under the control of the UN, but in reality it answers only to an ultra-secret committee of global power brokers known only as Seele (German for "soul"). This immediately suggests that Nerv and Seele are the executive management and power elites of yet another Japanese state-industrial body or juridical apparatus, a suspicion that seems to be confirmed when we learn that Ikari is the head of another project, running concurrently with Nerv but carefully separated and hidden away from the latter, called the Human Development Project ("jinrui hokan keikaku," with the connotation of perfection or completion) or, more simply, Instrumentality.

However, things are more complicated than this, mostly because the bodies of the Evas are not really the neonational symbols of robot samurai they seem to be. One of the most intriguing features of *Evangelion* is its steadfast and honorable stance of nonparticipation vis-à-vis Japan's one-party state and entrenched keiretsu elites. By rubbing the immanent registers of the former against the transcendental grain of the latter, Anno scandalously contradicts the single most prevalent form of identity politics of East Asian monopoly capitalism, an export-platform industrialism keyed to a heavily American-accented multinational consumerism. Anno will satirize this global industrialism with a planetary range of mythological references and theological quotations, ranging from the Sepharoticum and the Marduk Institute (referring to the Kabbalah and the Babylonian pantheon) to the Lance of Longinus (the mythical spear that a Roman centurion dipped in the blood of Christ), and from the Dead Sea Scrolls to the Egyptian pyramids. Intriguingly, while the Evas themselves are referred to with the English word *evangelions,* the angels are referred as *shito,* which means "apostle" (meaning the apostles of Christ, with the additional connotation of faithful servants; "angel" does, however, convey the necessary subtext of being a messenger or avatar of some higher power).

This heady brew of mythopoetic and theological signifiers is tied to a range of multinational and geopolitical tropes, all related to Tokyo-3's status as a new kind of global city or multinational urban space. Even Nerv's eye-catching logo—a red fig leaf outlined by a tongue-in-cheek quote from Robert Browning ("God's in His Heaven, All's Right with the World")—is a complex geopolitical pun, combining a British poet, a red leaf somehow reminiscent of the Canadian maple leaf, and a German noun.[9] In fact, the city's surface buildings are for the most part camouflage and delivery systems for the vast underground cavern of Nerv's "geofront" (yet another English neologism, referring to an underground living space). Shinji's first view of the geofront through the window of a bullet train is awe-inspiring. Washed in golden light from some artificial light source, Tokyo-3's retractable skyscrapers hang down from the ceiling like vast roots, while an enormous lake shimmers below. (A sonorous trumpet even echoes in the background, very much like the opening tag of the *Deep Space 9* TV series.) Nerv's central facility is located at the bottom of the geofront and consists of a curious kind of double pyramid: a vast depression, shaped like an inverted pyramid, directly adjacent to a smaller raised pyramid. Finally, there is a giant raised structure to the far right, suggesting nothing so much as an outdoor drive-in movie screen or the base of an early 1990s cellphone.

Over and over again, Anno will strike just the right balance between Yamashita's people-moving platforms, giant conveyor belts and Eva-related equipment, and Sadamoto's crisp, emotive character designs. During an early scene of "Evangelion 1," for example, Ritsuko (the head of Nerv's science team), Misato, and Shinji are silhouetted in an elevator against a glowing pink background, gloomily discussing the near-impossibility of ever getting the Eva to work properly. Suddenly the vast humanoid hand of Eva 1 materializes in the storage tank behind them. A similar technique is used when Shinji first confronts the gaze of Eva 1, whose segmented, eyeless face glares like a stylized demon out of Japan's storied theatrical tradition: Distant objects seem near, and near objects appear distant. All this culminates in the moment when Shinji is asked to pilot the Eva by his father, Gendou Ikari, whom he has not seen for three years. Gendou's face is shot against serried banks of video monitors, displaying multiple images of Shinji, ingeniously echoed by a close shot of Gendou's semitransparent glasses, which reflect these video images; these glasses will be a recurrent symbol throughout the series.

It is here that Anno transgresses against one of the fundamental features of the mecha narrative, by disrupting both its patriarchal gender codes and crude technological determinism. Unlike so many other anime, where the point is to show the son or daughter of the genius inventor dutifully carrying on the family lineage, Shinji actually *thinks* about his decision and starts shaking with rage at the thought of being treated as cannon fodder for an untried, experimental technology. Although Misato remonstrates with him, saying "You must confront your father, and you must confront yourself," he cannot bring himself to pilot the Eva. Finally Gendou has to call upon Rei to pilot the mecha; she is wheeled in on a stretcher, still badly wounded from a previous testing accident, accompanied by a haunting piano theme that will reappear at key moments later in the series. At this point one of the angel's power bolts tears loose debris from the roof of Tokyo-3, but just as a detached section of the roof threatens to crush Shinji, Eva 1 lifts up its massive armored hand *by itself* to protect him, batting the debris away in the direction of Gendou Ikari—who smiles grimly behind a shockproof glass wall, as if he had expected this turn of events all along. When Shinji finally agrees to pilot the Eva, it is out of compassion for Rei, who is obviously in bad shape, and not his father's wishes.

This is nothing, however, compared with the scandalous transposition of the battle sequence from the very beginning of "Evangelion 2" to the closing moments of the episode. We see the angel fighting with the Eva and apparently getting the upper hand by crushing the latter's left arm, when suddenly Anno cuts to Shinji waking up in the hospital. We only very gradually figure out he somehow won the battle, though at terrible cost. This transgresses against a general feature of East Asian media culture in the 1980s, namely, the video-boosted glorification of the physical bravery, dexterity, or athleticism of the martial arts hero or mecha pilot; something usually conjoined to the repressive micropolitics of the national police force, mythic warrior code, or state-developmental bureaucracy charged with battling comic book gangsters, rogue samurai, or corporate thugs. The battles with the angels are not contests of physical strength, however, but subjective and psychological tests of concentration and willpower. Eventually, they will become a kind of objective recorder or seismographic sensor, by which Anno will map out the fault lines of a postbubble Japan, slowly and painfully coming to grips with its past and present traumas.[10]

One of the most significant of these traumas is Japan's epic transformation from a predominantly agrarian society to an urbanized and industrial one. Britain took more than a century to become an urban society, and the United States and Western Europe accomplished the same feat in about seventy years; Japan did so in less than thirty years (1945–75). This tremendous achievement came at the price of enormous cultural dislocation, intergenerational conflict, and psychological stress, as ordinary Japanese had to cope with not just one or two but several cultural revolutions, all at once. It's no accident that the two leading cultural exports of Japanese cinema in the 1950s and 1960s—the Godzilla movies and the Kurosawa films—both put their finger on this precise contradiction. Toho's wildly successful monster epics deftly set the trauma of World War II and the utopia of Americanization in motion toward the monsters of humanity's thermonuclear Id, while Kurosawa's samurai thrillers and detective dramas did something similar with the antinomies of rapid urbanization and upward class mobility. At their outer limit, each paved the way for the multinational East Asian media culture of the future, in much the same way that the social tensions and conflicts of Japan's postwar boom anticipated those of other rapidly modernizing East Asian nations, most notably Taiwan and South Korea in the 1970s, and coastal China since the late 1980s. Certainly, one could argue that John Woo's Hong Kong blockbusters are the postmodern synthesis of the visual energies of the Godzilla spectacular and the scripting innovations of the Kurosawa film.

Evangelion records the generational aspect of this process in an unusually direct fashion: The "old men" of Seele represent the deeply conservative, immediate postwar generation, Gendou Ikari and Fuyutski hail from the technocratic generation of the 1970s, Misato and the other Nerv staffers represent the consumer-oriented 1980s, and the children incarnate the informatic 1990s. (Only fourteen-year-olds have the neural flexibility to pilot the Evas, a canny reference to the ability of the Nintendo kids to meld with a given technology far faster than any adult.) The clash of generations is also the crucial issue during Shinji's first face-to-face meeting with his father after the battle, when they run into each other in one of Nerv's elevators. A low-angle shot frames Gendou to the left of the screen and Shinji to the right. But neither can yet forgive the other, and after a tense moment of silence, like a standoff in some rural village, the door closes without either one saying a word. Anno will show us a range of similar scenes in the elevators, bullet trains, and skywalks of Tokyo-3, often using excruciatingly long shots to highlight the inner conflicts of the characters. Later, Misato takes Shinji to a scenic overlook, where they watch the skyscrapers of Tokyo-3 rise majestically from the ground at sunset, seconded by the same sweeping horn motifs that signaled Shinji's first glimpse of the geofront. The effect is like viewing a time-lapse photograph of postwar Tokyo, as one office tower after another rises up out of a sea of tenements and apartment buildings. Misato will complete the gesture by taking Shinji to one such apartment building, a new flat on the outskirts of town, in order to give him a home he can call his own.

This domestic space will allow Anno to quote a number of anime conventions, ranging from the registers of slapstick and domestic comedy, to the institution of the "service shot" (still shots of anime characters in vaguely suggestive or risque positions), all the way to the exaggeratedly *kawaii* (the Japanese word for "cute") series mascot or pet animal. The mascot in *Evangelion* is Pen-pen, a warm-water penguin with near-human intelligence, which has its own living quarters and even reads the newspaper. The penguin has been a significant mass-cultural symbol since Opus in Berke Breathed's classic 1980s comic strip, *Bloom County;* in the 1990s, the penguin became the icon of Linus Torvald's freeware PC operating system, Linux. Most of all, Anno inverts the usual gender stereotypes here: Not only is Misato a complete slob, but she has a habit of yelling out a war whoop after drinking a can of beer; that is, she is the complete antithesis of the docile Japanese housewife—in fact, Shinji ends up doing the cooking in the household. In "Evangelion 2," the obligatory service shots of Misato are even matched by a service shot of Shinji about to take a bath. When he discovers Pen-pen in the bathroom and runs screaming to Misato, totally naked, a beer can on the table strategically placed between our point of view and the lower part of his body; when Misato picks up the can of beer, a jar of toothpicks turns out to be in the way.

What does not quite ring true is Misato's latent aggression toward Shinji. In fact, later on in the series, Misato will become much more of a guardian figure, while Asuka will take on the role of the provocative, in-your-face tomboy. It is only in the solitude and quiet of his new home that Shinji begins to recall the shocking details of the battle sequence. After an extremely realistic close-up of Shinji's eye, brimming with multiple reflections on the cornea, Anno deploys a series of extremely fast cuts, each keyed to a crashing sound, which culminate in a full-scale flashback of the battle. The pilots of the Eva are enclosed in a shockproof "entry plug" (yet another English neologism) that looks like a guided missile, inserted manually into the Eva. This is the first in a series of quotations from William Gibson's classic *Neuromancer;* the entry plug is very much the fusion of the "coffin" hotel Case stays at in Tokyo (the actual term is "capsule hotels," and though they really are the size of a coffin, many have built-in TVs and alarm clocks), with the cyberspace deck (the Eva pilots wear trodes, which enable them to synch their brainwaves to the Eva).

The action scenes are superbly animated, conveying a sense of thermonuclear-strength battles with world-class editing, sound effects, and tracking shots. Anno not only borrows many of the stunt techniques of the Hong

Kong thrillers but intersperses close shots of the awed faces of Nerv personnel watching the action from their video monitors. After taking a terrible
pounding, the Eva seems to sense the danger to Shinji's life and miraculously
springs into action, howling like some primeval monster. The angel broadcasts an "AT field," or force field of mental energy to block it (keynoted by a
high ringing chime, a standard anime sound effect connoting surprise or
shock), but the Eva proceeds to regenerate its own arm and neutralize the
angel's AT field with its own field, before closing in for the kill. After the battle,
Shinji is looking outside at the Eva's blank, featureless eye socket, when suddenly tissue around the socket boils into existence, and a giant green eye slides
into view. Shinji's blue-gray eye freezes, as he realizes the Eva is *looking at
him*. He screams in horror, as the screen fades to black (a quotation of one
of the first great video tropes, the close shots of Sally's quivering eye in Tobe
Hooper's 1974 horror classic, *The Texas Chain Saw Massacre*).

What sharply distinguishes the Evas from the cyborgs, androids, and
genetically engineered bodies endemic to the anime genre, however, is the
fact that they are not really autonomous entities or a separate species. Rather,
like Stanislaw Lem's biologized aliens, the vanished Krell of *Forbidden Planet*,
or Gibson's curiously splintered AIs, they constitute the borderline or bound-
ary between the human and the nonhuman, or between the realms of social
history and natural history. In the earliest episodes of *Evangelion*, the social
and natural history in question is clearly that of postwar Japan: Thus in
"Evangelion 3" Shinji experiences the joys and sorrows of notoriety when
his high school classmates discover he is an Eva pilot; in "Evangelion 4" we
see the bullet trains, half-empty streets, and gorgeous natural scenery around
Tokyo-3; in "Evangelion 5" the spaces in question are the gray-in-gray concrete wasteland of postwar housing projects (identified with Rei) and the
high-tech laboratory (identified with Ritsuko); "Evangelion 6" illustrates the
Japanese national power grid via a satellite shot of Japan from outer space;
while "Evangelion 7" satirizes the arrogance of Japan's nuclear power lobby
and keiretsu business elites. Anno never allows these objective spaces to
overshadow the human drama of the characters involved; rather, the specific
tropes of the former are used to highlight the irreplaceable individuality of
the latter.

The very first of these dramas is Shinji's slow, painful process of adjustment to his new home, well worth describing in detail. While Shinji's classmates, Hikari, Touji, and Kensuke, are modeled on the duty-conscious class
monitor, the well-meaning but impulsive athlete, and the bespectacled science geek, all are complex, rounded characters in their own right.[11] In

"Evangelion 3," for example, Touji punches Shinji to the ground in revenge for his sister, who was critically injured in the battle with the angel (an act Touji will later regret terribly, when Shinji saves both him and Kensuke from the attack of the second angel). After being chewed out by Misato for disobeying orders, Shinji runs away from his new home, riding the rails of Tokyo-3, sleeping on benches and in a movie theater (ironically playing a grade-B science fiction movie based on the Second Impact), and dispiritedly wandering through the countryside, oblivious to the lush green fields, blue skies, terraced hills, and fog-shrouded valleys on every side. At last Shinji accidentally runs into Kensuke, who is camping out in the wilds in full camouflage gear and acting out the parts of the heroic, wounded captain and loyal lieutenant in a hackneyed war movie.[12] Shinji gradually warms to Kensuke when the latter reveals that he, too, lost his mother at a young age, and they strike up a friendship.

The next day, Nerv security agents take him in and present him with an ultimatum: either resign or return to full-time duty as a pilot. He opts to resign, in just one of several references to *The Prisoner*. (There is even a McGoohanesque shot of his Nerv ID card with his photo, stamped "resigned.") But before he leaves, Kensuke and Touji arrive, and Touji not only formally apologizes to Shinji but insists that Shinji punch him back to make sure they're even. After Shinji does so, they are reconciled, and they both praise him for his courage in piloting the Eva. This kindness completely unnerves Shinji, who is already deeply ambivalent about his status as a pilot and beginning to realize he will be leaving behind his newfound friends. At roughly the same time, Misato realizes that Shinji's flight is not a thought-out decision; it's the only way he knows of reaching out to others. This is capped by a significant scene at the railway station, when Misato roars up in her car, thinking she just missed him, before realizing he is still at the station. They stare at each other in silence, while the announcements of arriving and departing trains echo in the background, in a static shot lasting a full forty-eight seconds. ("I ... I'm home," stammers Shinji at last. Misato smiles and says, "Welcome home.")

After this wealth of character development, "Evangelion 5" proceeds to introduce Shinji's first key counterplayer, fellow pilot Rei Ayanami. Rei lives in a nondescript row of cement apartments, in a room overflowing with bandages and assorted junk. In fact, her only real personal possession is a broken pair of Gendou's glasses, still in their original case. Shinji's first visit to Rei is an explicit parody of the service shot. Not realizing Rei is home, Shinji puts on the glasses and is surprised by Rei, who emerges stark naked from the shower. Embarrassed, he tries to explain, while she unexpectedly reaches for the glasses, causing them to inadvertently fall on top of each other. If this were a normal service shot, Shinji would be slapped or otherwise called to account for his temerity. Here, however, Rei simply says quietly, "Will you get off?" and she gets dressed. Rei's general air of unearthliness is highlighted by her trademark blue hair, hardly an unusual sight in an anime series but a color that certainly meshes with the deeply introverted tenor of her personality. Rei is, however, capable of powerful emotional reactions, most notably in a later conversation with Shinji, when the latter angrily denounces his father; Rei steps forwards and slaps him, telling him he should have faith in his father.

Rei's appearance also coincides with the first explicit citation of neonational or cold war technological tropes, ranging from the positronic rifle Nerv requisitions from the weapons labs of Japan's Self-Defense Forces, to the alloy hull of a space shuttle Ritsuko uses as an improvised heat shield. (Gendou's broken glasses also return in one crucial shot, showing the glistening white screens of four computers piled up in Rei's room, an intriguing reference to information technology.) The enemy angel of "Evangelion 6" is a mirrorlike hypercube with an irresistible particle weapon beam, which knocks Eva 1 out of action with a single shot and begins drilling past the geofront's armor shields. Faced with an enemy that cannot be attacked directly, Misato improvises the clever strategy of downing the angel with a sniper shot, and Nerv proceeds to mobilize the entire national power grid of Japan to power the rifle. The sniper sequence begins with a magnificent series of shots of Tokyo-3 going dark, and then a vertical shot of Pen-pen staring into the night sky, followed by a satellite image of the entire Japanese archipelago blacking out, framed by the glowing arc of the Korean peninsula and coastal China. This geopolitical reference to East Asia accedes to a conversation between Shinji and Rei, highlighted by a brilliant sequence of frames:

SHINJI: *(Framed against eye of Eva 1.)* Ayanami, just why do you pilot this thing?

REI: *(Framed against her own Eva, thinks for a moment.)* Because I'm bonded to it.

SHINJI: You're bonded to it?

REI: Yes. It's a bond.

SHINJI: You mean, to my father?

REI: To all people. *(Slow pan from Shinji to Rei against the darkened valley, stars in background.)*

SHINJI: You're very strong, Rei.

REI: I have nothing else.

SHINJI: *(Framed against Rei.)* What do you mean, you have nothing else?

REI: *(Getting up.)* It's time. Let's go. *(She is silhouetted against an enormous close-up of the full moon.)* Good-bye, Shinji.

Powered by the entire energy grid of Japan, Shinji prepares to fire, but the angel senses their presence and launches its own energy pulse, throwing the shot off course. Rei then holds up the improvised heat shield against the withering blast of the angel, her Eva sustaining terrible damage in the process, until his second shot finally hits home. Afterwards, he wrests open the superheated entry plug of her battered Eva with his own hands, echoing a previous scene when his father opened Rei's superheated plug in the test chamber with his bare hands, badly burning himself:

SHINJI: *(Crying tears of relief.)* Don't ever say that. Just don't say that you have nothing else. Just don't say that. And don't say good-bye when we launch. It's just too sad. *(Cut to shot of half-melted entry plug in half-melted hand of Eva-01; medium shot of the two Evas reclining, their skins battered and seared by the angel's assault, almost as if they are talking.)*

REI: Why are you crying? . . . I'm sorry . . . I'm sorry, I don't know what to feel at times like this.

SHINJI: Just smile. *(Close shot of her eyes, Shinji's reflection in her pupils. Suddenly she draws in her breath, struck by his resemblance to Gendou Ikari. Slowly, hesitantly, she smiles.)*

This is just the first of many such extraordinary moments, where eye-popping visuals and gargantuan battles artfully embellish, rather than overwhelm, the subtlest of character interactions. Although Rei's inverted, rotating silhouette is the central motif of the series' closing tag, this is the first time she is explicitly identified with an extreme close-up of the moon, whose glowing circle is curiously replicated by the banks of outdoor floodlights that accompany several scenes in "Evangelion 4."

It's interesting that the last moment of the traditional mecha narrative ("Evangelion 7") marks Anno's first open critique of Japan's nuclear power lobby and keiretsu business elites. Misato and Ritsuko are called to attend a demonstration of an Eva-style robot by the Japan Heavy Chemical Industrial Cooperative—the difference being that this robot has its own internal nuclear power supply and is piloted by an onboard computer, not by a human pilot. Meanwhile, the corporate stooge in charge of the demonstration insults Nerv and its science team in the most obnoxious and sexist terms. ("It's [the Eva] like a hysterical woman, completely out of control.") Predictably, the supposedly failsafe robot goes haywire during its activation test and threatens to melt down in a populated region, forcing Misato to launch an emergency mission to stop it. There is one priceless scene of a corporate executive out on a golf course, trying to weasel out of responsibility for handing over the robot's password ("hope," a three-character kanji in Japanese) to Nerv. Although Shinji manages to catch up to the robot amid the rubble of Tokyo-2, Misato finds that the password doesn't work. In desperation she starts pushing in the neutron-absorbing safety rods manually, but at the last second the program finally activates, shutting down the reactor. This accident was, in short, no accident at all. In a later scene, Ritsuko reports to Gendou, saying everything went according to plan, except for Captain Katsuragi's operation—strongly hinting that they either aided or abetted the sabotage.

This pungent satire of the legendary turf battles between Japan's developmental state and its fiercely competitive corporations highlights one of the key weaknesses of the robot narrative and cybernetic technologies generally: its reliance on electronic control and communications subsystems (software). As befitting its status as an industrial semiperiphery, Japanese firms specialized for decades in medium-technology electronics and automotive goods, and did not start diversifying into high-end software, services, and broadcasting markets until the late 1980s (Sony's trajectory from a purveyor of cheap radios, to high-quality stereo and video equipment, and finally to video game platforms and media content is emblematic in this respect). The software industry is also marked by a striking multinational division of labor, such that the United States leads the world in PC software, the EU excels in enterprise resource planning (ERP) software, while Japan exports vast quantities of video game-related software.

Two new characters—the third pilot, Asuka Langley, and the intelligence operative, Kaji Ryouji—will mark the arrival of explicitly multinational and informatic signifiers in "Evangelion 8," by means of that oldest narrative of globalization of them all, the seafaring adventure. Not only does this episode manage to pastiche all the classic ocean adventures from *Moby Dick* up to *Jaws*. It also slyly alludes to Anno's own previous seafaring tale, *Nadia* (in the form of the crusty admiral, the spitting image of Captain Nemo). The bulk of the episode takes place on a supercarrier of the UN Pacific fleet, mobilized to protect the third Evangelion unit on its journey from Germany to Japan, a seemingly unlikely backdrop for the riotous physical comedy associated with Asuka and the emotional complications signaled by the suave Kaji (Misato's long-lost ex-boyfriend). Despite years of separation, Kaji still knows how to get Misato's goat: In one dinner scene, he playfully asks Shinji if Misato is still wild in bed, causing the children to gasp in shock and Misato to turn purple. What makes this especially funny is the incidental sound track of a B-grade, lurid soap opera running on the TV in the background, a technique Anno will repeat a number of times in the future.

In contrast to the self-abnegating Rei, Asuka is self-assertive, capricious, and that rarest of all things in anime, a female character with genuine emotional depth. She is also of mixed German and Japanese descent, frequently using choice German phrases in crisis situations, but displays a thoroughly Americanized individualism when piloting her Eva. When a sea-based angel suddenly attacks, sending ship after ship to the bottom of the sea with the unremitting fury of the White Whale itself, Asuka drags Shinji off to the cockpit of Eva 2 and launches without Misato's authorization. In one gorgeous sequence, Eva 2 leaps from ship to ship like so many stepping-stones, before landing on the deck of the supercarrier as if it were a giant surfboard. Although they successfully repulse the attack of the angel, the beast traps Eva 2 in its maw and drags them out to sea, reeling out the Eva's power cable behind it. This gives Misato the sudden inspiration to use the reel as a weapon, by sinking two battleships and using them as giant depth charges to blow up the angel from within. After fighting like cats and dogs, Asuka and Shinji manage to work together to make the plan succeed.

No episode of *Evangelion* would be complete without a devious plot twist to send a chill down our spine, and "Evangelion 8" does not disappoint. After the battle, Kaji delivers a mysterious package to Gendou back at Nerv. It is an embryonic life-form of some kind, encased in plastic, which Gendou calls Adam, "the first human being," the keynote of the mysterious Instrumentality project, and most likely the real provocation for the angel attack. This is actually the culmination of two earlier scenes: In "Evangelion 5," Ritsuko tells Misato and Shinji that the energy patterns of the angels are a 99.89 percent match to human DNA, while in "Evangelion 7" she reveals additional details of the Second Impact, saying that the catastrophe was caused not by an asteroid but by human contact with an angel.[13] This suggests that the Second and (potential) Third Impact are not really metaphors for World War II and a potential thermonuclear World War III. They refer to something specific to the post–cold war era, which we still need to identify.

The fundamental innovation Asuka brings to the story line is the element of subjective initiative and contingency, both in terms of her role as the popular foreign exchange girl, overwhelmed with attention from her classmates, and her status as a true psychological counterplayer for Shinji, someone who motivates him to break out of his Rei-like introversion. Put another way, Asuka's arrival marks the point at which the adults of *Evangelion* start acting like adults, and the children start acting like children—or more accurately, the moment when we begin to see how childlike adults can be, and how children wrestle with adult issues. One of the real achievements of Anno's scriptwriting here is his ability to balance Asuka's tempestuous friendship with Shinji—equal parts competition, friction, and growing empathy—with Misato's own stormy relationship with Kaji. There is one great moment in "Evangelion 9" when Asuka is sleepwalking and almost kisses Shinji. He leans forward, but she says, "Mama," in her sleep and he turns away, embarrassed. Elsewhere in Tokyo-3, Kaji is kissing Misato, as their old romance flares up again despite her protests to the contrary. "Which should I trust, your lips or your words?" he asks, devilish as ever. The upshot of all this is to add fresh layers of complexity to the various character interrelationships, most notably between Misato and Ritsuko. (For example, hanging out in a Tokyo-3 bar one night, Ritsuko suddenly asks, "So, still in love, huh?" as only an old friend can, causing Misato to choke on her coffee.) "Evangelion 9" is also the most explicit comic parody of the mecha, reveling in the chaos that erupts when Asuka and Shinji face off against what can best be described as the angel of karaoke, a creature that can replicate itself indefinitely and that can only be defeated by precisely timed choreography between Evas 1 and 2. Shinji and Asuka eventually learn to set aside their differences and cooperate, but not before treating us to their very own music video—a gorgeously choreographed one-minute videorecording of the battle, which manages to float effortlessly above the mecha genre, by citing the shot techniques of the televised sports event and Olympic gymnastics routine.

"Evangelion 10," on the other hand, is concerned not with the space of extended cultural consumption but with the space of production, relayed here by an embryonic angel found floating in the lava of a Japanese volcano. Although the volcano is one of the oldest metaphors for industrialization around, Anno manages to impart a fresh spin on the idea, by showing Nerv's attempt to capture the angel intact, in what amounts to the rewriting of J. R. R. Tolkien's military-industrial Mount Doom in a biological turn. Anno also subtly weaves the corporeal register of diving and the scientific one of thermodynamics into the story. Thus the high school class goes on a diving trip, Asuka shops for a swimsuit and goes diving in a pool at one point, the defeat of the angel is made possible by a creative application of a basic lesson of thermodynamics, and the episode ends with an appropriately comic moment at a volcanic hot springs. (On cue, Pen-pen shows up by package delivery.) All this is overshadowed by an unsettling moment, when Asuka and Misato are sitting by the hot springs and watching the sun set. Asuka notices

Misato's scar, a legacy of the Second Impact, and correctly surmises that Misato knows all about her past. ("It's my job," Misato reminds her gently.)

The motif of the fading sun is not an accident. This moment of relative equilibrium, where the various registers of comedy and tragedy, childhood and adulthood, society and technology all seem to coexist in relative harmony, will slowly disintegrate in future episodes, as *Evangelion* moves decisively beyond the mecha as a form and probes deeper and deeper into the terrible traumas of the past, not out of any desire to humiliate or punish its characters, but as the deepest and most necessary sort of healing. In the process, the neonational or Japanese motifs of the earlier episodes will gradually be rewritten into multinational and East Asian ones. Anno's first step is to mobilize the radical discontents of a post–cold war generation deeply dissatisfied with the asphyxiating monotony of the LDP one-party state, its xenophobic micropolitics, and its repressive gender roles, but unable, as yet, to formulate a coherent political or social project of resistance. This is signaled by "Evangelion 11," whose English subtitle, "The Day Tokyo-3 Stood Still," refers to the touchstone science fiction movie of dissent from the cold war, *The Day the Earth Stood Still.* Here, it is not the urban center of the Earth but the multinational urban space of Tokyo-3 that has been immobilized, only not by inimical aliens, but by human beings themselves. "I can't believe the first havoc wreaked upon our headquarters wasn't caused by some angel, but by another member of our own species," frets Fuyutski. Gendou responds philosophically, "Humanity is its own worst enemy."

The airing of the dirty laundry of the developmental state begins, appropriately enough, at a futuristic laundromat, where several Nerv staffers are picking up their laundry on their way to work. Hopping aboard the train, they meet their boss, Fuyutski, who is reading the morning newspaper:

> RITSUKO: You're quite early today.
>
> FUYUTSKI: Well, I have to go uptown as Ikari's representative.
>
> RITSUKO: I see. Isn't today the City Council's regular meeting?
>
> FUYUTSKI: It's a boring job. He always forces the most tedious work on me. Without the Magi's help, I couldn't do it.
>
> RITSUKO: Speaking of which, election day is coming up, isn't it?
>
> FUYUTSKI: The City Council has no authority at all. Actually, the Magi run everything now.
>
> MAYA: The Magi? You mean the three supercomputers?
>
> FUYUTSKI: Government by the majority decision of three computers. It's a sort of democratic system.

MAYA: And the council just obeys their decisions?

FUYUTSKI: *(Ironic.)* It's a most effective form of government.

MAYA: *(Wide-eyed.)* This truly is a City of Science. We're lucky to live in an era when Science reigns supreme.

SHIGERU: *(Rolls eyes to himself.)* That's so old-fashioned.

Maya's comment is less outdated than one might think. Simply substitute "Bill Gates, Larry Ellison, Andy Grove" for the three Magi and "Silicon Valley" for the City of Science and one could easily imagine some young U.S. tech professional of the 1990s bubble, dazzled by their inflated stock options, voicing the same opinion. What is interesting, though, is that Shigeru is not immediately identified with his most obvious U.S. counterpart, the hippie programmer or freeware guru. This is not, as one might assume, due to the belated development of the PC market in Japan (in fact, one of Gainax' main product lines in the early 1990s was made-for-PC software), but is meant to highlight the fact that Nerv is a kind of global frontier zone of free spirits, innovators, and visionaries, who would never fit into a buttoned-down corporate research program or official government lab.

More importantly, "Evangelion 11" shows Rei, Asuka, and Shinji interacting with one another for the first time. Finding that their subway cards have ceased functioning thanks to the blackout, Asuka leads them in the general direction of Nerv headquarters, only to end up practically running into the new angel in the process (a giant spider with a central acidic eye). The angel's form is no accident, but perfectly complements a jaw-dropping shot involving the mechanical eye of a subway card reader. We see a huge blob trailing across the screen, which turns out to be Asuka's thumb rubbing the scanner, as if filmed from the perspective of a spider located behind the scanner plate! The angel's crawling method of locomotion is also replicated by the children, who have to crawl through underground service ducts to get to their Evangelions, and then crawl through yet more ducts to get to the scene of the battle. Along the way, Asuka and Rei repeatedly clash, displaying a mutual antagonism that makes Asuka's run-ins with Shinji look like purest harmony, if not indeed a romantically tinged jealousy. (Asuka whispers to Shinji, in a true case of the pot calling the kettle black: "This First Child [Rei] isn't someone to mess with. She'll do anything to accomplish her objectives. She's a real self-righteous bitch.") Working for the first time as a trio of equals, they finally defeat the angel, leading to this intriguing postbattle meditation:

They stare up into the Milky Way, the night sky perfectly clear thanks to the blackout.

SHINJI: It's ironic . . . without electricity and artificial light, the sky can look so
   beautiful.

ASUKA: But without the lights, it's as if there weren't any people there. *(Lights
   come back on in city, block by block.)* See? I feel so much better this way.

REI: *(Poetically.)* Human beings fear the Darkness and drive it away with Flame,
   in order to survive.

ASUKA: *(Dismissively.)* Philosophy!

SHINJI: Is that what makes humankind a special species? Is that why the angels
   keep attacking us?

ASUKA: What are you? Stupid? Who knows what they think?

Here at last *Evangelion* finds the ultimate narrative synthesis between
Rei's lyric neonational interiority and Asuka's pragmatic multinational
exteriority. This is the global frame of Shinji's explicitly aesthetic cognition. The extraordinary power of this move will become apparent only in
"Evangelion 12," when Anno begins to provide this global frame with content. The episode begins with a flashback to the year 2000. We see the blue
marble of the Earth rise above the cratered surface of the moon, and then a
bright light flashes near the South Pole. The next shot is of the blasted ruins and howling winds of the Second Impact, punctuated by a brief shot of
the very first angel (Adam) radiating in the background like the thermal pulse
of an A-bomb. Misato's father, badly wounded, is carrying his unconscious
daughter to a safety capsule (an interesting early version of the entry plug).
She awakens briefly when a drop of his blood falls on her cheek, saying,
"Father," just as the capsule closes. Safely out at sea, Misato's capsule opens,
and she stares at the Apocalypse. A high, electronic sound resounds, like the
whinny of an angel, whilst a terrible pair of stylized double wings rises far
off, as some unknown energy source blasts Antarctica into nothingness. The
scene cuts to 2015, when Misato is getting dressed, and we finally see a frontal shot of the scar across her chest. This is more than just the negation of
the sexist service shot; It is also the savage repudiation of that cold war sex
symbol par excellence, the *bikini* (named after Bikini Atoll, the Pacific reef
vaporized by an H-bomb), as well as the ingenious rewriting of the signature atomic mushroom cloud into a planetary or ecological register.

As if to second this, Fuyutski and Gendou Ikari carry on the following
quasi-theological conversation during a secret mission at the tip of the South
Pole, onboard an aircraft carrier making its way through a poisoned, radio-
active sea, sprinkled with residual ice or rock formations poking out of the
luminous pink water:

FUYUTSKI: Nothing alive can exist in this world of death, Antarctica . . . or should we just call it Hell?

GENDOU: And yet we human beings stand here, as living beings.

FUYUTSKI: Because we're protected by science.

GENDOU: Science is the power of humanity.

FUYUTSKI: That arrogance caused the tragedy of the Second Impact fifteen years ago. This is the result. The punishment is too harsh, considering what we've done. . . . It's like the Dead Sea.

GENDOU: And yet it's a purified world, washed clean of sin.

FUYUTSKI: I prefer worlds where human beings can live, regardless of how steeped in sin.

The next angel, a weirdly bulbous creature with a vast central eye, chooses this inopportune moment to attack. Satellite recon photos show its first two blasts landed harmlessly in the Pacific Ocean, while the next hits land. (It is unclear whether it lands in southern Japan, the Korean peninsula, or elsewhere in Southeast Asia.) Whereas the satellite image in "Evangelion 6" conveyed a primordial East Asian form, via the identical power grids of China, South Korea, and Japan, these images hint at a nascent East Asian identity: that of fellow victims, as the A-bombs and atmospheric H-bomb tests uncannily converge with the airborne devastation of Korea and Vietnam during the cold war. Misato's off-the-cuff plan is for the children to catch the angel as it falls from the skies, using their AT fields like giant nets. She bluntly tells them their chances aren't good, and even asks them if they want to write a will. ("I have no intention of dying," shoots back Asuka.) The references to the era of the H-bomb continue to multiply when, at one point, she promises them a steak dinner if they succeed, and they pretend to jump for joy. Once she's gone, Asuka delivers the great line: "Does she really think that children nowadays care about a steak dinner? Second Generation people are so *cheap*," and she starts thumbing through a tourist guide, trying to find the most expensive steak house in town. Even more interesting is a moment when Shinji, waiting in Eva 1 to engage the angel, thinks back to his conversation the previous day with Misato. They were standing at the edge of Tokyo-3, watching the sun set behind the buildings, when suddenly she began to talk about her past:

MISATO: Shinji, yesterday you asked me why I joined Nerv. My father was a man who put everything into his research, into his dreams. I've never been able to forgive him for that, and in fact I even hated him.

SHINJI: Just like my father.

MISATO: He never took care of me, my mother, or the family. People said he was
very sensitive and delicate, but the truth was that he was just a weak person
who didn't want to face reality, the reality called his family. He was like a little
kid. So I agreed with my mother when she decided to divorce him, because she
was always crying. He was depressed about it, but I laughed at him because he
deserved what he got. *(Close shot of the cross hanging from her neck.)* But he
sacrificed himself to save my life during the Second Impact. I didn't know
whether I hated him or loved him. The only thing that was clear to me was that
I wanted to destroy the angels who had caused the Second Impact. That's why
I joined Nerv. It could be I'm trying to take revenge for my father, in order to
finally become free of him. *(Montage in Shinji's mind of childhood themes of
abandonment, news headlines, Eva-1, finally the thought: I mustn't run away, I
mustn't run away, I mustn't run away. He returns to consciousness in the entry
plug of Eva-1.)*

SHINJI: *(To himself.)* I must *not* run away.

In yet another eye-popping sequence, scored to a Spanish aria reminiscent of Leone's spaghetti Westerns, Shinji manages to intercept the angel
with his own AT field, enabling Asuka and Rei to arrive just in time to neutralize the angel's AT field and knock out its core. Misato's powerful meditation on gender, the first moment of a revolutionary micropolitics, is seconded by the postbattle briefing, when Ikari praises his son in front of the
others for the first time (an unusual moment in a culture that, even today,
tends to recognize group achievement rather than individual merit).

It is only now that a genuinely informatic politics will take wing, as Anno
decisively moves away from the cybernetic and nuclear tropes of the cold war
and toward the biological and silicon tropes of the information age. The plot
of "Evangelion 13" turns on the invasion of the informatic space of the Magi
system, rather than the physical invasion of Tokyo-3 and the geofront. One
early scene shows banks of computer screens, and various semitransparent
computer screens projected onto the windows of the water-filled test chamber. This is perhaps the place to emphasize the extraordinary aesthetic
beauty of Nerv's instrument panels, which exhibit an inexhaustible wealth
of richly detailed graphical displays, warning decals, logos, and symbols,
each with its own subtle visual stylization and sound effect. The invading
angel is not a Godzilla-sized monster but a kind of biological microproces-
sor or nanomachine, which at first appears to be some harmless corrosion
near a "protein wall," which quickly spreads to the vicinity of the test chamber and then eats into the "Pribnow box" surrounding headquarters, before
hacking into the Magi directly. All these terms are drawn, by the way, from

real-life genetics research (the Pribnow box, for example, is a DNA sequence that repeats in a certain way), and one could argue that "Evangelion 13" is to that extent the biological reappropriation of silicon cleanroom technology. The scene where Nerv plots its counterstrategy is surely one of the transcendental moments of late-twentieth-century science fiction, perfectly balancing the objective discourses of nanotechnology, programming, ecological niches, and evolution against the subjective motivations of its characters:

> RITSUKO: This angel must be composed of "micro-machines" [in English], each the size of viruses. In a very short period of time, they have exponentially evolved to form a sophisticated intelligence circuit.
>
> FUYUTSKI: Evolved!
>
> RITSUKO: Exactly. They're continuously changing to form the best system to cope with any environment.
>
> FUYUTSKI: It's this angel's survival mechanism.
>
> MISATO: *(Determinedly.)* Against an enemy that constantly evolves to overcome its weaknesses, the only effective countermeasure is to eliminate the host and let the parasite die with it. The only option is to order the Magi to self-destruct. I propose the physical elimination of the Magi.
>
> RITSUKO: *(Parries.)* Impossible. Destroying the Magi means destroying headquarters itself.
>
> MISATO: *(Heatedly.)* Then I'm officially requesting it on behalf of the Operations Division.
>
> RITSUKO: Rejected. This situation is the responsibility of the Technology Department.
>
> MISATO: Why are you being so mule-headed?
>
> RITSUKO: This situation is the result of my carelessness.
>
> MISATO: Why do you always have to be like this? You're always taking all the responsibility on your own shoulders to avoid depending on anyone else.
>
> RITSUKO: *(Thinking furiously.)* As long as this angel keeps evolving, we still have a chance.
>
> IKARI: *(With sudden insight.)* Expedite its evolution?
>
> RITSUKO: Yes, sir.
>
> IKARI: The end of evolution is self-destruction: death itself.
>
> FUYUTSKI: Thus we just need to accelerate its evolution.
>
> RITSUKO: If the angel considers it the only practical means of survival, it may choose to coexist with the Magi system.
>
> MAKOTO: But how do we do that?
>
> RITSUKO: If the angel is a computer itself, we can do a reverse hack by connecting Caspar to the angel and upload a self-destruct program. However . . .

MAYA: *(Finishes thought.)* . . . at the same time we'll be turning off the barrier to
   the angel.

IKARI: So either Caspar or the angel, whichever is faster, will win.

RITSUKO: Yes.

MISATO: Can this program be ready in time? If Caspar is taken over, it'll be all over.

RITSUKO: *(Glances at her, looks away.)* I keep my promises.

Ritsuko's stubbornness is due not to any technocratic arrogance but to
her deeply ambivalent relationship to her mother, the late Naoko Akagi, a
brilliant scientist who created the Magi years ago and wrote its basic programming. The interior of the Magi system turns out to be a massive cube
of tightly coiled, bulbous data pipes, looking eerily like biological organs.
Deep in an access hatch, they discover the scrawled developers' notes left
by Naoko and the original Magi team (one even says "Ikari, you idiot!"),
which will enable them to utilize the Magi's backdoor systems to launch their
counterattack. When the faceplate of the Magi system is removed, we see the
folds of what looks like a human brain, but that is really an electronic recording mechanism. The core of the Magi system, as Ritsuko explains to Misato
while she works, is a personality transplant operating system similar to the
one that powers the Evas. The three Magi are each semiautonomous AIs,
constantly battling for dominance, each one based on the three aspects of
her personality as a scientist, as a mother, and as a woman—a clever gender-
bend of the patriarchal trinity of the Father, the Son, and Holy Ghost.
Ritsuko eventually succeeds in launching the program, and with one second
to spare they defeat the angel. In the aftermath, Ritsuko finally reveals her
feelings about her mother to Misato: "As a scientist, I respected her. As a
woman, I hated her." Though she omits the precise reason for that hatred,
we do learn that Caspar was the AI implanted with the program of her as a
woman; it was this AI that resisted the angel to the bitter end. ("How totally
like my mother," concludes Ritsuko.)

It's no accident that many of the themes of "Evangelion 13" are borrowed
wholesale from *Neuromancer,* ranging from recorded personality constructs
(the Dixie Flatline) and AIs all the way to Naoko herself, who is clearly
modeled after *Neuromancer*'s Marie Tessier-Ashpool. Marie was the enig-
matic programmer who created the AIs, only to be murdered by her megalomaniac husband, Ashpool, in an internal power struggle within the Tessier-
Ashpool corporation; we will see later how Anno ingeniously rewrites
Gibson's straightforward allegory of global rentiers usurping the rule of
developmental engineers into the much more disturbing set of circumstances
surrounding Naoko's tragic death in "Evangelion 21."

The multinational subjectivities in "Evangelion 12" and the information society in "Evangelion 13" finally converge in "Evangelion 14," the narrative hinge and turning point of the series, wherein *Evangelion* finally breaks free from its neonational moorings and floats, ever so gently, into the multinational reaches of cyberspace. This is signaled by Gendou's secret report to Seele, recapitulating each of the battles to date, which creates an uproar when he baldly states that the invasion of the informatic angel never happened. The committee threatens and blusters, but since they cannot afford to do without Gendou as head of the project, they have little choice but to accept his version of events for the time being. At the same time, a subsequent activation test with Rei radically departs from any Eva sequence we have heretofore seen, suggesting that not only is Nerv growing restive under the thumb of Seele but that the Evas are beginning to develop a mind of their own, too. When Rei pilots Shinji's Eva, Unit 1, for the first time, feedback from the Eva suddenly filters into Rei's consciousness. The result is an astonishingly beautiful dream sequence, scored to a haunting sound track halfway between a vocal chorale and a string instrumental, which rewrites all the known rules of video in the course of two minutes. Due to the extreme complexity of the sequence, Rei's musings are collected in the left-hand column, while the images cycling through the dialogue are on the right:

VOICEOVER	IMAGE
Mountains. Heavy are the mountains. Things that change over time.	*Misty mountain ravine.*
Sky. Blue sky. Which your eyes can't see.	*Blue summer sky, framed by two clouds.*
Which your eyes can see.	*Green ricefields in the sun.*
Sun. That which is only one.	*Shot of valley, then blinding shot into sun.*
Water. That which is comforting. Commander Ikari?	*Lake illuminated by sunlight.*
Flowers. So many are alike.	*Field of radiant sunflowers, against a*
So many are useless.	*glowing, yellow sky.*
Sky. Red, red sky.	*Purple sky turns red.*
The color red. I don't like red.	*Vertical pan of Eva 1 in bright pink storage fluid.*
Flowing water.	*Glass beaker.*
Blood.	*Hand smeared with blood.*
The smell of blood. A woman who never	*Field of red neon stars rushes past us.*

bleeds. Human beings are created from the red earth. Human beings are created by man and woman.

City. A human creation.

Eva, a human creation as well.

What are humans? A creation of God. A human creation. The things I have are my life and soul.

'Entry Plug' [in English], the throne of a soul.

Who is that? That's me.

Tokyo-3 at night.
Close shot of Eva Unit 1's faceplate.
Enormous moon, rendered in photo-graphic detail, over surface of water.

Close-up of Rei's eye, which blinks.

Who is this me? What am I?

What am I? What am I.

[question reverberates]

Long pan across a long line of identical images of Rei, extending into a night sky filled with stars.

This physical body is me. This is the form which creates me.

Yet it feels as if this is not myself.

Strange. I feel as if my body is melting.

I can no longer see myself. My shape is fading. I feel the presence of someone who is not me.

Who is there, beyond me here?

Orange sky, Rei's inverted silhouette scrolls downwards.

Sun shines from behind silhouette.

Another close-up of her eye.

Shinji?

Blurred shot resolves into close-up of Shinji.

I know this person. She is Doctor Akagi.

Other people.

Blur-and-resolve on Misato.

Normal close-up of Ritsuko.

Close-up of Kensuke and Touji.

Classmates.

The pilot of Unit 2.

Commander Ikari?

Who are you?

Who are you?

Close-up of Hikari.

Close-up of Asuka.

Close-up of Ikari's glasses.

Shot of Rei herself.

Eva with faceplate removed, one of its green eyes staring at us.

Who are you?

Who are you?

Close-up of Eva's eye.

False-color image of a human eye.

"Who is No. 1?" was the refrain of *The Prisoner,* and "Who am I?" is the key line of Heiner Müller's magnificent 1973 play, *Germania Death in Berlin,* which chronicled the irresistible decay of the Eastern bloc nomenklatura into just another Eurobourgeoisie. Here, though, Rei asks the objective "What am I?" followed by the subtly plural "Who are you?"[14] The multiple images of Rei are certainly reminiscent of the clones and androids endemic to 1970s science fiction, while the entry plug is called the throne of the soul, the ironic negation of the soulless machinations of Seele. The images suggest a spectrum from classic East Asian mythology, from the creation of Monkey in *Journey to the West* by the union of Heaven and Earth (sky and mountains), to a series of photographic and painted surfaces (the sun, rippling reflections in the water, a field of flowers radiating Van Gogh-like intensity), and thence to tropes of bodily circulation (red sky, red earth, water, and blood), and finally spaces of corporeal production (the human creations of cities, Evas, and of course the children themselves).

Although Rei seems capable of interfacing with Eva 1 to some degree, Shinji is not compatible with Unit 0, and the attempt to interface between the two causes Eva 0 to run amok, forcing an immediate shutdown. We already know Asuka and Rei are diametric opposites, but it's interesting that Anno deftly avoids the logical third possibility here: What might happen when Asuka and Shinji switch Evas? That, of course, is precisely what will happen at the conclusion of *Evangelion,* but to understand why this is so, we first need to look more closely at the Evas and their relation to a certain micropolitics of the body.

> Song is the highest achievement of Lillim culture.
>
>> —Kaoru Nagisa speaking to Shinji Ikari
>> after humming the Chorale of Beethoven's
>> "Ode to Joy" in "Evangelion 24"

Our first clue that the bodies of the Evas are not quite what they seem is Rei's spine-tingling vision of Eva 1's head during her dream sequence in "Evangelion 14": a giant green eye peers from a bizarre skull that is not quite a series of flesh grafts, but not really a molded plastic or metal shell either. In the back of the skull are coils of circuitry and mechanical plates, while a tyrannosaurus-sized lower jaw studded with primeval teeth juts below. While the jaw and the circuitry are fairly explicit references to the 1960s Godzilla spectacular and the 1980s cyborg thriller, the giant green eye cites one of the most subversive video tropes of them all: the flashing green electronic eye of No. 1 in the finale of McGoohan's *The Prisoner*. But where McGoohan located No. 1's eye in the armature of the cold war symbol of the rocket booster, Anno situates the machinery of video in the post–cold war technology of the entry plug (several close shots of the entry plugs even make them look like rocket boosters, a clever homage to McGoohan). We have already been told that Eva 2 is the first mass-produced Evangelion. Given that Rei's entry plug is marked "Prototype" (in English), while Shinji's entry plug is marked "Test type" (also in English), this strongly suggests an informatic division of labor, wherein Eva 0 symbolizes the space of the R&D lab, Eva 1, the leading-edge information commodity, and Eva 2, the affordable or mass-produced spin-off of such. Each of these spaces will be subsequently set in motion toward a scandalously multinational content. Rei thus becomes a key figure of the Instrumentality project and the global technology of genetic engineering, Shinji will project the dissident micropolitics of Japan's postbubble generation, and Asuka herself will be centrally associated with the geopolitical space of the European Union.

Probably the single most impressive symbol of this multinational content is the external design of the Evas. Traditionally the mecha consisted of stacks of mechanical boxes and tubes that approximate a human figure, creating the profile of the robot samurai or cybernetic sumo wrestler. By contrast, the Evas look and move like quasi-living creatures, thanks to extensible necks, tapered waists (very similar to anime characters themselves), gracefully elongated arms and legs, and unusually thin shoulder guards. The effect is to streamline the baroque complexities of the battle mecha in much the same way that Tokyo-3's luminous buildings, airy vistas, and half-deserted streets negate the tenebrous, supercrowded cities typical of 1980s anime: Less turns out to be more. It's worth noting this didn't occur all at once. Rather, just as Anno greatly revised and expanded the script during the course of *Evangelion,* so too did Yamashita and Anno gradually refine their mecha designs. For example, at the beginning of the series, Eva 0's armor is a dull orange, in what was perhaps meant to be the logical inversion of Eva 1's purple armor. Later episodes, however, show Eva 0 is blue with a white trim, the polar opposite of Eva 2's bright red exterior and orange trim (red plus blue equals purple, nicely correlating with Shinji's intermediate position between the irreconcilable antipodes of Rei and Asuka). Anno injects an additional layer of complexity to this color scheme by means of the plug suits of the pilots: Rei's suit is white; Shinji's suit matches Eva 0's external armor, that is, blue body with white trim; and Asuka is dressed in a red suit with green trim (Eva 1's armor has an identical green trim). This does seem to tally with our previous identification of Rei as the avatar of a blank neonational interiority and Asuka as the locus of an outrageous multinational exteriority.

There are intriguing parallels between Anno's strategy and that other great document of multinational culture, Kieslowski's 1993–94 *Three Colors* trilogy, which set the geopolitical spaces of Poland (*White*), France (*Blue*), and Switzerland (*Red*) in motion toward the technological infrastructures of the Central European metropole. Arguably, Anno pushes this logic in the opposite direction, by setting the multinational technologies of the East Asian region in motion toward their corresponding geopolitics. One of the first great examples of this is encoded in the facial features of the Evas: Eva 0 has one central eye, glowing redly like James Cameron's Terminator, as well as an empty or nonfunctional eye socket in the top of its head. Eva 1 has two silhouetted eyes, crisscrossed with lines that give it a more than slightly demoniac look, and framed by a prominent lower jaw and a horn vaguely reminiscent of a unicorn. Eva 2 has four green eyes (two on each side of its face) and a doubled mouth, with jagged white bands in lieu of teeth. Once again, Anno subtly quotes one of the key symbols of *The Prisoner,* Rover's technologies of surveillance and control, via the decorative white circle on Eva 0's faceplate. In retrospect, Rei's white plug suit, eerily blank personality, and attachment to Gendou's reflective glasses all begin to make sense as tropes of recorded media. Eva 1, on the other hand, radiates a video Ur-subjectivity that can no longer be recontained in the neonational forms of the Godzilla and space mecha narratives, signaling the arrival of a genuinely East Asian identity politics. Eva 2's doubled eyes and doubled mouth suggest, in turn, some sort of multinational object or infrastructure somehow equidistant from the spaces of the electronic recording and East Asian micropolitics alike.

   This, however, is to anticipate themes better dealt with in the framework of *Evangelion*'s awe-inspiring finale. For now, we need to specify the precise coordinates of those recordings and identities. "Evangelion 15" gives us an important hint by negating the mediatic cliché of the family snapshot and the science fiction cliché of the mad scientist, in a scene when Shinji visits his mother's grave with his father:

> *Shots of graves stretching into the distance, marked by obelisks with rounded tops.*
> GENDOU: It's been three years since the last time we came here together.
> SHINJI: I ran away then, and haven't been back since. My mother is resting here.
>   . . . I don't really believe that. I don't even remember her face.
> GENDOU: People survive by forgetting their memories. But there are some things
>   you should never forget. Yui taught me about the irreplaceable things. I come
>   here to confirm that.
> SHINJI: You have no pictures of her?
> GENDOU: There are none. This grave is merely a decoration, too. There are no
>   remains.
> SHINJI: So the teacher was right. You threw them away.
> GENDOU: I keep everything in my heart. That is enough. *(Silence. Roar of a*
>   *hovercraft. Gendou turns to depart.)* It's time. I'm leaving now. *(Shinji glimpses*
>   *Rei in a window of the craft.)*
> SHINJI: *(Suddenly.)* Father! . . . Well . . . I'm glad . . . we could talk today.
> GENDOU: *(Pause.)* Indeed. *(Gendou and Rei roar off in craft, as Shinji watches*
>   *from ground.)*

   Shinji's precocious insight into his father's motivations is matched by Gendou's tacit acknowledgment to his son that the wounds of the past still afflict him. One senses, suddenly, how alike they are, and on some level they must realize it, too, because their village stand-off has now become a tentative truce. It's no accident that "Evangelion 15" (whose English title, appropriately, is "Those women longed for the touch of others' lips and thus invited their kisses") marks the moment that romances suddenly begin to blossom between the various characters—a serious one in the case of Misato and Kaji, who renew their old affair, and a teenage one between Shinji and Asuka. At one intriguing moment, we hear Shinji playing what looks like a cello, the first time we have seen him in the role of a cultural producer, greatly impressing Asuka. Later, she manages to goad him into kissing her, a scene played for great comic effect when Pen-pen (that unlikely Cupid) wanders into the background. When Kaji and Misato renew their affair, the background in question is a gentle piano version of *Fly Me to the Moon.* Anno gives us another hint when Hikari begins to angle for Touji, of all people. Hikari's older and younger sisters are named Kodama and Nozomi—a clever reference to the bullet train lines linking Tokyo to Osaka (the Kodama line is the slowest, Hikari is faster, and Nozomi is the ultra-high-speed line).

In fact, *Evangelion* practically overflows with references to trains, train stations, and maglevs or magnetic levitation carriages, ranging from the surface lines of Tokyo-3 to the catapult system that launches the Evas to the surface. All this will be highlighted during the battle with the next angel in "Evangelion 16," which is less a physical antagonist than a conceptual one. At first the creature seems to be a strange moire-patterned sphere floating above Tokyo-3. Suddenly, Eva 1 is swallowed up by a vast circular shadow on the ground, the angel's nanometer-thin "body," which is really a hyper-dimensional Dirac sea. (The moire-globe is merely its three-dimensional shadow, Ritsuko explains.) This is a reference to one of the oldest computer tropes of them all, the graphics programs of the very first home computers. In fact, *Neuromancer* makes use of moire patterns in a remarkable scene where Case is trying to break free from a neural trap set by one of the AIs.[1] Similar to Case, Shinji's real struggle is not with the angel but with the reflections and refractions of his own mind:

> *Fish-eye view of train window. Sound of train. Fish-eye view of Shinji seated in train, illuminated by setting sun.*
>
> SHINJI: *(White vertical tone band against black background.)* Who's that? *(The chimes that signal arriving or departing stations at Japanese train stations resound, then doppler-shift away.)* Who's there? *(Haunting score, the same as in Rei's dream sequence in "Evangelion 14.")*
>
> YOUNGER SHINJI: *(White horizontal tone band against black background.)* Shinji Ikari.
>
> SHINJI: *(Vertical band.)* That's me.
>
> YOUNGER SHINJI: *(Horizontal band.)* I'm you. Everyone has another self inside them. The self consists of two selves.
>
> SHINJI: *(Vertical band.)* Two?

YOUNGER SHINJI: *(Horizontal band.)* The self which exists for others, and the self which you see in yourself. The Shinji Ikari in your own mind. The Shinji Ikari in Misato Katsuragi. The Shinji Ikari in Asuka Souryu. The Shinji Ikari in Rei Ayanami. The Shinji Ikari in Gendou Ikari. All these Shinjis are different from one another, and yet every single one of them is the true Shinji Ikari. You are afraid of these other Shinjis.

SHINJI: *(Vertical band.)* I'm afraid of being hated.

YOUNGER SHINJI: *(Horizontal band.)* You're afraid of being hurt.

SHINJI: *(Fish-eye close-up.)* Who is bad? Father is. *(Horizontal band.)* The father who left me. *(Hospital close-up.)* I can't do anything.

(Flashbacks with close-ups of speakers.)

ASUKA: You're always saying you're worthless! You're just punishing yourself.

SHINJI: Damn it, I can't do anything.

MISATO: Or do you just think you can't do anything?

REI: *(Slapping him.)* You don't trust your father?

SHINJI: *(Half-turned.)* I hate my father. But now I'm not sure.

(Tone band forming a jagged line that moves down, then right, then down, at right angles.)

GENDOU: Good work, Shinji.

SHINJI: *(Image of father's shadow, Shinji at phone.)* Father called my name. *(Shinji remembering praise of "Evangelion 12.")* He praised me.

(Flashbacks end. Scene returns to inside of train as before.)

YOUNGER SHINJI: Will you spend your life regurgitating and redigesting those few pleasant memories?

SHINJI: Damn it, as long as I have these few words, then I can go on living.

YOUNGER SHINJI: Aren't you lying to yourself? *(Cut to medium shot inside train, younger Shinji seated to left silhouetted by sun, older Shinji to right.)*

SHINJI: But everyone does it, right? Lie to themselves in order to live.

YOUNGER SHINJI: You can't go on living any more, if you think you can't change yourself.

SHINJI: This world is too painful for me.

YOUNGER SHINJI: You can't swim, for example?

SHINJI: *(Protesting.)* Human beings aren't made to float.

YOUNGER SHINJI: You are deceiving yourself.

SHINJI: I don't care what you call it.

YOUNGER SHINJI: You've closed your eyes and ears to what you don't want to know.

(Second series of flashbacks.)

KENSUKE: *(When Touji punches Shinji.)* Sorry, but your little sister was— *(Brief shot of Eva 1's skull without faceplate.)*

MISATO: *(Silhouetted.)* It's not your job to take care of others!

(A simultaneous vertical and horizontal tone band, crossing in *upper left of screen, then close shot of Shinji to left of screen.*)

GENDOU: *(Direct shot of his face. Angrily.)* Go home! *(Very rapid burst of images: an angel, a hand-drawing suggesting tangled threads, Shinji wandering in forest, Rei in bandages, false-color image of city, Shinji's bulging eye. End of flashbacks, return to train as before.)*

SHINJI: No . . . I don't want to hear that.

YOUNGER SHINJI: So you're already running away again. No one can live by stringing together one pleasant experience after another like beads. And especially not me.

SHINJI: *(Voice rising along with background of railway chime, ending in a scream.)* I've found something that I can do to feel good. Something I want to do! What's wrong with that?!

This sequence simply pulverizes the mold of any animated feature ever made in the twentieth century. Anno ingeniously transforms the public space of the train into a kind of video theater, wherein Shinji's dialogue with what seems to be a future self runs counterpoint to a complex set of flashbacks, garnished with luminous halos and dreamlike reverb effects. Each of the four flashbacks in "Evangelion 16" mobilizes a slightly different set of images: The first cycles through faces, while the second quotes antagonistic or hostile images (Touji, his father, an angel, Rei in bandages) tied to the space of Tokyo-3. The third zeroes in on newspaper headlines dealing with the mysterious accident that apparently killed his mother, as well as a curious set of frames that enclose the receding silhouettes of his father and Misato, very much like receding windows or snapshots. The fourth displays a dazzling childhood memory of Shinji's mother. The tone bands, on the other hand, suggest a crude electronic recording technology, like a cross between early videotape and an analog oscilloscope.

"Evangelion 16" also contains the series' last explicit reference to the cold war, Ritsuko's desperate scheme to airdrop the planet's entire stock of N2 mines simultaneously to try to blast the angel apart. (We even see the jet trails of the bombers gathering in the sky.) This harebrained scheme is forestalled by Eva 1, which senses that Shinji's onboard life-support systems are failing and takes matters into its own hands. The shadowy surface of the angel shudders, roils, and then erupts, as the Eva rips apart the creature from the inside, throwing spectacular gouts of blood and angel flesh in all directions. This is the shocking birth of a whole new geopolitical subject, as unexpected as the fall of the Berlin Wall or the emergence of the European Union out of a supposedly washed-up collection of semiperipheral social democracies and derelict Eastern bloc economies. But where Kieslowski's *Red* followed Valentine's trajectory from fashion plate model to avatar of the Eurostate, mediated by the agency of the global news service, Eva 1's rebirth signals the arrival of a genuinely East Asian subjectivity, red in export-platform tooth and silicon claw, its eyes glowing with the demonic industrial energies of the Pacific Rim.

Later, while Nerv personnel rinse down Eva 1 in its docking station, Ritsuko nervously asks Gendou whether the Evas are really on humanity's side. Gendou remains noncommittal. The reason is that Seele has become extremely worried about the direction of the Eva project, to the point of applying pressure on various members of Nerv for inside information, for reasons that are not yet clear. It cannot be an accident, however, that Anno chooses this moment to highlight one of the fundamental economic shifts of the late twentieth century, namely, the irresistible decline of the U.S. industrial base, and the corresponding rise of Japan and the EU to twin workshops of the world. This is subtly relayed by the catastrophe of Second Branch of Nerv, located at a secret base in the U.S. state of Nevada, which is completely wiped out by a Dirac sea during a test experiment. This moment is strikingly reminiscent of the breathtaking post–cold war scenario of *Half Life* (1998), unquestionably the single greatest PC videogame of the 1990s, which portrays a similar catastrophe at a mythical Black Mesa Research Facility somewhere in Arizona. (The game designers even pay subtle homage to the mecha, in the form of Gordon Freeman's signature hazard suit.) But where *Half Life* concentrated on the post–cold war character trope of Gordon Freeman's information guerrilla, *Evangelion* shines a spotlight on the social geography of the post–cold war era, by revealing that the catastrophe occurred during the installation of a mysterious "S2 engine," designed and manufactured in Germany. This mobilizes the geopolitical reality of the supercharged East Asian and EU machine tools industries directly against the speculative ideology of the Wall Street rentiers.[2] This in turn may explain one of the stranger aspects of the angel of "Evangelion 16," the fact that it physically swallowed some of the skyscrapers of Tokyo-3, a suggestive gloss of the real-life deflation of Japan's overpriced real estate market after the post-1990 collapse of the bubble economy.

This triple denunciation of the Wall Street rentiers, the U.S. military-industrial complex, and Japan's bubble financiers is the flip side of an equally stinging critique of East Asia's indigenous industrialism. Probably the greatest single example of this is a "dummy plug" system in "Evangelion 17," a digitized personality construct that serves as a crude automatic pilot for the Evas. What seems at first to be a fail-safe or backup technology reveals a much more ominous dimension, however, when we glimpse Rei floating in an LCL capsule amid a vast assemblage of quasi-biological tubes and wiring, extending deep into the Magi system. Eerie mechanical breathing issues from the sound track. The room is dark, backlit only by two glowing lines of symbols in neon green: These are actually strings of the English letters G, C, A, and T, the symbols for the base pairs of nucleotides that form DNA. This is the logical antipode of a hair-raising scene late in "Evangelion 15," when Kaji showed Misato a secret chamber in the deepest recesses of Nerv's headquarters, containing a lifeless angel nailed to a cross and pierced by a curious lance. The lower half of the angel's body is missing. Its face, however, is identical with Seele's symbol (seven eyes set against an inverted pyramid). Strangest of all, what at first glance seem to be internal organs hanging from its midriff are not entrails at all but *human legs*—almost as if the creature were composed of multiple beings fused into a single organism. Kaji calls the creature "Adam," suggesting it is the mature form of the embryo he delivered in "Evangelion 8." Significantly, the angel seems to be bleeding some sort of fluid, hinting that it functions as a kind of biochemical factory.

This terrifying vision sets all our alarm bells ringing about Seele's real agenda. Unexpectedly, Anno takes this opportunity to emphasize that Gendou is *not* the stereotypical mad scientist or Bond-style techno-villain of yore. In fact, Fuyutski's conversation with Gendou on the subject of Tokyo-3 reveals an unexpected vein of humanity in Shinji's father:

> *Fuyutski and Gendou are seated to the left and right in a subway car, watching the urban panorama of Tokyo-3's surface buildings, glowing in the red sunset, passing by.*
>
> FUYUTSKI: The city, a paradise made by the hands of human beings.
>
> GENDOU: Driven from paradise, humanity fled into the world, on the edge of death. Created by the frailest of all beings, created from the sapience garnered from that weakness, we created our own paradise.
>
> FUYUTSKI: This paradise was created to protect ourselves from the fear of death, to satiate us with happiness. *(Close-up of buildings scrolling by.)* This city is truly a paradise, outfitted with weapons to protect us.
>
> GENDOU: A city for cowards, who flee from the world outside, filled with enemies. *(Window goes dark, as subway enters geofront.)*
>
> FUYUTSKI: Cowards live longer. That's one good thing.

Gendou has the crucial insight that if humanity is to have any future at all, it must be one *without* fortresses, weapons, and enemies, and that To-kyo-3 is merely a stepping-stone in that direction. This is part and parcel of a significant recasting of the gender roles in the story, such that Kaji begins to take on a fatherly role toward Shinji, at the same time that Shinji and Asuka draw closer together. (During one school recess, when Shinji forgets to make Asuka lunch and they go at each other with hammer and tongs, Touji's apt comment is, "The husband and wife are fighting!"). Still later, Kaji shows Shinji his secret garden in the geofront, where he grows watermelons, a cru-cial clue that the geofront is not merely an underground living space but also the symbolic global ecology of Tokyo-3's multinational city. In "Evangelion 18," Shinji asks Kaji about Shinji's father.

> KAJI: The fact is that people don't understand themselves, let alone each other. Understanding 100 percent of anything is impossible. That's why we spend so much time trying to understand our own motivations and those of others. That's what makes life so interesting.
>
> SHINJI: *(Innocently.)* Does that mean you can't understand Misato either?
>
> KAJI: *(A bit taken aback by Shinji's quick-wittedness.)* The kanji that we use for the word *she* literally means "a woman far away." No matter how hard we try, women will always be on the distant shore of a great gulf of misunderstanding. The current that separates men and women is broader and deeper than the ocean itself.
>
> SHINJI: I don't understand what it's like to be an adult.

One of the grimmest realities of adulthood, market competition against one's peers, will become an issue when the United States ships an experi-mental Eva to Japan for testing. Misato doesn't have the heart to tell Shinji about the pilot selected for the new Eva, who turns out to be Touji, of all people. The latter expresses no great enthusiasm for the task, agreeing to be a pilot only if Nerv's hospital takes special care of his injured sister. Alas, the Eva goes haywire during the activation test, when an angel somehow takes it over from within. Though the bestial roar, prominent backbone, and earthquakelike tread of this angel are unmistakable references to Godzilla, the creature's hide (dark with white flanges) is modeled after Touji's trade-mark dark sweatshirt with white stripes. The angel is also framed against a setting sun reminiscent of the Japanese flag, suggesting a multinational con-stellation of the global sports or sports apparel industries, the Japanese monster film, and the Pacific Rim export-platform economy. This is a dead ringer for John Woo's Hong Kong thrillers, and the conclusion will subtly quote Woo's trademark theme of warring brothers or battling doubles. Shinji realizes he is fighting another Eva, piloted by a child just like himself, and refuses to fight back. Faced with the imminent loss of Eva 1, Gendou orders Shinji's nerve connection terminated and the dummy plug system put into operation. It works only too well: Eva 1 springs to life, throttling the angel and gruesomely ripping it apart, splattering gore in all directions a la *The Killer*, while Shinji can only watch in horror.

Miraculously, Touji survives, albeit badly wounded, but Shinji is crushed by his father's psychological double cross. At the beginning of "Evangelion 19," he once again resigns from Nerv, bound and determined never to pilot an Eva again. But before he can depart from the train station, Tokyo-3 is assailed by the most powerful angel yet. This time around, though, Eva 1 displays a mind of its own, refusing to synchronize with Rei or with the dummy plug. On the battlefield, Asuka and Rei prove to be no match for the angel, which rips apart their Evas in short order and blasts its way into the heart of Nerv's headquarters. In the midst of the battle, Shinji runs into Kaji in the geofront, who reveals that if the angel comes into contact with the body of the deceased angel buried deep beneath the geofront, Third Impact will occur, destroying the entire human race. More important, he says the crucial words that Gendou cannot bring himself to say: "Shinji, the only thing I can do is stand here and water. But you, you have something that you can do. That only you can do. Nobody is forcing you. Think for yourself and make the decision by yourself." Only a freely chosen subjectivity, the Ur-form of solidarity, can answer for the catastrophe of unbridled market competition. Shinji returns to confront his father (framed by banks of video monitors, exactly as in "Evangelion 1") and for the first time in the series, lays claim to an explicit identity: "I . . . I . . . I am the pilot of Evangelion Unit 1! I am Shinji Ikari!"

As if to underline the double-edged micropolitical connotations of this moment, the angel crashes straight through Nerv's central viewscreen, before Eva 1 arrives in the nick of time to repulse the creature. The angel strikes back, severing the Eva's left arm, but Shinji gamely wrestles the angel to a nearby catapult, which launches them both to the surface of the geofront. Just when it looks as though Eva 1 might be getting the upper hand, though, its damaged battery pack suddenly runs out of power, and the angel closes in for the kill, pounding on a strange, luminous red core in Eva 1's belly with its metallic arms. Trapped in the entry plug, Shinji desperately hits against the controls, imploring the Eva to move, his voice rising to a scream in a tremendous piece of voice acting by Megumi Ogata. At the last possible moment, a heartbeat pulses. Roaring like some preternatural beast, the Eva awakens at last. With a single blow, it shreds the angel's arms and uses the mangled tissue as a graft to regenerate its left arm (a double-jointed reference to Luke Skywalker's cybernetic arm in the *Star Wars* trilogy, as well as to the machining and cutting implements of the global machine tools industry), before smashing its opponent senseless. Science fiction posthistory suddenly converges with primeval prehistory, as the Eva begins to *feed* on the still twitching corpse, ingesting the angel's power core (what we later learn is the S2 engine) with a suddenly bared set of white teeth. Framed against the thick forests on the floor of the geofront, the Eva suddenly stands up, its faceplate a dead ringer for Darth Vader's ominous mask, its swelling muscles bursting its armor. Even more shocking is Ritsuko's awed revelation to the others that this armor is not what it appears to be: "Those are restraints that allow us to control the Eva's power. But now the Eva is removing the web that binds it to our will." Eva 1, the colossal incarnation of the East Asian metropole—Asiazilla in the flesh—defeats the Angel of Export-Platform Industrialization and arrives on the stage of world history at last.

While Nerv hastily reconstructs its headquarters, Nerv's science team discovers the terrible blood price of this transformation: Shinji has been physically absorbed into the Eva. All that remains is his empty plug suit, floating in the entry plug, forcing Ritsuko and the others to scramble over the next few weeks to try to find Shinji's wave pattern within the Eva and return it to physical form. "Evangelion 20" features two extraordinary shots of Eva 1 swathed in bloodied white bandages, grinning like some gigantic mummy that has finally reclaimed its jeweled treasure (the iridescent red orb of the S2 engine, glistening from its belly). The first shot frames Misato and Makoto against the background of a frontal shot of the Eva's bandaged face, its vast right eye staring sightlessly at us, sporting two rows of realistic white teeth. The second silhouettes Ritsuko, Maya and Misato against a side shot of Eva 1, its green eye still staring straight at us, the scene ingeniously framed by three gleaming spotlights in the upper right corner. Clearly, the Eva is now watching *us*.

Somewhere within the Eva, Shinji experiences four dream sequences during his struggle to free himself, each of which differs in subtle but significant ways from the four flashbacks of "Evangelion 16." The shot pacing of the first sequence, for example, is dramatically accelerated, and images cycle in against a luminous white background, creating a vibrant visual rhythm that matches the subtle techno loop of the sound track. At the same time, the national tropes of the national train system and newspaper headlines are replaced by the global ones of the seashore and by written kanji characters in various fonts, captioned on each image (service shots, if you will, of the angels themselves):

SHINJI: *(His empty bodysuit floats in the LCL-filled interior.)* What's that? Where am I? The entry plug of Unit 1? There's nobody here. Not even myself. *(Several rapid shots of waves lapping at a seashore, only with bizarre, false-color images suggesting outer space scenes where one would expect to see sand.)* What is this? What is this? What is this? *(Waves accede to rapid close-ups of everyone in the series, their faces cycling in and out, while a faint techno beat loops from the sound track.)* I don't understand. These people. Yes, they're people I know. People who know me. I understand now. This is my world. *(Scene shifts to an underwater perspective.)* What's this? I don't know this, but it's part of my world. An image from outside. A hostile image? That's right. An enemy. *(Close-ups of angels cycle just as quickly as the faces of the characters did, interspersed with white-and-black shots of various kanji fonts of the word for "enemy.")* Enemy, enemy, enemy, enemy. . . . Our enemies are something called angels, they have the names of the angels, too. They are the targets of Nerv and the Evas. *(Close-up of Shinji as a young boy.)* This is our revenge for the death of Misato's father. Why do I fight? Despite all the pain and suffering?

ASUKA: What are you? Stupid? An unknown enemy is attacking us. Of course we have to fight them!

SHINJI: Am I odd to try to find a reason to fight? Am I not supposed to think about it? *(Scene shifts to quick zoom shots of angels, which cycle as rapidly as before. Shot of Tokyo-3 at sunset.)* Enemy. Enemy. Enemy. . . . All are my enemies! Us . . . that which threatens us is the enemy. *(Cut to Eva launching from its service tunnel.)* Of course, how can I be faulted for protecting my own life and those of others? *(Scenes of angels now interspersed with shots of Gendou Ikari.)* Enemy . . . enemy. . . . *(Sound of metal door slamming shut, shot of Shinji facing his father.)* Damn it, damn it, damn it. . . . You injured Touji and killed Mother! Father! *(He screams, shot of Eva 1 lunging with progressive knife. Silence. Sudden flashback to conversation with Rei on escalator.)*

REI: Why don't you like your father?

SHINJI: No one could get along with a father like that!

REI: Don't you understand your father?

SHINJI: Of course not. I've hardly ever seen him.

REI: And that's why you don't like him?

SHINJI: Yes. Father doesn't need me, he abandoned me.

REI: And am I his substitute?

SHINJI: *(In bodysuit, framed by silhouette of father on the left.)* Exactly. That's what it must be! He left me because of Rei!

(Silhouette of father fades to close-up shot of Shinji's face, while his previous image is replaced by Rei, shown here as a young child.)

REI: As if you didn't run away all by yourself.

Rei is evidently taking on the role of Shinji's internalized conscience, the arbiter of a complex set of Oedipal conflicts and psychological ambivalences. The seashore will return late in the second dream sequence, which briefly cites the hallucinogenic train and tone band themes of "Evangelion 16," before quoting a genre quite specific to the manga tradition, *hentai* (the word means "perverted," but refers to explicitly erotic manga as well as unauthorized, underground versions of official anime and manga characters):

> *Shot of seashore. This time we see the sand. All subsequent shots shine with dreamy light.*
>
> MISATO: *(Over multiple tape loops of her naked, approaching Shinji as if leaning over him, each loop repeating after each sentence.)* I'm nice to you. Tell me, Shinji, do you want to become one with me? To be of one body and mind? It could be so nice. Ask me any time. I'm ready.
>
> ASUKA: *(Over similar tape loops.)* Hey, Shinji, you blockhead! Don't you want to become one with me? To become of one mind and body? It could be very, very nice. You ought to appreciate your good fortune. Come on!
>
> REI: *(Over similar tape loops.)* Ikari . . . do you want to become one with me? To become of one mind and body? It could be very, very nice. Ikari . . .
>
> MISATO: *(Single loop.)* Do you want to become one with me?
>
> ASUKA: *(Single loop.)* To become of one mind and body?
>
> REI: *(Single loop.)* It could be so pleasant. *(They merge into a single blurred image.)*
>
> MISATO/ASUKA/REI: Relax and release your soul. *(Fade to black, single drop of water falls in darkness.)*

It should be emphasized that Misato, Asuka, and Rei are not really informatic Norns or weavers of temporal destiny, so much as three distinct corporealities that coexist within a single temporality. Misato's role is evidently that of the motherly provider, while Rei addresses Shinji by his last name, Ikari, a formal reference to the realm of family ties or bonds. Only Asuka is genuinely seductive, airily tossing her hair, flashing her eyes, and urging him to actually *do* something instead of bemoaning his fate.

The third dream sequence consists mostly of glowing, multicolored kanji of the names of the characters cycling in the darkness, serenaded by the distorted voices of the characters calling out "Shinji," suggesting a synthesis of the angel captions and dream faces into a series of neon scripts. During the fourth and last dream sequence, the key scene is a subtle rewriting of Shinji's farewell to Misato at the train station, just before the angel's attack. In his dream, Misato tells him that only he can decide his future. He finally grasps what Misato really said: that she would always care about him, regardless of whether he was a pilot or not. The next shot is a simple pencil sketch of a child at its mother's breast, accompanied by the imaginary voices of Gendou and Yui, Shinji's mother. Gendou is fretting about raising a child in the aftermath of the Second Impact, but Yui says simply, "Anywhere can be heaven if you try to live" (possibly a reference to Kurosawa's classic 1956 *Ikiru*, which means "to live"). They decide to name the child either Shinji or Rei, depending on its gender. This suggests, in turn, that Rei incarnates the space of an interiorized micropolitics, in the same way that Asuka represents the realm of an externalized geopolitics.[3] This is followed by a brief quotation of the opening tag, contrasting bluish watery reflections and a blue star field against red reflections and a red star field, until the light pulse of the opening tag orchestrates the utopian merger of the two. Just as the Eva was reborn from the nonspace of the angel, so too is Shinji reborn from the Eva's S2 engine: Kieslowski's children of the euro are matched by the children of Asiazilla.

Seele is now thoroughly frightened, confirming what we already suspected, that the Eva's unexpected absorption of the S2 engine has given it godlike powers of autonomy. During "Evangelion 21" they go so far as to kidnap and interrogate Fuyutski, trying to determine whether Gendou will try to subvert their plan. Instead of the committee members we saw before, Seele now appears as a circle of faceless black obelisks, their voices electronically obscured, like a cross between *2001* and Stonehenge. Sitting in the semidarkness, memories of Nerv's earliest days flood over Fuyutski, as he recalls the moment when he ran into Yui Ikari, a brilliant young biologist, and Yui's future husband, Gendou Nokubungi (he would later take his wife's last name). Yui's tragedy is recounted, ironically enough, from the perspective of Ritsuko's mother, Naoko Akagi, via a letter she is writing to her daughter. One day Yui brought her son Shinji, at that time a little boy of four or five, to watch an experiment at the UN artificial evolution laboratory, when catastrophe struck. In Naoko's words: "A freak accident wiped her from this existence, just as I had hoped it would. What a disgusting woman I am. Ritsuko, after that day, Commander Ikari completely changed."

Now, at last, we can begin to understand the dream image of Shinji's younger yet somehow older self in "Evangelion 16," as well as Ritsuko's antagonism toward her mother (she accidentally glimpses Naoko embracing Gendou). What is not quite clear is why Fuyutski accepted Gendou's Mephistophelean offer to join the Evangelion project, though we are given the significant clue that the geofront is a natural creation, not a human one. This is not the last tragedy associated with the birth of Nerv, however. The project's original name was Gehirn (the German word for "brain") and changed to Nerv following a dreadful incident in 2010 involving Naoko and Rei. Naoko is already deeply suspicious of Rei, due to the latter's eerie resemblance to Yui, her romantic rival. Late one night, just as she is preparing to leave the Magi installation, Naoko spots Rei watching her from a corner. But not only does Rei coldly rebuff her friendly overtures; she repeats, dronelike, that Naoko is an "old hag." Furious, Naoko tells her Gendou will hear about her behavior, whereupon Rei reveals that she is simply repeating what she heard Gendou constantly saying about her ("The old hag is stubborn, we don't need the old hag anymore"). In a fit of rage and jealousy, she strangles Rei, crying out, "You little bitch! Don't you know you're replaceable, too, Rei? Replaceable just like me." Suddenly realizing what she has done, she leaps from the balcony, killing herself.

If Rei was strangled in 2010, then the Rei of 2015 is clearly some sort of copy or clone, hinting that the secret of Instrumentality is some sort of applied genetic engineering. It's no accident that each of Nerv's technological advances is paid for by some form of corporeal sacrifice: Asuka's mother in the case of Eva 2; Yui in the case of Eva 1; and Naoko and the first Rei in the case of the Magi system and Eva 0. Alas, the Evangelion project will claim one more victim in this episode, when Kaji arrives and frees Fuyutsuki without Seele's authorization, in exchange for the secret of the Evangelion project. Shortly afterwards, Kaji is indeed gunned down by an unknown assailant (mostly likely, one of Seele's goons). This leads to one of the most heartbreaking scenes of the entire series, which deftly employs the humble answering machine in much the same way that Kieslowski employed the telephone: Misato hesitantly presses the play button and listens, eyes quivering, to Kaji's final message. "If I ever see you again, I'll say the words that I couldn't say eight years ago," concludes Kaji, in a sparkling piece of voice acting by Yamadera Koichi. In the background, we see a pencil sketch of Kaji slowly fade away. Sobbing, Misato falls to her knees, her tears spilling on the table, as slow, mournful piano music traces out the theme from *Fly Me to the Moon*. In his room, Shinji cradles his head in his arms, trying not to listen.

It would be easy to assume, given the scope of these devastating revelations, that *Evangelion* could not possibly surprise us anymore, and that the series will now wind down via the standard climactic battle with a super powerful opponent, followed by a denouement that tidies up the remaining plot strands. But Anno not only refuses to slow down but he *accelerates* the series toward its revolutionary conclusion. Whereas the previous angels still exhibited latent associations with cold war technologies or geopolitical events, the last three angels are the purest ciphers of the information age imaginable. "Evangelion 22," for instance, rewrites the space of the hospital and the childhood toy into Asuka's black-and-white memories of her mother, hospitalized after being driven insane by a contact experiment. A pair of doctors, a man and a woman, carry on a lugubrious conversation, the high point of which is the woman saying bitterly, "Human beings create dolls in their own image. If God exists, it's possible that we're all just dolls to Him." The trope of the doll will be cited incessantly in "Evangelion 22," ranging from Ritsuko's black-and-white figurines of cats to Asuka's scolding of Eva 2 ("You're my doll, so move like I tell you to and don't argue!") all the way to Asuka's fight in the elevator with Rei. This latter is a static shot that lasts an impressive fifty seconds, with Rei in the foreground left and Asuka to the right. When the tension has reached the boiling point, Rei says matter-of-factly, "If you don't open your mind [heart, soul] to her, your Eva won't move." Naturally Asuka explodes, and as she backs out of the elevator, she castigates Rei as a windup doll. ("I am not a doll," states Rei quietly, causing Asuka to slap her.)

The real issue is that Asuka's sync ratios are dropping disastrously, which means she is losing her ability to pilot Eva 2. Given her own doll-like appearance and overcompensating vanity, it's difficult not to conclude that she is beginning to subconsciously rebel against her own internalized sexism, that is, the noxious gender ideology of the mecha. This is confirmed when a new angel arrives from outer space, a luminous winglike entity that overwhelms Asuka with some sort of mind-ray, gorgeously choreographed to the music of Handel's *Messiah*. One of the many deliberate ironies of this episode is Anno's insistence that beautiful images can be pure poison, while the ugliest of images can be a healing salve. Although Tokyo-3 is shadowed in pouring rain, the angel shines like a blistering sun, flooding the screen with light; similarly, the glorious sound track signals a terrible violence, in the mold of Kubrick's *A Clockwork Orange*. In Eva 2, Asuka screams over and over again, as heavily distorted kanji and stark white German words crash into her mind (the words are shown too quickly to be read at normal viewing speed, and consist of the Japanese and German words for "no," "strangled," "hatred," "misery," "shame," and "death"). Later, during an extended dream sequence, these word-images will be complemented by successive pans through stylized doors in the darkness, which open up to reveal hallucinogenic, false-color backgrounds; the sound track is a dialogue of Asuka battling the dream memory of her mother: "I'm not Mama's doll! I'll think for myself, and I'll live for myself!" Whereas Shinji's dream sequence focused on his struggle to redefine himself in dialogue with a future self, Asuka seems to be wrestling with the fallout of her nightmarish past. To save Asuka, Gendou orders Rei to descend into Central Dogma and get the Lance of Longinus. Deep underground, Rei wrests the lance from the body of the crucified angel Misato discovered in "Evangelion 15," a weirdly flexible double-stranded javelin, wrapped like a coil of DNA. This is the canny rewriting of the graphical map that displays the sync ratios of the Eva pilots to Nerv's staffers, which looks very much like a two-dimensional outline of DNA. In effect, the subjectivity of the Eva pilots accedes to a new kind of object. Back on the surface, Rei grits her teeth, exhibiting the first moment of genuine rage we have ever seen. As the *Messiah* counts down to its finale, Eva 0 leaps forward, hurling the Lance into the heavens and smiting the angel from the sky.

This epochal moment is much, much more than just the savage denunciation of the unutterably vile sexism permeating so many anime series. According to medieval mythology, Longinus was the Roman centurion who wounded Christ while on the cross; the Lance, also known as the Spear of Destiny, was supposedly one of the sacred treasures of the Knights Templar. But it is the location of the Lance—Central Dogma—that gives the game away here. "Central Dogma" is not a theological term but a biological one; it is the cardinal theorem of genetics, the notion that DNA switches on RNA (a process called transcription) and that RNA in turn switches on proteins (a process called translation). In its original version, Central Dogma was very much a monopoly-capitalist model of human biology (CEOs give orders to managers who give orders to line workers), but a vast amount of subsequent scientific research has shown that proteins reciprocally influence RNA and powerfully influence which DNA codes are activated and which are not.

Given that the Evas incarnate the social history of the East Asian region, this suggests that the angels embody its logical counterpart, natural history. The Lance of Longinus, anointed not in the blood of Christ but in the blood of the crucified angel (whose real identity will not be revealed until "Evangelion 24"), is therefore the Ur-symbol of an abstraction that controls or dominates nature: not technology per se, but the hegemonic commodity form of multinational capitalism, or what we call *information*. Rei's act, in other words, marks the moment when micropolitics storms the Gates of Informatic Creation, and a revolutionary sisterhood smashes the patriarchal consumerism broadcast from the orbiting satellites of late capitalism. This is confirmed by a subsequent shot of the Lance drifting in outer space, its vertical form silhouetted against the horizontal curvature of the Earth: Information wants to be free, but will settle for a lunar orbit.

This is also Seele's ultimate nightmare scenario, the breaking of their monopoly over the Lance, which was probably not primarily designed to destroy angels but was in all likelihood their trump card against the Evas. Before Seele can move to dismiss Gendou or otherwise retake control of Nerv, however, the next angel arrives in "Evangelion 23." Appropriately enough, this creature is a gigantic humming double helix of neon DNA, cycling continuously in midair. Uncoiling, the whiplike end of the angel lashes out with the speed of a bullet train, puncturing Rei's AT field and driving into Eva 0's flesh. Even worse, the angel begins to bioassimilate Rei, transmitting cords of angel flesh directly through her body. Alas, Asuka is still shell-shocked from the last battle and cannot pilot her Eva effectively, while the sheer speed of the angel seems to be too much even for Shinji. What saves them is Rei's quick-wittedness: During the process of bioassimilation, the angel makes mental contact with her. In a curious dream sequence, Rei sees her own mirror image (the angel) knee-deep in the same orange liquid we saw splashing at the base of the crucified angel, and she seizes this chance to communicate her own subjectivity to the creature invading her. The more the angel becomes exactly like Rei, the more it absorbs her pain, loneliness, and sorrow, until eventually it acts exactly as she would: It retreats within itself, temporarily releasing her consciousness. Rei awakens to find she is shedding the first tears she can ever remember. She quickly seizes the opportunity to initiate the self-destruct sequence of Eva 0 and destroy the angel trapped inside her, at the price of leveling half of Tokyo-3 in the process. (The whole scene recalls the tragic moment in *Moby Dick*, when Ahab's infinitely precious tear falls into the sea.)[4] In the hellish thermal pulse of the explosion, we glimpse Unit 0's torn midriff, ironically echoing the body of the crucified angel. The disasters of natural history are replicated by the catastrophes of social history.

How, then, could Rei have possibly survived the explosion? Misato discovers why when she employs Kaji's last gift, a chip containing the passcode to the ground floor of Central Dogma. Together with Shinji, she commandeers Ritsuko at gunpoint, determined to learn the truth. (For reasons of her own, Ritsuko agrees to take them to Central Dogma.) In one scintillating distance shot, the elevator slides downwards through a chassis consisting of a glowing, DNA-like double coil, set against a background of several such coils tilted diagonally. Ritsuko shows them the spartan room where Rei was raised, and then unveils the remains of early Eva test models, their skeletal bodies piled up in a vast antechamber like medieval hecatombs. Finally, at the very core of Central Dogma, Rei's secret is revealed:

MISATO: Is this the source of the dummy plug?

RITSUKO: Let me show you the truth. *(Presses button, aquariumlike tanks fill with light; clones of Rei float inside. Sorrowful string music fills the sound track.)*

SHINJI: *(Wide-eyed.)* Rei Ayanami?

MISATO: *(Horrified.)* Impossible! Eva's dummy plug is . . .

RITSUKO: Right, this is the production factory for the core of the dummy plug.

MISATO: This is?

RITSUKO: These are all dummies. Nothing more than replacement parts for Rei. Humans found a god and tried to obtain it. As a result, humanity was punished. That was fifteen years ago. The god that they found vanished. However, humanity tried to create God anew and that's how Adam was born. From Adam, human beings created what resembles God, Itself. That is Eva.

SHINJI: So . . . they're human?

RITSUKO: Yes, they're human. We put supposedly mindless souls in Eva. All the souls were salvaged souls. Rei is the only container that can hold the souls. The souls are born only in Rei. The Room of Guaf is empty. These are merely empty containers. They have no souls. *(Close-up on Ritsuko.)* So I want to destroy them, because I hate them. *(Presses self-destruct and the clones dissolve into fluid, crying out feebly. Tanks turn purple, as if filling with blood.)*

MISATO: *(Gun raised.)* Do you know what the hell you're doing?

RITSUKO: Yes, I do. I'm destroying them. They're not human beings. They're things with human form. But I lost to these dolls! I couldn't win him! *(More and more emotional.)* I could stand any humiliation for him. I didn't care how wretched I became! But . . . but he had chosen . . . he chose. I knew this, but . . . *(Breaks down completely.)* I'm such an idiot. Both mother and daughter are idiots. Shoot me if you want to. I'd rather die.

MISATO: *(Lowers gun.)* That won't release you from your agony. *(Ritsuko collapses to floor, sobbing. Misato thinks to herself.)* The tragedy of the Eva Project is its people. *(Narrows her eyes.)* But I'm one of them, too.

The Room of Guaf is the mythical chamber where the souls of the unborn await their earthly bodies. Rei is indeed replaceable, just as Naoko said, but the logical consequence of the extended reproduction of bodies in late capitalism is that everyone becomes as exchangeable as Rei, mere accessories of blind, uncontrolled accumulation. The terrible truth shining from the wreckage of German porcelain dolls, American fashion mannequins, and Japanese robots piling up before us like the Storm of Progress in Walter Benjamin's parable of the Angel of History is that *everyone* is victimized by late capitalism.[5]

The often overlooked corollary of this grim state of affairs is that everyone is a potential source of resistance to the total system, regardless of whether they are aware of this potential or not. "Evangelion 22" thus transcends the noxious consumerism of the global mass media by means of the solidarities of a global feminism, while "Evangelion 23" turns the android and cyborg narratives of the 1980s against themselves, uncovering the grisly realities of the informatic factory. "Evangelion 24" will push both insights still further, by setting Asiazilla (the mutated Eva 1) in motion toward its leading geopolitical counterplayers, Wall Street neoliberalism and Euroindustrialism. It's no accident that the English title of "Evangelion 24" is "The Beginning and the End or, Knockin' on Heaven's Door," in homage to a memorable Bob Dylan song, while the Japanese title, "saigo no shisha" (literally, "the final messenger"), deliberately puns the word *shisha,* which can mean a sacrifice or casualty as well as a messenger or courier. The sacrifice in question is that of transience or temporality, something underlined by Asuka's dream sequence at the beginning of the episode, which reveals what lay behind the endless doors we glimpsed in "Evangelion 22": the corpse of her mother, hanging from the ceiling. Sunk into a suicidal depression, unable to pilot her Eva anymore, Asuka languishes in Hikari's abandoned apartment in the ruins of Tokyo-3, while Shinji meditates gloomily next to the artificial lake created by the implosion of Eva 0.

At this point, Shinji hears someone humming the Chorale from Beethoven's Ninth Symphony (the "Ode to Joy"). A young boy calling himself Kaoru Nagisa (another pun—his name means "Kaoru of the Seashore") introduces himself as the fifth Eva pilot to Shinji, and delivers the immortal line, "Song is the highest achievement of Lillim culture, don't you think?" Performances of the so-called Dakei or "Big Nine," as the Ninth Symphony is called, are a staple of New Year's celebrations in Japan, but the reference to the Lillim is Anno's own idiosyncratic rewriting of the medieval myth of Lilith (the most common version is that Lilith was Adam's ex-wife who refused to put up with Adam's iron-fisted rule and ran off to mother broods of demons). The Lillim are, literally, the nonhuman children of Lilith, but Kaoru is using the term to describe the human race in general, hinting that he himself is not quite human. The effect is heightened when we learn that Kaoru has truly unearthly powers of synchronization vis-à-vis the Evas, making him the most proficient pilot of them all. Unlike the angels, however, Kaoru does not exhibit any overt signs of destructiveness, but seems genuinely compassionate toward others. After a long day of activation tests, Kaoru runs into Shinji outside the test chamber, and they have the following conversation in the shower:

Giant viewscreen overhead cycles between a postcard snapshot of Mt. Fuji and
Nerv's logo. Steam fills the shower.

KAORU: You avoid any sort of direct contact with people. Are you afraid of
reaching out to others? So long as you ignore others, you won't be betrayed or
hurt. Yet you are never free of the feeling of loneliness. A person cannot remove
sorrow forever. Everyone is alone. But human beings can forget, that is why
they can live. *(Shower stops.)*

SHINJI: Uh . . . it's time.

KAORU: Already?

SHINJI: We have to go to bed.

KAORU: *(Innocently.)* With you?

SHINJI: *(Embarrassed.)* No . . . uh . . . they must've given you your own bed.

KAORU: *(Innocent.)* Hmm . . . The hearts of human beings are full of pain. A heart
can be wounded so easily. This makes life difficult. And your heart especially is
as fragile as glass.

SHINJI: Mine?

KAORU: You deserve the empathy of others.

SHINJI: Empathy?

KAORU: I mean, I like you.

The subtle apposition between the premier national pictorial symbol of
Japan (Mt. Fuji) and Nerv's multinational logo is matched by an equivalent
oscillation of the registers of natural history and social history, relayed subtly by Kaoru's alternating usage of the otherwise interchangeable terms
Lillim and *human beings.* To make matters even more interesting, the term
like is, if anything, even more ambiguous than its English counterpart, and
could indicate almost any degree of affection one might name. In fact, Anno
is quoting one of the most popular subgenres of manga culture, namely, explicitly gay or gender-bending comics known as *yaoi,* which run the gamut
from outright pornography to extremely stylized and aestheticized same-sex
romances.[6] The utopian homoeroticism invoked here, however, is the gentle
corrective on the compulsory heteroeroticism of Shinji's warming relationship with Asuka, and it's worth pointing out that Asuka's physical absence
from "Evangelion 24" actually *increases* her structural importance to the
story. The reason is that Seele is now plotting the total destruction of To-
kyo-3, in order to ensure the fulfillment of its apocalyptic scenario. We learn
that Kaoru is indeed the very last angel, whose mission is to neutralize Eva
1, eliminate Gendou and forestall Nerv's impending rebellion against Seele.
Instead of mutating into some tentacled monster, however, Kaoru merely
steps into the air, levitating in place and synchronizing with Eva 2 from out-

side of the entry plug by sheer mental effort: "Come, Adam's alter ego and Lilith's minion!" As the full-scale orchestral version of the "Ode to Joy" erupts from the sound track, Kaoru uses Eva 2 as a battering ram to smash his way into the heart of the geofront, forcing Nerv to launch Eva 1 in a desperate bid to intercept him.

Anno's choice of music is truly an aesthetic masterstroke, comparable in its brilliance perhaps only to Beethoven's invention of the melodic theme of the "Ode" in the first place. The libretto is a poem by Schiller that celebrated the national revolutions of America and France with the striking phrase, "Alle Menschen werden Brüder / Wo dein sanfter Flügel weilt" ("All people become brothers/ Underneath your gentle wing"). Anno takes care to counterpoint every single motif of Schiller's text with an antithetical content: divine joy with human sorrow, the daughters of Heaven with the angels of Seele, the highest reaches of Heaven with the deepest recesses of the geofront, and the joyous sparks of the gods ("Götterfunken") with the earth-shattering clash of the Evas. The reason is that the "Ode to Joy" is not merely the musical pinnacle of Beethoven's art; it is also—since 1995—the official anthem of the European Union! With a thunderbolt of insight that makes the brain reel, the true significance of Asuka's German heritage, the S2 engine, the Third Branch of Nerv in Germany, and Kaoru's own comment on the sublimity of song flashes into view. The irrepressible beauty of song is that it is the most transient and fleeting of human creations. Eva 2 is not merely a multinational form. It has a temporal content as well, and what we are witnessing is not the foundation of the nation-state but the *beginning of its end.* The symbolic avatars of two mighty transnational armatures materialize before our astonished eyes: Eva 2, also known as Euroeva, temporarily lacks a guiding will to survive and has been hijacked by Kaoru, while Eva 1, also known as Asiazilla, has Shinji's desperate will to survive but not the sheer muscle to defeat Eva 2. The stakes of this battle, however, are not merely the survival of Tokyo-3, Japan, or even East Asia, but the unimaginable destiny of humankind:

> KAORU: *(Thoughtfully, while hovering out of reach of Eva 1.)* Evas, made from Adam, creatures abhorrent to humankind. And yet the Lillim try to survive by employing them. I do not understand why.
>
> SHINJI: *(Fighting in Eva 1 against Eva 2.)* Kaoru, stop! I don't understand!
>
> KAORU: Eva is of the same tissue as I. For I am created of Adam as well. If the unit has no soul, then I can unite with it. And now that the soul of this unit is in hiding . . . *(Shinji's mecha lunges at Kaoru with the progressive knife, but a force field blocks him.)*

SHINJI: *(Stunned.)* An AT field!!

KAORU: Yes, that's what you Lillim call it. That holy realm in which no one else
may intrude. The Light of the Soul. You Lillim should know . . . you should
know about the AT field, the Armor of the Soul, which everyone has.

SHINJI: *(Desperate.)* I don't understand!! Kaoru!!! *(Evas 1 and 2 continue to
descend toward Terminal Dogma, locked into ferocious battle.)*

Everyone has an AT field and is capable of resisting the assault of the
angels and potentially piloting the Evas, an amazing insight into the plebeian nature of global micropolitics. We already know the entry plug of the Evas
is the throne of the soul, but if everyone has an AT field (that is, engages in
global micropolitics, whether conscious of the fact or not), then the Evas
themselves must incarnate the geopolitical space of that micropolitics. Thus
where Asiazilla symbolized the bursting of the symbolic fetters binding the
East Asian developmental states to the dominion of the American empire,
Euroeva's subalternity is clearly an allegory of the Maastricht monetarism
that hijacked the otherwise commendable project of European unification
in the early 1990s for its own destructive ends.[7] If this is so, then Kaoru of
the Seashore can be nothing other than a cipher of neoliberalism, the Angel
of Global Speculation.

Back at headquarters, Misato and Makoto are grimly preparing to self-
destruct the entire geofront in order to prevent Kaoru from entering Terminal Dogma and setting off Third Impact (one clever self-referential scene
shows a map of the complex behind the silhouettes of Makoto and Misato,
displaying the battling Evas passing level number 24—the exact number of
the episode). Suddenly, Kaoru generates the most powerful AT field ever
measured, as the battling Evas crash spectacularly through Terminal
Dogma's roof, falling into an icy field reminiscent of the poisoned ruins of
Antarctica. "It is human fate," thinks Kaoru to himself. "The hope of humanity is hung with the thread of sorrow." Passing easily through the final safety
lock, he approaches his final destination: the crucified angel of "Evangelion
15." But just when all seems lost, another AT field shows up out of nowhere,
blocking and then recontaining Kaoru's field. The savior in question turns
out to be Rei Ayanami:

KAORU: *(Approaches the crucified angel.)* Adam, our mother creator. One who is
born from Adam must return to Adam. Although it could destroy all humanity?
No! This is Lilith. I see now. I understand the Lillim! *(Eva 1 smashes Eva 2 to
the ground, enters Terminal Dogma, and grabs Kaoru with its mighty glove.
"Ode to Joy" continues in background.)*

KAORU: Thank you, Shinji. *(Shot of Eva 2, sprawled on ground.)* I wanted to give you Unit 2. Otherwise, it would've lived on with her.

SHINJI: Kaoru, why?

KAORU: It was my destiny to live forever, even though it would bring destruction to humanity. I would prefer to die here. To be or not to be makes no difference for me. In my death is my ultimate freedom.

SHINJI: What are you? I don't understand what you're talking about! Kaoru!!

KAORU: My last words. Now please destroy me. Otherwise, you will be destroyed. Only one life-form can evade the destruction and inherit the future. And you are not the existence that should die. You need the future. *(He looks up at Rei and smiles. She gazes back, steely and unflappable. Kaoru turns back to Shinji.)* Thank you. I am glad to have met you. *(Static shot of Unit 1 holding Kaoru, as music swells in background, holding for sixty-four seconds. At last Shinji acts.)*

Lilith is the symbol of an enchained natural history, not of an enchanted social history. Kaoru, Seele's Angel of Global Speculation, is thus countermanded by Rei, Nerv's humanly constructed Angel of History. The destructive potential of the former is precisely matched by the constructive energies of the latter. Only Shinji, however, has the power to tip the balance one way or the other. He chooses the future, and monopoly-national temporality falls into global space. Kaoru relinquishes his stranglehold over the machinery of the Eurostate, at the same time that Asiazilla sheds the mask of an unbridled East Asian industrialism. This is subtly relayed by the close-up of the unconscious Eva 2, its faceplate pierced by Eva 1's knife, and the final scene of Eva 1, Eva 2's knife still stuck in its body armor: This is the symbolic negation of the multinational mask and Lilith's crucified corporeality alike in the form of Asiazilla's mighty hand. This is the classic symbol of laboring bodies, the repudiation of the invisible hand of the marketplace by the agency of a billions-strong East Asian proletariat.

This is indeed the Gospel of a New Century, only one not in the service of Wall Street neoliberalism, keiretsu corporatism, or Euroindustrialism, but serving rather that global proletariat presently reinventing its own ideologies, organizational structures, and modes of class struggle on a transnational scale. This is confirmed by a final shot of Eva 1 back in its storage chamber, where Gendou and Rei watch Nerv personnel wash Kaoru's blood from its hands, a subtle rewriting of the end of "Evangelion 16," when Ritsuko expressed her doubts to Gendou about the Frankenstein she helped to create. This is an explicit class alliance between rebellious high-tech professionals and Asiazilla, mediated by the Angel of History—the perfect symbol of the pro-democracy movements, feisty unions and powerful civic groups that rocked the military dictatorships and repressive one-party regimes of East Asia to their very foundations in the 1980s and 1990s.

No gospel would be complete without a suitably mind-bending set of final revelations, and *Evangelion's* two-part denouement does not disappoint. "Evangelion 25" begins with a complex dream sequence in which Shinji, Asuka, and Rei relentlessly question themselves (and each other) about their choices and motivations, their individual comments interspersed by graphical quotes set in stark black and white. Their own individual self-destructive tendencies are subsequently linked with those of society as a whole, in the form of Gendou's apocalyptic vision of an Instrumentality that would definitively fill in humanity's existential void (Seele's agenda). This vision terminates, as one might suspect, in total destruction, drawing Misato's stinging rebuke: "And so you'll just crush everyone's minds together to fill the gaps? How dare you presume to make the entirety of human existence into an experiment to prove your theory?!"

More important, "Evangelion 25" draws extensively on theatrical tropes—spotlights, character monologues, and simple stage props—borrowed from East Asia's thriving theater culture.[8] During Misato's own moment of self-reflection, for example, her childhood photograph is shown repeatedly, each time looking slightly more torn and frayed than before, creating the same jarring effect Heiner Müller employed in *Hamletmachine:* The stage directions call for a photograph of Müller himself to be torn up onstage, the critical self-reflection of the cultural superstar. Something similar applies to Misato's flashback of her affair with Kaji. Shinji silently watches them from *within* the flashback, accompanied by the steady rocking of a subway or train and the ringing railway chime familiar from Shinji's previous dream sequences in the Eva. We see shots of a whirring fan and hear the sound of a crowd cheering, followed by an eerie synthesizer sound, like electronic breathing.[9] Asuka's own self-reflection centers on the theatrical symbol of her childhood teddy bear, which bursts open by itself at one point, its soft cotton contents eerily reminiscent of Lilith's protohuman entrails. Later, she transforms her childhood trauma into words for the first time: "Then my momma was hanging from the ceiling. She looked so happy. But I hated how she looked." It is only by coming to terms with the past that we open the door to the future. With this realization, the stage lights go on, and Shinji realizes he has been watching a series of performances (including his own).

"Evangelion 26" proceeds to fill in this theatrical space with a multinational content. The dialogue becomes densely polyphonic, featuring static shots of each of the characters asking Shinji simple yet profoundly subtle questions, for example, am I happy, why do I feel pain, what value do I have as a person, and so forth. (Here is a sampling of one such sequence: Kensuke says, "You're not the only one who gets hurt, Shinji." Touji continues: "Everyone feels pain. You aren't the only one." Hikari concludes: "It's just easier for you to think that's true, isn't it?") Much of this dialogue is scored to black-and-white photos of plastic chairs, cables, electrical equipment, and other assorted junk, while a techno loop pulses subtly in the background, recalling to mind the industrial noir of Shinya Tsukamoto's wild and woolly 1990 science fiction film *Tetsuo* ("Iron Man"). This is followed by a terrific shot of Shinji drawn in black-and-white, set against a bright red background; his hand-drawn body is filled in with full-color images drawn from the entire series that cycle rapidly in place, creating the effect of a reverse silhouette.

This moment signals the emergence of Shinji's own critical reflexivity: "This is a representation," he thinks, "Everything is merely a description, not my real self. Everything is simply a shape, a form, an identifier to let others recognize me as me. But then, what am I?" Still later, he sees his own hand-drawn image floating in a white void, backed by the angelic sound track of the dream sequences of "Evangelion 20." The world of unrestricted freedom is a world of complete emptiness. It is not until Gendou says at one point, "Let me give you a restriction," and draws a horizontal line that Shinji can orient himself properly. (He begins to walk, punctuated by the Nintendo-like beeping of an early video game.) Next, Shinji free-associates a series of stripped-down versions of the basic visual symbols of *Evangelion* (spirals, eggs, stars, planets, angels, a cross, fire, waves, and an eye) before envisioning a series of stick figures and outlines of human forms. Finally, we see a recursive visual loop of one human outline ceaselessly enclosing another. This is not the mythic repetition of the same but a display of infinite complexity and variation, as one unique outline gives way to another.

Suddenly, Asuka shakes Shinji awake, and to our surprise, we see the perfectly ordinary bedroom of an ordinary Tokyo teenager in the humdrum year of 1995. What follows is an uproarious slice of domestic comedy, as the end of *Evangelion*—very much like the conclusion of *The Prisoner* and the finale of the *Three Colors* trilogy—self-reflexively rewrites its own beginning. In this reality-based version of events, Yui, Shinji's mother, is alive and well and happily married to Gendou, who hides himself behind the morning newspaper just like any other father. Pen-pen is a plastic doll, not a real-life penguin. Asuka is Shinji's obstreperous girlfriend, just as we always suspected she was, while Rei is simply a new kid in the neighborhood, whom Shinji accidentally crashes into on the way to school. Even Misato briefly returns, this time in the role of the popular classroom teacher who introduces Rei as the new girl, sparking a hilarious shouting match between Asuka and Rei.

As the camera pans back, revealing color sketches and penciled-in editing directions, we see Shinji looking out at a model replica of Tokyo-3 (the vantage point of Godzilla, recast as our own reflexive position as media consumers), realizing that this is one possible future among many. A piano version of the opening theme song of *Evangelion* then begins to cycle in the background, as the voices of the entire cast circulate around Shinji, telling him that there are as many truths as there are people and that everyone has the power to define their own truth. At last Shinji draws the logical conclusion.

> SHINJI: *(Seated in mist.)* I'm cowardly, sneaky, and weak.
> MISATO: *(Close-up from dream sequence of "Evangelion 20.")* If you know yourself, you can be kind to others.
> SHINJI: I hate myself. *(Voices of Misato, Rei, Asuka, and Shinji speak the same line, all at once.)* But maybe I could love myself.

This collective voice is the key: The precondition for the genuine development of each individual is the full development of every other individual.[10] True subjective freedom can only be realized objectively, that is to say, by a freely chosen collective solidarity among individuals. Following this insight, the machinery of the stage tumbles to pieces all around him, revealing a graduation ceremony wherein each of the characters congratulates Shinji (Anno's own scripted coda: "To my father . . . Farewell to my mother . . . To all the children: congratulations!").

Which version, then, is the real one, the domestic comedy of 1995 or the mecha tragedy of 2015? The irresistible conclusion is that *both* are true and that the individual happiness of the former is the flip side of the collective praxis of the latter. In an era when an unfettered global marketplace enriches a tiny, unaccountable, and self-interested elite while submerging billions in the cruelest poverty; in a world system that promises boundless wealth while perpetuating the most agonizing misery; in a rapacious business culture where people are reduced to mere financial objects and financial abstractions are venerated as people—human beings have no choice but to pilot the Evangelions of multinational class struggle against Seele's apostles of neoliberalism. If the Nintendo children dream worlds of East Asian socialism, then the children of Asiazilla, together with the children of the euro, dream cosmologies of revolution; at no lesser stakes are *Evangelion*'s video aesthetics to be understood.

Notes

Introduction

1. For those unfamiliar with the term, *death matching* refers to on-line video games such as Quake, Half Life, and Unreal, played via modem by individuals or teams. They combine eye-popping graphics with visceral gameplay and pulse-pounding excitement.

2. Theodor Adorno, *Minima Moralia* (Frankfurt am Main: Suhrkamp, 1951), 55.

1. Video and Interpretation

1. The World Bank defines low-income as annual per capita income of $755 or less, middle-income as $756–$2,995, and high-income as $2,995 and above. The middle-income countries have the greatest share of the world population, 2.7 billion residents; by contrast, 2.4 billion live in low-income and 891 million in high-income countries. *The 2000–2001 World Development Report,* 174–75, 311–12.

2. Although the World Bank and the IMF publicly insist that the poor have made great progress under their tutelage, the World Bank's own statistics prove otherwise. Despite heavy regulations and strong state intervention in the economy, the Second and Third World grew very rapidly indeed from 1945 to 1980. Since then, most of these countries have been subjected to punishing structural adjustment packages by the IMF. The typical prescription is fiscal orthodoxy, a decline in real wages, deregulation of the financial sphere, abolition of national tariffs, and lush subsidies for well-heeled foreign investors. The results bespeak a planetary developmental disaster: Annual per capita growth in consumption in low-income countries declined to only 1.4 percent between 1980 and 1998. In middle-income countries, per capita growth was 2.2 percent, which at first glance seems comparable to that of high-income countries (also 2.2 percent). These figures, however, include India and China, which grew at 2.7 percent and 7.2 percent rates, respectively, between 1980 and 1998. Both of these countries pursued economic policies that broke every rule in the IMF's neoliberal playbook: They rejected fiscal austerity, emphasized state-owned enterprises, carefully regulated financial markets, and protected domestic markets. Excluding these two, 95 out of the remaining 107 countries listed in the World Bank report saw per capita consumption levels fall (in some cases, quite drastically) relative to those of the richest countries. If this is success, one shudders to think of what failure might look like. *The 2000–2001 World Development Report,* 277.

3. In *Negative Dialektik* (Frankfurt am Main: Suhrkamp, 1970), Theodor Adorno's classic formulation of the vocation of a negative (read: multinational) dialectics poses this issue in terms of the antipodes of the micrology and the macrology:

> Immersion into the particular, dialectical immanence raised to an extreme, requires as one of its moments the freedom to step out of the object, too, the freedom that the claim of identity cuts off. Hegel would have abjured this; he relied upon the

complete mediation in objects. In the praxis of cognition, the resolution of the irresolvable, the moment of such transcendence of thought comes to light in that solely as a micrology does it employ macrological means. The demand for committalness [Verbindlichkeit] without system is that for thought models. These are not of a merely monadological sort. The model strikes the specific and more than the specific, without dissolving it into its more general master concept. To think philosophically is so much as to think in models; negative dialectics is an ensemble of model analyses. (39, my translation)

4. Applying this insight to the rise of cultural studies more generally, it is no accident that new literary fields such as New Criticism, existentialism, and the canon of Western European modernism all emerged in the 1950s, at the exact moment that the post–World War II English and literature departments were confronted with the task of educating swelling numbers of undergraduates. The transformation of the theoretical field was part and parcel of an intergenerational struggle between professors, administrators, and educators, caught up in the transition away from the Ivy League model of training a narrow, privileged elite, and toward the publicly funded, heavily militarized mass research university. One can observe a similar dialectic at work in the 1960s, where the rise of structuralism, semiotics, and micropolitics went hand in hand with the mediatization, multiculturalization, and, of course, repoliticization of the university system.

5. As Adorno stated in *Negative Dialektik:*

Theory and intellectual experience require their reciprocal effect. This does not contain answers for everything, but reacts to a world which is false to its innermost core. Theory would have no jurisdiction over what would be free of the bane of such. The ability to move is essential to consciousness, not an accidental characteristic. It signifies a double procedure: that of the inside out, the immanent process, the authentically dialectical, and a free one, something unfettered which steps out of dialectics, as it were. Neither of them are, however, disparate. The unregimented thought has an elective affinity to dialectics, which as critique of the system recalls to mind what would be outside of the system; and the energy which dialectical movement in cognition unleashes is that which rebels against the system. Both positions of consciousness are connected to one another through each other's critique, not through compromise. (42, my translation)

It is one of the most hopeful signs of the late 1990s that a wide range of intellectuals and activists are starting to take Adorno's point very seriously indeed. Postcolonial theorists such as Gayatri Spivak, Homi Bhabha, and Aijiz Ahmad are beginning to ask the same unsettling questions about multinational culture and identity as First World gender theorists such as Judith Butler and Eve Sedgwick, while the work of economic critics such as Doug Henwood and Patrick Bond in critiquing Wall Street neoliberalism is increasingly informing (and being informed by) the theoretical insights of sociologists such as Boris Kagarlitsky, David Harvey, and Pierre Bourdieu.

6. My own feeling, shared by many hip-hop cognoscenti, is that the real musical innovations of the 1980s and 1990s were made by hip-hop artists, such as Public Enemy's album *It Takes a Nation of Millions to Hold Us Back,* Cypress Hill's eponymous first album, and Kool Keith's *Dr. Octagon.* Unfortunately, no comprehensive musicology of late-twentieth-century hip-hop has yet been written.

7. Ella Shohat and Robert Stam, *Unthinking Eurocentrism* (New York: Routledge, 1994), 329–31.

8. Stephen Teo, *Hong Kong Cinema* (London: British Film Institute, 1997).

2. Mapping the Global Village

1. Brooks did not contribute to *Get Smart* beyond its first season, but he was instrumental in launching the basic idea and scenario.

2. The opening tag of the very first episode, "Arrival," is somewhat less formatted and dense than the remaining ones, which have been carefully streamlined. For example, the scenes of the parking ticket machine and whatnot are later eliminated, a significant clue that McGoohan was as canny an editor as he was a scriptwriter, actor, and producer.

3. It should be emphasized that this is a critique of the Bond films, not of Barry's scores, which are some of the best ever written for the cinema. (Barry was responsible, incidentally, for scoring the trademark Bond guitar strum, which first appeared in *Dr. No.*) The sound track keynoting the outer space sequences in *You Only Live Twice,* for example, which combined an arresting trumpet theme with a spine-tingling low bass march quoted from Puccini's *La Bohème,* would remain unequaled in the action-adventure genre until Hideaki Anno's quotation of Beethoven's Ninth Symphony in an episode of *Evangelion.* Barry would go on to win five Oscars for his work as a composer, writing the scores for other Bond films as well as *Out of Africa* and *Dances with Wolves.*

3. The Information Uprising

1. Alain Carrazé and Hélène Oswald, *The Prisoner: A Televisionary Masterpiece* (London: W. H. Allen, 1990), 213–14.

2. Jean Genet, *Les Nègres* [The Blacks] (Décines: Barbezat, 1963), 99.

3. It should be noted that McKern's haggard expression and decrepit mannerisms during this final scene were by no means mere histrionics. As McGoohan would recount to an interviewer on Canadian television, while working on the final episodes McKern suffered a mental breakdown, very similar to the one that transpired in the episode itself. Although he recovered and would finish the series, the episode highlights the extreme production pressures weighing upon the cast and crew during the final episodes. Not only were the crew kept in the dark as to the true identity of No. 1, but McGoohan reportedly wrote the bulk of the final script in a single forty-eight-hour stretch of crazed inspiration, suggesting that the final episode stands in the same relation to the rest of the series as the 1968 rebellions did to the social forces unleashed by the 1960s consumer culture, that is, the moment when quantity turns into quality.

4. This seems to be a peculiarly British symbol of the televisual sphere, whose true genesis was the palantir or magical crystal ball of J. R. R. Tolkien's *Lord of the Rings* trilogy, written in the late 1940s and early 1950s. The villain of the series, Sauron, never puts in a personal appearance. He consists solely of a terrifying Eye, a disembodied gaze that sees but cannot be seen, and that bends hapless viewers to its will (a nice intuition of the ideology behind the CBS logo, really, and one could argue that Tolkien's career as a professional philologist of some renown made him unusually sensitive to the homogenization and deadening of language by the mass media). The time-crystal episodes in the 1970s *Doctor Who* series are a much later version of the same trope, albeit cast in a more conventional, melodramatic plotline. By contrast, American fantasy and science fiction have tended to emphasize the more pragmatic or technological aspect of the mass me-

dia, as with E. E. Doc Smith's Lens (a kind of mental telephone, fax machine, and computer all in one) in the classic Lensman space operas of the late 1930s and early 1940s.

4. Krzysztof Kieslowski's Eurovideo

1. In *Communism, Capitalism, and the Mass Media* (London: Sage, 1998), Colin Sparks writes:

> According to Radio Free Europe, which had some direct experience of interference, television seems never to have been jammed, even when Western signals were quite widely available. In Hungary, where 30 percent of the population is able to receive terrestrial Austrian and Yugoslav signals, there had never been any attempt to prevent reception. In the case of video, there were no political moves to control the import either of Western technology or programmes, although the customs service operated tariffs that had the effect of rationing such items through price rises. Nevertheless, in 1984, according to official sources, between 500,000 and 600,000 people out of a population of around 10 million had access to video recorders, although some estimates were for a much lower figure of around 120,000 adults with recorders in their own homes.
>
> Video recorders do not appear ever to have been illegal in Poland. The restriction on their ownership was largely economic. To buy them required a large sum of scarce convertible currency. Apart from authorised outlets, they were often acquired as an investment by Poles travelling abroad, who then resold them inside the country at a profit. (60–61)

2. As Kieslowski remarked in Danusia Stok's *Kieslowski on Kieslowski* (London: Faber and Faber, 1993):

> The initial idea was for a film which takes place in a courtroom. About the lawyer who's dead, and about the woman he leaves behind who realizes that she loved him more than she thought when he was alive. I didn't know anything more about the film. The film is terribly diffuse, of course, since it is three films in one, as it were. And you can see that—the stitching's not very subtle. The film doesn't fuse together to form a whole. A part of it, the discursive part, is about a young worker. A part of it is about the widow's life (the widow is played by Grazyna Szapolowska). Then there's the most metaphysical part, that is, the signs which emanate from the man who's not there any more, towards all that he's left behind. And these three films don't really want to come together. Of course, they do mix all the time, threads and thoughts constantly interweave, but I don't think we managed to bring it together. (131)

Kieslowski consciously tried to compensate for the incompatibility of the ghost thriller, the existential thriller, and the documentary drama by means of editing techniques. Some of these work surprisingly well, as with the brief montage of the interior of Urzsula's car, when the engine stalls. Others fall flat, most notably the glaring and unmotivated jumpcut in the midst of the bedroom scene with the British stranger.

3. Stok, *Kieslowski on Kieslowski*, 136–37.

4. Annette Insdorf, *Double Lives, Second Chances: The Cinema of Krzysztof Kieslowski* (New York: Miramax Books, 1999), 65–66.

5. Kieslowski himself gives us this broad hint:

> A great deal in life depends on who smacked your hand at breakfast when you were a child. That is, on who your father was, who your grandmother was, who your great-grandfather was, and your background in general. It's very important. And the person who slapped you at breakfast for being naughty when you were four, later put that first book on your bedside table or gave it to you for Christmas. And those books formed us—at least, they did me. They taught me something, made me sensitive to something. The books I read, particularly as a child or a boy, made me what I am. (Stok, *Kieslowski on Kieslowski,* 5)

6. In his lecture to the university seminar, Krzysztof concludes by saying: "This device, which seems to differentiate between zero and one, has not only a kind of intelligence, it *selects.* That makes it capable of choice, perhaps even an act of will. In my opinion, a properly programmed computer may have its own aesthetic preferences, a personality." Kieslowski even flags this cyborg narrative with an appropriate moment of poststructuralism: Previously Krzysztof had explained to the class that language operates via flexible Saussurean relays of meaning, rather than fixed definitions. His example is a complex chain of associations that gradually resolves into the term "under-Judas-ment," a word that doesn't exist but one that, he reminds the class, everyone immediately understands—an unmistakable dig in the direction of the censors and secret police.

7. As Adorno notes in *Negative Dialektik:*

> The moment, however, in which history and nature become commensurable is that of transience; this is the central cognition of Benjamin's *Origin of the German Tragedy-Play.* Nature hovered before the Baroque poets, so they say, "as eternal transience, in which alone the Saturnine glance of that generation recognized history." Not only of theirs; natural history was ever in the canon of historical-philosophical interpretation: "Where history wandered into the scenery of the tragedy-play, it did so as script. On the countenance of Nature stood 'History' as the signification of transience. The allegorical physiognomy of Nature-History, which was introduced to the stage through the tragedy-play, is truly contemporary as a ruin" [*Origin of the German Tragedy-Play,* 199]. That is the transmutation of metaphysics into history. It secularizes metaphysics into the secular category pure and simple, that of decline. Philosophy points to that signification, the always new Menetekel, in that which is smallest, the fragments struck loose by decline and which bear objective meanings. (353, my translation)

8. Note that there is a precisely analogous moment in John Woo's film *The Killer,* when the camera does a slow semicircular pan around the police officer, played by Danny Lee, during a scene in which the officer recognizes the hitman's girlfriend from the cover of a compact disc and a photograph. The closest analogy of the semicircular pan in the musical field was the electronically boosted bass pulse of early 1990s hip-hop, which DJs converted from an objective marker of the rhythm into an independent voice in its own right, usually in the breaks between lyrical passages, where the bass line would pulse up or down the space of a half-note, accompanied only by a drum brush or musical scratch. Whereas the blues bass line symbolized railroad technology and the R&B bass referenced an automotive mobility, the hip-hop bass pulse signified the aerospace sublime, the thunder of jetliners, rockets, and other heavy transport equipment.

Among other interesting similarities, both Kieslowski and Woo regularly feature all manner of jetliners, airports, and other aerospace signifiers in their work.

5. Velvet Television

1. The character of Mr. Halloran, the African American chef victimized by Jack Torrance in Stanley Kubrick's 1980 film *The Shining,* is a much later variation on the same theme. Where Fellini, Bergman, and other European auteurs mobilized the innovations of European theatrical modernism to combat a hegemonic Americanization, Kubrick locates the resistance to the freezing reification of the Overlook Hotel and the image-culture of Thatcherism in the collective traditions and solidarities of African American culture, with its unique ability to read the traces of the past (as well as anticipate the future).

2. To emphasize the point, Kieslowski splices in brief clips of a bicyclist far in the distance and a horse in a nearby field during the bloody struggle, in other words, modes of transportation; the horizon of the outdoor scenes never fails to register at least one distant smokestack or industrial building. There is a strikingly similar moment in John Woo's 1992 *Hard-boiled,* where an automobile assembly plant is transformed into a battlefield between rival gangs and undercover police. Bullets ricochet and airborne bodies fly across, around, and even *through* the half-finished shells of compact cars and exploding motorcycles, in what amounts to the symbolic ballet of export-platform industrialization.

3. This scene also makes a passing reference to one of the most stereotypical narratives of the Eastern bloc culture-industry, the collective farm drama, which Heiner Müller successfully pastiched in his 1961 play, *The Settlers.* Kieslowski offers a somewhat grimmer version of the same moment:

> JACEK: Yes, there were three places. Mary and father are there and one place is left. Mary is there . . . five years now. Yes, five years ago she was run over by a tractor back home. She was still at school. She was twelve. The school year had just begun. The driver of that tractor, he was my pal. We'd been drinking vodka and wine just before it happened. After, he left and ran her over in the meadow by the forest. There was a meadow there, by the forest. . . . I always kept thinking that . . . if only she could have stayed alive, things would be different. Perhaps I wouldn't have left home, I'd have stayed. I had three brothers, but she was the only sister. I was her favorite. She was my favorite, too. Perhaps everything would have been different.
>
> PIOTR: Perhaps it wouldn't have come to this?
>
> JACEK: Perhaps I wouldn't be here now.
>
> OFFICER: *(Interrupting them.)* The Chief and the Prosecutor ask if you're ready.
>
> PIOTR: *(Gets up.)* Tell them I'll never say I'm ready.
>
> OFFICER: *(Repeats dully.)* You'll never say you're ready. *(Piotr sits back down.)*
>
> JACEK: We bought the grave plot. *(Officer stares at them through keyhole, in a curiously voyeuristic pose, unwittingly giving them a few more seconds, before going off to assemble the execution squad.)*

4. Murder rates and the incidence of violent crimes in the European Union are among the lowest on the planet, according to Interpol statistics; comparable figures for Eastern Europe are a bit higher, but not significantly different from those of the Euro-

pean semiperipheries (Greece, Ireland, and Spain). By contrast, the United States continues to lead the industrialized world in executions, violent crime, and incarceration. An astonishing 3 percent of the U.S. adult population is currently either locked up, on probation, or otherwise supervised by the criminal justice system. (This does not include ex-felons or those who have fully served their sentences.)

5. Žižek provides a stirring analysis of the filmic codes that "Decalogue 6"'s video tropes adroitly redeploy, but because he lacks a theory of video adequate to its content, he ends up recycling a schematic, Deleuzian model of rhizomatic flows of desire, rather than ascending to the concrete multinational content of the aesthetic material. As Žižek explains in "There Is No Sexual Relationship," *Spectator* 16, no. 2 (spring/summer 1996):

> When, upon their becoming acquainted, Maria asks Tomek what he effectively wants from her, a mere kiss, or a full sexual act, his resolute answer is "nothing." This "nothing," of course, is the unmistakable index of true love: Tomek is not to be satisfied with any positive content or act (going to bed with him, for example) by means of which Maria could reciprocate his love. What he wants her to offer in return is the very "nothingness" in her, what is "in her more than herself"—not something that she possesses but precisely what she does not have, the return of love itself. . . .
>
> . . . the true enigma of the film is Tomek's change from the loving one into the object of Maria's love. So how does he succeed in substituting his position of the loving one with the position of the beloved? How does he capture Maria's desire? The answer, of course, resides in the very purity and absolute intensity of his love: he acts as the pure $, the subject whose desire is so burning that it cannot be translated into any concrete demand—this very intensity, because of which his desire can only express itself in the guise of a refusal of any demand ("I want nothing from you"), is what makes him irresistible. This second metaphoric substitution is not simply symmetrical to the first one: their difference hinges on the opposition of "to have" and "to be." In the first case, we are in the dimension of having (the loved one doesn't know what he has in himself that makes him worthy of the other's love, so in order to escape this deadlock, he returns love), whereas in the second case, the loving is (becomes) the beloved object on account of the sheer intensity of his love.
>
> What one has to reject here is the notion that Tomek's love for Maria is authentic and pure, spiritual, elevated above vulgar sensitivity, whereas Maria, disturbed by this purity, intends to humiliate him and later changes her attitude out of a feeling of guilt. It is, on the contrary, Tomek's love which is fundamentally false, a narcissistic attitude of idealization whose necessary obverse is a barely conceived lethal dimension. That is to say, *A Short Film on Love* ["Decalogue 6"] should be read against the background of slasher films, in which a man observes and harasses a woman who traumatizes him, finally attacking her with a knife: it is a kind of introverted slasher in which the man, instead of striking at the woman, deals a blow to himself. (136–37)

The whole point of the episode, though, is that Tomek's cinematic gaze is superseded by Magda's multinational window of viewpoints. The real issue is the emergence of that strange new beast, equal parts speculative calculation and multinational image-consumption, otherwise known as Euroconsumerism.

6. This is explicitly spelled out in a later dialogue:

ELZBIETA: What do you teach your students? How they should live?

ZOFIA: No, not that. I try to help them discover themselves.

ELZBIETA: Why?

ZOFIA: Because goodness exists. I think it exists in every human being. Situations release good or evil. That evening did not release the good in me.

ELZBIETA: And who is evaluating it?

ZOFIA: He who is in all of us.

ELZBIETA: I didn't find God in your works.

ZOFIA: I do not go to church. I don't use the word *God.* But one can know, be without doubts, without using the words, that people are free, they can choose. If they wish, they can leave God behind.

6. Neon Genesis Evangelion

1. Alice Amsden, *Asia's Next Giant: South Korea and Late Industrialization* (New York: Oxford University Press, 1989); Michael Gerlach, *Alliance Capitalism* (Berkeley: University of California Press, 1992); Robert Wade, *Governing the Market: Economic Theory and the Role of Government in East Asian Industrialization* (Princeton: Princeton University Press, 1990). The classic text on Japan's developmental state is Chalmers Johnson's *MITI and the Japanese Miracle: The Growth of Japanese Industrial Policy, 1925–1975* (Stanford: Stanford University Press, 1982). For an excellent restatement and critique of the developmental state thesis, see Meredith Woo-Cumings, ed., *The Developmental State* (Ithaca: Cornell University Press, 1999).

2. Federal Reserve statistics show that the United States has become the biggest debtor country in the world, running vast trade and current account deficits (meaning that it must import capital from abroad to finance its economy), and owing Japan and Europe $2 trillion on its net international investment account.

3. Here are the Japan Bank for International Cooperation's figures for Japan's total financial assistance to Southeast Asia from July 1997 through December 1998, the worst period of the Asian crisis (at an exchange rate of 110 yen = $1 U.S.):

Country	Total assistance	Percentage of country's GDP
Thailand	$10.2 billion	6.2
South Korea	6.01 billion	1.3
Indonesia	5.89 billion	3.2
Malaysia	2.90 billion	3.6
Philippines	2.73 billion	4.9
Singapore	1.67 billion	2.1

4. Note that one should not confuse the *Evangelion* TV series with the theatrical films by the same name (*End of Evangelion* and *Evangelion: Death and Rebirth*) produced after the series. The films are visually stunning but aesthetically deficient works, which Gainax created mostly as a way of cashing in on *Evangelion*'s runaway success. (This is somewhat comparable to the two full-length films Kieslowski created based on the fifth and sixth episodes of *The Decalogue,* which were also not quite as good as the originals.)

5. Note that these are the original versions of the series, not the later, less interesting sequels of such (e.g., *Dirty Pair: Flash* and *Bubble Gum Crash*). Currently the best

English-language source of anime information, links, and analyses on the Web is the Anime Web Turnpike at <http://www.anipike.com>.

6. Though fairly conventional in terms of its plot—it is essentially a sea-based version of the American TV show *Wild Wild West,* featuring a late-nineteenth-century setting saturated with improbably advanced technology—the visual designs of *Nadia* do show intriguing hints of what was to come. For one thing, Nadia herself is a moody character who looks and acts distinctively Southeast Asian, pointing to a powerful undercurrent of multiculturalism. She is also the spitting image of Misato Katsuragi. Likewise, her compatriot Jean will later reappear as *Evangelion*'s tech geek, Kensuke; the vain, supercilious Grandis is clearly a protomorphic Asuka; and the curiously reserved first officer of the Nautilus, Electra, is an embryonic Ritsuko. *Nadia* also features wonderfully literate scriptwriting; for example, the America ship that hunts the Nautilus is named Abraham (as in Lincoln) while its captain is Melville (in reference to Herman Melville). One could also point to the scenes of the underground Atlantis midway through the series as the prescient model for the Nerv geofront.

7. William S. Burroughs, *Nova Express* (New York: Grove Press, 1964), 132.

8. In fact, the opening sequence is constructed almost completely from extended quotations of the Godzilla movies. The more noteworthy examples include Shinji's instantaneous, dreamlike vision of Rei in the distance (reminiscent of the miniature twin sisters from Monster Island); the white flash of an explosion annihilating a streetcar (a Hiroshima trope); the explicit destruction of UN tanks and helicopters (read: U.S. military forces) by the angel; and the spectacular atomic shockwave of the N2 mine.

9. The quote is from Robert Browning's *Pippa Passes,* a poetic drama written in 1841. At one point Pippa, the main character, sings the following song:

> The year's at the spring
> And day's at the morn;
> Morning's at seven;
> The hill-side's dew-pearled;
> The lark's on the wing;
> The snail's on the thorn;
> God's in His heaven—
> All's right with the world!

From *Complete Works of Robert Browning* (New York: AMS Press, 1966), 114.

10. Shinji's painful struggle to grow up will reprise one of the most fundamental tropes of Japanese aesthetic modernism, as evinced by this extraordinary passage from Natsume Soseki, which set the modernist antihero in motion toward an alien mass culture all the way back in the 1910s:

> Ichizo's disposition is one that coils inwardly whenever he comes in contact with the world. Whenever he receives an impulse, it turns round and round, driving itself in more and more deeply and carving itself more and more finely into the recesses of his mind. And it distresses him that this encroachment upon his mind continues, knowing no bounds. He's so worried about it that he prays for any escape whatever from this inner activity, but he's dragged on by it as though it were a curse beyond his power to drive out. The time is going to come when he'll inevitably collapse, totally alone, under his own mental exertion. He's going to come to dread that

moment. When it happens, he'll be exhausted, like a madman. This is the great misfortune lying at the very core of his life. In order to turn it into a blessing, there's no other way except to reverse the direction of his life and to make it uncoil outward. We must get him to use his eyes so that instead of carrying outside things into his head, he can look with his mind at things as they exist outside. He should find one thing under heaven—and a single thing is enough—which is so great or beautiful or gentle that it will engross his entire being. In a word, he has to become frivolous.

From Natsume Soseki, *To the Spring Equinox and Beyond,* trans. Kingo Ochiai and Sanford Goldstein (Rutland, Vt., and Tokyo: Charles Tuttle, 1985).

11. Unlike U.S. high schools, where at the end of each class each student goes to a different class, in Japan it is the individual teachers who typically walk from classroom to classroom, while the students remain together as a group for most of the day. The Japanese school year is also longer than its U.S. equivalent, resulting in a much deeper sense of class camaraderie. The class monitor typically has the task of calling for order at the beginning of each class, taking attendance, and organizing after-school cleanup activities. The notorious "exam hell" many Japanese students endure is not a product of high school per se but the result of after-school cram schools and the entrance examination system for universities. The high schools themselves have done a commendable job of creating one of the most literate and highly skilled workforces in the world, thanks to plentiful funding, a deep-seated cultural respect for education of all kinds, and highly trained, capable, and motivated teachers.

12. It should be noted that this has nothing to do with any lingering militarism in Japanese culture, but is part of a general tendency in postwar Japan to reproduce certain aspects of U.S. culture in extremely precise detail, ranging from baseball to Hollywood movies and from country-and-western bars to pop songs.

13.

> RITSUKO: Fifteen years ago, in Antarctica, humanity discovered the being known as the first angel. In the middle of the investigation, however, for unknown reasons, the angel exploded. *(Blast of air ruffles Misato's hair.)* This is the real truth behind the Second Impact.
>
> SHINJI: Then the things we're doing here are to—
>
> RITSUKO: To prevent a probable Third Impact from happening. That is the purpose of Nerv and the Evangelions." ("Evangelion 7")

14. One minor point: ADV's subtitled version of this sequence slightly skews part of Rei's dialogue. At one point the titles don't quite match up to the Japanese words being spoken. The above transcript is the correct, original version, that is, the dialogue on the left is uttered exactly when the images on the right appear.

7. Dawn of the East Asian Metropole

1. As William Gibson states in *Neuromancer* (New York: Ace Books, 1984): "There was a gray place, an impression of fine screens shifting, moire, degrees of half tone generated by a very simple graphics program. There was a long hold on a view through chainlink, gulls frozen above dark water. There were voices. There was a plain of black mirror, that tilted, and he was quicksilver, a bead of mercury, skittering down, striking the angles of an invisible maze, fragmenting, flowing together, sliding again" (244).

2. The 2001 edition of the *Gardner Report,* a trade publication that tracks world machine tool production, shows that in the year 2000 Europe produced 47 percent of the world's machine tools by value, the East Asian region produced 38 percent, whereas the United States produced a paltry 11 percent (http://www.gardnerweb.com/consump/ produce.html). As a result, the United States had to import almost 43 percent of all its machine tools in 2000. This is important, because machine tools are the DNA of an economy, the machines that produce all other machines. One of the most important subsets of the overall machine tools market is the robotics industry, and here, too, U.S. market share has been largely stagnant while the European Union has been catching up with Japan. Here are the total operational stocks of industrial robots as percentages of world stock in the three major economic zones (East Asia equals Japan plus Singapore, Taiwan, and South Korea). Germany makes up about 46 percent of the EU total, and Japan makes up 90 percent of East Asia's total.

Region	1985	1990	1995	1999
EU	12.7%	14.2%	18.6%	23.7%
East Asia	55.1%	61.9%	67.1%	60.3%
U.S.	11.3%	8.6%	10.8%	12.5%

Source: *World Robotics 2000* (New York and Geneva: United Nations/Economic Commission for Europe and the International Federation of Robotics, 2000), table A-3.

IFR statistics on yearly shipments of industrial robots as a percentage of world robot production show a broadly similar trend. Germany makes up about 42 percent of the EU total, and Japan makes up 91 percent of East Asia's total.

Region	1985	1990	1995	1999
EU	13.8%	15.0%	21.2%	30.8%
East Asia	68.8%	76.6%	61.2%	48.2%
U.S.	16.2%	5.3%	14.2%	18.5%

Source: *World Robotics 2000,* table A-4.

3. This synthesis is matched by the appearance of two new multinational forms: the mass media therapist or counselor and the mature adult romance. The first appears when Misato and Ritsuko drive home shortly after Shinji's rebirth, while a talk show host on the car radio describes the stages of psychological development: "I know a lot of guys like that, and from your letter, you're just like them. I feel sorry for your girl-friend. She can't be your mate and your mother." This is followed by an explicitly sexual scene between Misato and Kaji, where they gently tease each other about their respective professional roles. In response to her queries, Kaji finally gives her a mysterious capsule, a gift which, he says gloomily, may be his last. This is not quite accurate; his last gift will be the message he leaves her shortly before he is killed, which motivates her to open the capsule.

4. As Herman Melville wrote in *Moby Dick* (New York: Norton, 1967):

> Slowly crossing the deck from the scuttle, Ahab leaned over the side and watched how his shadow in the water sank and sank to his gaze, the more and the more that he strove to pierce the profundity. But the lovely aromas in that enchanted air did at last seem to dispel, for a moment, the cankerous thing in his soul. That glad, happy

air, that winsome sky, did at last stroke and caress him; the stepmother world, so long cruel—forbidding—now threw affectionate arms round his stubborn neck, and did seem to joyously sob over him, as if over one, that however wilful and erring, she could yet find it in her heart to save and to bless. From beneath his slouched hat Ahab dropped a tear into the sea; nor did all the Pacific contain such wealth as that one wee drop. (443)

Ahab's shadow, drifting away into the sea, is replicated by Rei's last moment of consciousness: a snapshot of Gendou, without his glasses, smiling warmly at her, fading away into the detonation that takes her life.

5. Walter Benjamin, in *Über den Begriff der Geschichte* [Theses on the Concept of History] (Frankfurt am Main: Suhrkamp, 1974), writes:

There is a painting by Klee called Angelus Novus. An angel is depicted there who looks as though he were about to distance himself from something which he is staring at. His eyes are opened wide, his mouth stands open and his wings are outstretched. The Angel of History must look just so. His face is turned towards the past. Where *we* see the appearance of a chain of events, *he* sees one single catastrophe, which unceasingly piles rubble on top of rubble and tosses it before his feet. He would like to pause for a moment so fair [a reference to Goethe's *Faust*], to awaken the dead and to piece together what has been smashed. But a storm is blowing from Paradise, it has caught itself up in his wings and is so strong that the Angel can no longer close them. The storm drives him irresistibly into the future, to which his back is turned, while the rubble heap before him grows sky-high. That which we call progress is *this* storm. (ix, my translation)

6. The term *yaoi* is an abbreviation of the Japanese phrase "yama nashi, ochi nashi, imi nashi," which means "no mountain [peak, climax], no point, no meaning." Gay-oriented manga are also known as *june* (pronounced jou-nay).

7. This is subtly confirmed by Asuka's plug suit: flaming red with a prominent green stripe. This is a clear reference to the Red-Green political alliances that led the resistance to Maastricht monetarism and the assault on the European welfare states, and swept to power in the EU in the late 1990s. *Evangelion* was completed in early 1996, at the cusp of the December 1995 strikes in France, before popular discontent turned into active resistance to neoliberalism, but it is remarkable that Anno recognized the quintessential symbol of the multinational Left as early as he did.

8. Anno's inspiration here was probably Tokyo's so-called Little Theater boom during the mid-1970s, when avant-garde directors such as Hideki Noda created a lively theatrical postmodernism. In the late 1990s, Noda created intriguing works such as *Aka-Oni* (Red Demon), a multicultural fable performed in Thai by Thai actors on the stage but narrated in Japanese to a Japanese audience via headphones.

9. Note that the English-language dubbed version of *Evangelion* distributed by ADV inexplicably garnishes this scene with an almost pornographic sound track. The point, however, is to emphasize emotional intimacy over sexuality per se, like a romantic encounter witnessed on a train or in the street.

10. Alas, ADV's dubbed version not only misses this crucial point but compounds the original error by mistranslating Misato's words into ". . . now you can take care of

yourself," when the Japanese original clearly states kindness to *others* (fortunately, the subtitled version gets it right). It should be noted that, all things considered, ADV's translators and English-language voice actors do a commendable job throughout the series; Tiffany Grant's voice-acting for Asuka, for example, is simply outstanding.

Bibliography

Publications

Adorno, Theodor. *Minima Moralia*. Frankfurt am Main: Suhrkamp, 1951.

———. *Negative Dialektik* (Negative dialectics). Frankfurt am Main: Suhrkamp, 1970.

Amsden, Alice. *Asia's Next Giant: South Korea and Late Industrialization*. New York: Oxford University Press, 1989.

Beckett, Samuel. *Endgame*. New York: Grove Press, 1958.

Benjamin, Walter. *Über den Begriff der Geschichte* (Theses on the concept of history). Frankfurt am Main: Suhrkamp, 1972.

———. *Ursprung des deutschen Trauerspiels* (Origin of the German tragedy-play). Frankfurt am Main: Suhrkamp, 1972.

Bourdieu, Pierre. *Homo Academicus*. Paris: Les Éditions de Minuit, 1984.

Browning, Robert. "Pippa Passes," part 1. In *Complete Works of Robert Browning*. New York: AMS Press, 1966.

Burroughs, William. *Nova Express*. New York: Grove Press, 1964.

Carrazé, Alain, and Hélène Oswald. *The Prisoner: A Televisionary Masterpiece*. London: W. H. Allen, 1990.

Genet, Jean. *Les Nègres* (The blacks). Décines: Barbezat, 1963.

Gerlach, Michael. *Alliance Capitalism*. Berkeley: University of California Press, 1992.

Gibson, William. *Neuromancer*. New York: Ace Books, 1984.

Henwood, Doug. *Wall Street*. New York: Verso, 1997.

Insdorf, Annette. *Double Lives, Second Chances: The Cinema of Krzysztof Kieslowski*. New York: Miramax Books, 1999.

Jameson, Fredric. *Late Marxism*. New York: Verso, 1990.

———. *Postmodernism, or the Cultural Logic of Late Capitalism*. Durham: Duke University Press, 1991.

———. *Signatures of the Visible*. New York: Routledge, 1990.

Johnson, Chalmers. *MITI and the Japanese Miracle: The Growth of Japanese Industrial Policy, 1925–1975*. Stanford: Stanford University Press, 1982.

Johnson, Rheta Grimsley. *Good Grief! The Story of Charles M. Schulz*. New York: Pharos Books, 1989.

Melville, Herman. *Moby Dick*. New York: Norton, 1967.

Müller, Heiner. *Germania Tod in Berlin*. Berlin: Rotbuch, 1977.

———. *Mauser*. Berlin: Rotbuch, 1978. (Contains *Philoktet, Hamletmachine*).

Mulvey, Laura. *Visual and Other Pleasures*. Bloomington: Indiana University Press, 1989.

Pynchon, Thomas. *The Crying of Lot 49*. Philadelphia: Lippincott, 1966.

———. *Gravity's Rainbow*. New York: Penguin Books, 1995.

Sembène, Ousmane. *The Money-Order*. Trans. Clive Wake. London: Heinemann, 1972.

Shohat, Ella, and Robert Stam. *Unthinking Eurocentrism.* New York: Routledge, 1994.

Soseki, Natsume. *To the Spring Equinox and Beyond.* Trans. Kingo Ochiai and Sanford Goldstein. Rutland, Vt., and Tokyo: Charles Tuttle, 1985.

Soyinka, Wole. *The Lion and the Jewel.* London: Oxford University Press, 1963.

Sparks, Colin. *Communism, Capitalism, and the Mass Media.* London: Sage, 1998.

Stok, Danusia. *Kieslowski on Kieslowski.* London: Faber and Faber, 1993.

Teo, Stephen. *Hong Kong Cinema.* London: British Film Institute, 1997.

United Nations/Economic Commission for Europe (UN/ECE) and the International Federation of Robotics. *World Robotics 2000.* New York and Geneva: United Nations, 2000.

Verne, Jules. *Twenty Thousand Leagues under the Sea.* Trans. Emanuel J. Mickel. Bloomington: Indiana University Press, 1991.

Wade, Robert. *Governing the Market: Economic Theory and the Role of Government in East Asian Industrialization.* Princeton: Princeton University Press, 1990.

Woo-Cumings, Meredith, ed. *The Developmental State.* Ithaca: Cornell University Press, 1999.

World Bank. *The 2000–2001 World Development Report.*

Žižek, Slavoj. "There Is No Sexual Relationship." *Spectator* 16, no. 2 (spring/summer 1996).

Videos

Battle of Algiers. Dir. Gillo Pontecorvo. Casbah/Igor Film, 1965.

A Better Tomorrow. Dir. John Woo. Cinema City Film, 1986.

Blade Runner. Dir. Ridley Scott. Warner Brothers, 1982.

Blind Chance. Dir. Krzysztof Kieslowski. Film Polski, 1982.

Blue. Dir. Krzysztof Kieslowski. Miramax, 1994.

Bubble Gum Crisis. Dir. Katushito Akiyama and Hiroki Hayashi. Youmex/Artmic, 1990.

Camera Buff. Dir. Krzysztof Kieslowski. Polish TV, 1979.

Chinatown. Dir. Roman Polanksi. Paramount, 1974.

City of Lost Children. Dir. Marc Caro and Jean-Pierre Jeunet. Sony Pictures, 1995.

A Clockwork Orange. Dir. Stanley Kubrick. Warner Brothers, 1971.

The Day the Earth Stood Still. Dir. Robert Wise. Twentieth Century Fox, 1951.

The Decalogue. Dir. Krzysztof Kieslowski. Polish TV, 1988.

Delicatessen. Dir. Marc Caro and Jean Jeunet. Miramax, 1991.

Dirty Pair. Dir. Koichi Mashimo. Sunrise, 1985.

Diva. Dir. J. J. Beineix. United Artists Classics, 1981.

The Double Life of Veronique. Dir. Krzysztof Kieslowski. Miramax, 1991.

Dragonball Z. Dir. Daisuke Nishio and Akira Toriyama. Toei, 1996.

Enter the Dragon. Dir. Robert Clouse. Warner Brothers, 1973.

Faust. Dir. Jan Svankmajer. Zeitgeist Films, 1994.

Forbidden Planet. Dir. Stanley Wilcox. MGM, 1956.

Godzilla: King of Monsters. Dir. Inoshiro Honda and Terry Morse. Toho, 1956.

The Good, the Bad, and the Ugly. Dir. Sergio Leone. United Artists, 1966.

Gunbuster: Aim for the Top! Dir. Hideaki Anno. Gainax, 1989.

Hard-boiled. Dir. John Woo. Golden Princess Film and Milestone Pictures. Fox Lorber, 1992.

Ikiru. Dir. Akira Kurosawa. Toho, 1952.

Jaws. Dir. Stephen Spielberg. MCA/Universal, 1975.

The Killer. Dir. John Woo. Golden Princess, 1989.

Krzysztof Kieslowski: I'm So-So. Dir. Krzysztof Wierzbicki. First Run Features, 1995.

Man of Iron. Dir. Andrzej Wajda. Film Polski, 1980.

Man of Marble. Dir. Andrzej Wajda. New Yorker Video, 1990.

Memories of Underdevelopment. Dir. Tomás Gutiérrez-Alea. El Instituto Cubano del Arte e Industria Cinematográfrica, 1968.

Nadia: Secret of Blue Water. Dir. Hideaki Anno. Gainax, 1990.

Nausicaa: Valley of the Wind. Dir. Hayao Miyazaki. Studio Ghibli, 1984.

Neon Genesis Evangelion. Dir. Hideaki Anno. Gainax, 1995.

No End. Dir. Krzysztof Kieslowski. Film Polski, 1984.

North by Northwest. Dir. Alfred Hitchcock. MGM/UA Home Video, 1983.

The Omen. Dir. Richard Donner. Twentieth Century Fox, 1976.

One Flew over the Cuckoo's Nest. Dir. Milos Forman. United Artists, 1975.

Princess Mononoke. Dir. Hayao Miyazaki. Studio Ghibli, 1997.

The Prisoner. Dir. Patrick McGoohan. MGM/UA, 1967.

Psycho. Dir. Alfred Hitchcock. Universal, 1960.

Rear Window. Dir. Alfred Hitchcock. MCA/Universal, 1954.

Red. Dir. Krzysztof Kieslowski. Miramax, 1994.

Red Sorghum. Dir. Yimou Zhang. New Yorker Films, 1987.

Run, Lola, Run. Dir. Tom Tykwer. Sony Pictures, 1999.

The Shining. Dir. Stanley Kubrick. Warner Brothers, 1980.

Solaris. Dir. Andrei Tarkovsky. New York: Fox Lorber, 1991.

La Strada. Federico Fellini. Embassy Home Entertainment, 1986.

Tetsuo. Dir. Shinya Tsukamoto. Fox Lorber, 1990.

Texas Chain Saw Massacre. Dir. Tobe Hooper. New Line Cinema, 1983.

Touch of Evil. Orson Welles. MCA/Universal, 1958.

2001. Dir. Stanley Kubrick. MGM/UA, 1968.

Underground. Dir. Emir Kusturica. New Yorker Films, 1996.

Wargames. Dir. John Badham. MGM/UA, 1983.

Weekend. Dir. Jean-Luc Godard. Grove Press, 1968.

White. Dir. Krzysztof Kieslowski. Miramax, 1994.

Wings of Honneamise. Dir. Hiroyuki Yamaga. Gainax, 1987.

You Only Live Twice. Dir. Lewis Gilbert. United Artists, 1968.

Z. Dir. Costa-Gavras. Cinema V, 1969.

Recorded Music and Videogames

Cypress Hill. Cypress Hill. Sony Records, 1991.

Doom. Id Software, 1993.

Dr. Octagon. Kool Keith. Bulk Recordings, 1996.

Electric Ladyland. Jimi Hendrix. Warner Brothers, 1968.

Exodus. Bob Marley and the Wailers. Island Recordings, 1976.

Half Life. Valve Software. Sierra, 1998.

It Takes a Nation of Millions to Hold Us Back. Public Enemy, 1988.

Legend. Bob Marley and the Wailers. Island Records, 1976.

Never Mind the Bollocks, Here's the Sex Pistols. Sex Pistols. Warner Brothers, 1977.
Quake. Id Software, 1996.
Quake 2. Id Software, 1997.
Quake 3. Id Software, 2000.

Index

Dennis Redmond earned his doctorate in comparative literature from the University of Oregon. His research interests include media culture, multinational economics, and the process of European integration. His essay "Adorno as Multinational Marxist" is forthcoming in *Critical Theory and Globalization*, edited by Max Pensky, and other selections of his writing are available online at www.efn.org/~dredmond.